How Long
Will I Cry?

Published by
Big Shoulders Books
DePaul University

Chicago, Illinois

Fourth Edition

ISBN: 978-1-62890-155-9
Library of Congress
Control Number 2013949113

Cover photo by Carlos Javier Ortiz
www.carlosjortiz.com

Big Shoulders Books logo design
by Robert Soltys

**BIG SHOULDERS
BOOKS**

**DEPAUL
UNIVERSITY**
**COLLEGE OF LIBERAL ARTS
AND SOCIAL SCIENCES**

How Long will I Cry?

BOOK CLUB

VOICES OF YOUTH VIOLENCE

Miles Harvey
Editor

Chris Green and Jonathan Messinger
Associate Editors

Lisa Applegate and Molly Pim
Managing Editors

**Bethany Brownholtz,
Rachel Hauben Combs and
Stephanie Gladney Queen**
Associate Managing Editors

Becky Maughan
Copy Editor

Published by Big Shoulders Books
DePaul University

About Big Shoulders Books

Big Shoulders Books aims to produce one book each year that engages intimately with the Chicago community and, in the process, gives graduate students in DePaul University's Master of Arts in Writing and Publishing program hands-on, practical experience in book publishing. The goal of Big Shoulders Books is to disseminate, free of charge, quality anthologies of writing by and about Chicagoans whose voices might not otherwise be shared. Each year, Big Shoulders Books hopes to make small but meaningful contributions to discussions of injustice and inequality in Chicago, as well as to celebrate the tremendous resilience and creativity found in all areas of the city.

The views and opinions expressed in this book do not necessarily reflect those of DePaul University or the College of Liberal Arts and Social Sciences, and should not be considered an endorsement by DePaul for any purpose.

About This Book

THIS BOOK IS FREE. The editors ask that by taking a copy, you agree to support groups working on anti-violence efforts in Chicago. Please donate money—or your time—to one of the organizations listed at the end of this volume. When you're done, pass the book along to someone else (for free, of course), so that he or she can give. It adds up

To learn more: bigshouldersbooks.com

About Our Funders

This fourth edition was made possible by the William and Irene Beck Charitable Trust, which also helped finance the previous printings. Additional support came from the Vincentian Endowment Fund at DePaul, as well as from Steppenwolf Theatre Company and Now Is The Time, a citywide call to action against youth violence. Funding for Now Is The Time was provided by the Hive Chicago Learning Network, through the Smart Chicago Collaborative, a joint project of The Chicago Community Trust, the John D. and Catherine T. MacArthur Foundation and the City of Chicago.

The Richard H. Driehaus Foundation provided funding for educational programming connected to this book.

Additional financial, logistical and/or administrative support was provided by the following organizations at DePaul University:

Irwin W. Steans Center for Community-based Service Learning

Egan Urban Center

Beck Research Initiative

Women's and Gender Studies Program

Office of Institutional Diversity and Equity

Department of English

College of Liberal Arts and Social Sciences

The following DePaul University students participated in this project:

Emily Ce Anderson
Lindsey Anderson
Mickie Anderson
Leah Andrews
Ruben Anzures Oyorzabal
Lisa Applegate
Steve Barclay
Zachary Baron
Nicole Bartoloni
Meredith Boe
Ashley Bowcott
Ashley Braun
Bethany Brownholtz
Nathan Brue
Kevin Cahalin
Borja Cabada Anon
Matthew Caracciolo
Mariah Chitouras
Adam Cohen
Rachel Hauben Combs
Teresa Cronin
David Cueman
Emma CushmanWood
Mollie Diedrich
Anna Dron
Jerae Duffin
Lynneese Duckwiley
Rose Gregory
Mellissa Gyimah
Shawn Haynes
Bridget Herman
Bethanie Hestermann
Timothy Hillegonds
Maria Hlohowskyj
Rachel House
Stefanie Jackson-Haskin
Tannura Jackson
Megan Jurinek
Olivia Karim
Haileselassie Keleta

Bryan Kett
Danielle Killgore
Marc Leider
Christopher Lites
Brittany Markowski
Genna Mickey
Adrienne Moss
Ashley Mouldon
LaDawn Norwood
Miriam Ofstein
Michael O'Malley
Sara Patek
Molly Pim
Robin Posavetz
Stephanie Gladney Queen
Sydney Riebe
Ariel Ryan
Jacob Sabolo
Genevieve Salazar
Tyler Sandquist
Amy Sawyer
Samantha Schamrowski
Jason Schapiro
Kristin Scheffers
Monica Schroeder
Michael Shapiro
Barbara Sieczka
Erika Simpson
Kendall Steinle
Annelise Stiles
Ann Szekely
Molly Tranberg
Jaida Triblet
Danielle Turney
Michael Van Kerckhove
Sarah Vroman
James Walsh
Colleen Wick
Alexis Wigodsky
Nora Williamson
Kaitlyn Willison

For those who died and those who are still bleeding.

CONTENTS

Welcome to a publishing phenomenon.

When the first copies of *How Long Will I Cry?: Voices of Youth Violence* rolled off the press in the fall of 2013, the book's chances of success seemed relatively small. For one thing, it covered a topic many Americans would rather not think about—the ongoing slaughter on the streets of marginalized urban neighborhoods. For another, it was full of people whose stories almost never get told, including kids in gangs, kids risking their lives to stay out of gangs, parents and siblings who've lost loved ones to street violence, and adults who've been part of that violence and now must live with their actions. These stories, moreover, were largely collected and edited by a bunch of inexperienced college students. And if all that wasn't enough, *How Long Will I Cry?* was being released by a brand-new publishing company.

Oh, and there was one other big roadblock on the path to success (albeit one we erected ourselves). From the start, we were determined to make the book available to readers free of charge.

With a business plan like that, who could have guessed *How Long Will I Cry?* would turn out to be a hit? Certainly not the book's editor, who predicted that, with a little luck, we might go through a couple thousand copies. Well, I'm delighted to say I was wrong. Very wrong. As the book goes into its fourth edition, more than 20,000 copies have been distributed nationwide. Requests have poured in from at least 43 states (we've lost count), and the book has been put to use in such far-flung locales as Germany, the United Kingdom, Australia, Nigeria, Morocco, Bolivia, Mexico and the Virgin Islands. On the day I'm writing this, in fact, we received an order from Algeria.

How Long Will I Cry? would easily qualify as a best-seller, if not for one key fact. We've never sold a single copy. At Big Shoulders Books—a new publishing entity at DePaul University—we're interested in something more important than money. We ask readers to take action. We ask readers to connect with other people. We ask readers to change their communities. We ask readers to transform their own lives.

And finally, because we believe in the power of storytelling, we ask readers to tell us about themselves. Each day, as we check orders placed through our website (bigshouldersbooks.com), we find more and more inspirational tales from ordinary people, many of them struggling to stop the killings on our streets. We want to share a few of those stories here. They are the true measure of the power of the voices in this book.

When I requested the book, I had no idea that the Michael Brown shooting would occur in nearby Ferguson, Missouri, and that it would have such an impact on my students. Your book has been an excellent vehicle to use as we examine the case and all of the circumstances surrounding it. It has become a model for how we can express our thoughts and feelings in a creative and productive way. I am so grateful that we had How Long Will I Cry? *as a model.*

—Kimberly A. Moody, St. Louis

I'm from Sandy Hook, Connecticut, from the neighborhood where the massacre at the elementary school started in 2012. I promised myself that weekend, for the sake of my family, to do everything I could do to save even one life and create a safer society for them to live. I'm working on a national violence awareness project called SODINA with The Avielle Foundation whose mission is to prevent violence and build compassion in communities by fostering brain science research, community engagement and education. I heard about how powerful the book is from one of our project advisers. I just gave away my remaining copies in a meeting last night. It would be great if you could send me 10 more!

—Lee Shull, Sandy Hook, Connecticut

I used the book in my reading class at Kennedy King College. My students love the stories so much they don't want to give it back. I think the book is doing for us what the authors wanted it to do.

—Michelle Yisrael, Chicago

I am currently a Master of Social Work student, interning inside of a correctional facility. I recently gave a copy of the book to a resident in our substance abuse program who has not been following his treatment plans. I gave him a homework assignment to read three stories and he said they spoke to him. He has not picked up a book while being incarcerated, so this was a huge step for him. He read the other residents a chapter of the book and it has become a part of the group sessions.

—Anjelica Roman, Chicago

I'm currently teaching this book in three of my English 101 (freshman composition) classes. My students are incredibly engaged by the stories, and even though we're reading this book in Los Angeles, my students feel close to it. They begged to keep their books, and I didn't have the heart to take them.

—Katelyn Cunningham, Fullerton College, California

I hold informal sessions with my residents, both individual and group formats, in which we collectively read the interviews and have brief discussions afterward. The residents have been quite eager to read about others that have experienced similar histories of violence and trauma. Residents who aren't typically interested in reading have shown great interest in having their own personal copies of the book. It has been quite useful in my efforts to promote and develop empathy in the residents within our facility. Additionally, they seem to develop a greater insight into the impacts of their actions on their families, their neighbors and their greater communities.

—Spencer Washington, Burnett Bayland Rehabilitation Center, Houston, Texas

I taught a unit in my English II class last year and used this book. This was a powerful unit for the kids, and I want to continue to share these stories and what you have created with this amazing book!

—Claire Florine, Chicago

I teach "Violence in America" at Aurora University and used your book last semester. Students were required to read three chapters of their choice; most students were so inspired that they read the entire book. End-of-semester student feedback indicated overwhelmingly that reading this book impacted them more than any of the other assignments during the semester. Many were then motivated to initiate change in their communities.

—Lora Windsor, Aurora, Illinois

I am a caseworker here at the Cook County Juvenile Temporary Detention Center in Chicago, and I have been using How Long Will I Cry? *in a book club. My goal is to offer hope to the youth by modeling true integrity and providing them with resources and social skills that will assist them in achieving a better future. This incredible book has changed the lives of these young men and women.*

—Ezell Smith, Chicago

We understand that growing up in violent communities can have a traumatic impact on the development of many of the young people in our care. How Long Will I Cry? *is an important tool we utilize to engage in meaningful discussions about the emotional impacts of violence and about finding lasting pathways to peace and healing.*

—Marc Velasquez, Mercy Home for Boys and Girls, Chicago

Before I became a juvenile probation officer, I was employed as a GED instructor at Cook County Jail. I struggled to find material that interested the students (maximum-security detainees). Some of them were hesitant about reading How Long Will I Cry? *because they believed that they could not change the violence that existed within their communities, but as time went on the students realized that their stories and thoughts were important. Once they read and realized the impact of their actions and words, I had the students write reflections on the stories that they read. Students in the program all wanted a copy of the book to keep and pass the book forward to other people. I plan to continue to use the book in my current position as a juvenile probation officer. I would like to think this book has acted as an agent of change for the students that I taught. The students can relate and envision a future that does not involve so much violence or pain. I look forward to reading the next book!*

—Nicole Roman, Chicago

I am a high school English teacher in the Pilsen neighborhood of Chicago, and many of my students have been affected by or know someone who has been affected by violence. We read this book together and talked about the choices that were made and the choices that could have been made with a different result. My students are becoming better human beings as a result and want to make changes in their own communities. This book has created great classroom discussions and my students are realizing that violence is not the answer.

—Nicole Agee, Chicago

My teacher recommended this book to me in class and I was very entranced by the whole thing. It really inspired me to want to contribute to society more and to help people out, and I want to keep it because it seems like a book worth remembering.

—Ayesha Kahn, Lincolnwood, Illinois

If you're reading *How Long Will I Cry?* for the first time, we hope that you, too, will find it to be a book worth remembering. This fourth edition—like the ones that came before it—would not have been possible without the support of the William and Irene Beck Charitable Trust. Bill and Irene's generous financial backing of Big Shoulders Books has only been surpassed by their collaborative spirit, strategic vision, ceaseless energy and inspirational approach to life. My gifted colleague David Welch, the managing editor of Big Shoulders Books, also played a central role in the production of this fourth edition. And finally, a special thanks to editorial assistant M.M. Gray, who revised and edited parts of this book.

As I write this, local media outlets are reporting that 12 people were killed and at least 44 people wounded by gun violence across Chicago this past weekend. In Baltimore, there were nine murders and nearly 30 shootings during that same time, bringing that city's monthly homicide toll to its highest point in more than 15 years. In New York City, 23 people were killed or injured in 16 separate shooting incidents. The bleeding continues, but we hope that the powerful stories you are about to read will be, as one reader puts it, "a healing balm."

--Miles Harvey

May 26, 2015

INTRODUCTION

By Miles Harvey

This book began with a brutal murder, a viral video and a cup of coffee.

The murder took place on Sept. 24, 2009, in the Roseland neighborhood on Chicago's Far South Side. On that Thursday afternoon, a fight broke out between two groups of students from the nearby public high school, Christian Fenger Academy High School. There had been a shooting outside the school earlier in the day, and now tensions exploded into a wild melee near a local community center. Acting "out of impulse," as one of the participants later put it, about 50 young people swarmed toward each other, a few of them wielding huge pieces of lumber as weapons.

Somebody slammed one of those boards into the skull of a 16-year-old named Derrion Albert; somebody else punched the honor student in the face; somebody else swung another board down on him like an ax; somebody else stomped on his head and left him to die; somebody else shot a video, laughing while he filmed. And when that video went viral on the Internet, it caused a national uproar. U.S. Secretary of Education Arne Duncan described the killing as "terrifying, heartbreaking and tragic," while Attorney General Eric Holder, who traveled to Chicago with Duncan shortly after the incident to call for a "sustained national conversation" on youth violence, claimed the murder had left an "indelible mark" on the American psyche.

I normally don't pay much attention to the platitudes of politicians, but by that time I was beginning to realize that Derrion Albert's death had left an indelible mark on my psyche, too. Chicago is the most racially segregated city in the country,[1] and it's easy for those of us who live here to think of other neighborhoods as distant planets. Before that video, I had pretty much viewed youth violence as someone else's problem. But now I could no longer turn away. I wondered how such carnage could happen in my own city, and then I began to wonder how I could stand around and *let* it happen. But what was one white, middle-aged creative-writing professor supposed to do about it? What was *anybody* supposed to do, for that matter? The problem just seemed too big and scary and complex.

Then one day I happened to have coffee with Hallie Gordon, an old friend. As the artistic and educational director of Steppenwolf for Young Adults, Hallie produces plays aimed at teenage audiences. She spends a lot of time with young people, and she's passionate about their problems. Like me, she was frustrated and angry about Derrion Albert's death; unlike me, she had a plan. Her dream, she explained, was to produce a documentary theater piece about youth violence in Chicago, a production that would weave together the real stories of real people, told in their own words. The trouble, she said, was that she didn't have anyone to go out and do the interviews. For me, it was one of those *aha!* moments. "What would you think," I asked her, "about the possibility of my students doing those interviews?"

Our plans were modest at first, but things quickly snowballed. Before long, Hallie had not only received the enthusiastic backing of Steppenwolf Artistic Director Martha Lavey, but she had also enlisted the support of other arts and cultural organizations in Chicago. The result was Now Is The Time, a citywide initiative aimed at inspiring young people to make positive change in their communities and stop youth violence and intolerance. Partner organizations eventually included the Chicago Public Library, Facing History and Ourselves, and more than 15 of Chicago's finest theater companies.

The administration at DePaul, meanwhile, proved equally enthusiastic, allowing me to set up special courses for both graduates and undergraduates and providing the project with financial and logistical support through the Irwin W. Steans Center for Community-based Service Learning, the Egan Urban Center, the Beck Research Initiative, the Vincentian Endowment Fund and other programs.

Soon my students started coming back with stories—amazing, heart-breaking, brutal, beautiful stories, far more stories than we could fit into a single play. Long before *How Long Will I Cry?: Voices of Youth Violence* premiered at Steppenwolf Theatre on Feb. 26, 2013, we knew we needed to collect as many of those stories as possible in a book.

The interviews for this volume were conducted over the course of two years. While more than 900 Chicagoans were being murdered in 2011 and 2012, creative-writing students from DePaul fanned out all over the city to speak with people whose lives were directly affected by the bloodshed.

Most of the interviews lasted one or two hours, after which students took their audio recorders home and transcribed the entire session word-for-word, a hugely time-consuming task. Whenever possible, the student then went back for a second interview, attempting not just to firm up facts but to pin down whatever it was that made the participant tick, even if it was hard for that person to articulate.

Often, these second interviews produced remarkable results. Young people who had denied gang involvement in the first interview, for example, opened up about their lives on the streets—and about their anxieties. Parents of victims began to talk more frankly about their murdered children. Community activists and public officials set aside their well-rehearsed talking points and spoke from their hearts.

Once the interviews were complete, students began shaping the raw transcripts into narratives for this book—a process that the legendary oral historian Studs Terkel once likened to "the way a sculptor looks at a block of stone: inside there's a shape which he'll find, and he'll reveal it by chipping away with a mallet and a chisel."

In our case, it wasn't just one sculptor at work, but a team of artisans. All the narratives in this book have gone through several rounds of careful revision and editing by graduate students—a gifted group that included Lisa Applegate, Bethany Brownholtz, Rachel Hauben Combs, Stephanie Gladney Queen, Molly Pim and the members of Professor Chris Green's editing course. Our goal was always the same—to make every piece as coherent and compact as possible, without losing the poetry of the speaker's voice.

One of the trickiest issues we struggled with was dialect. It was true, for example, that some of the African-Americans we interviewed said "ax" instead of "ask." But it was equally true that white interviewees, with their nasal Chicago accents, often pronounced the same word "ee-yask." And if we used a phonetic spelling of one ethnic group's pronunciation of a word, shouldn't we do the same for all groups? Linguists, after all, insist that *everyone* speaks with a dialect. Keeping this in mind, I urged my students to steer clear of nonstandard spelling and try instead to capture the cadences, speech patterns, inflections and slang of their subjects. Nonetheless, we found that some words and phrases sounded too formal in standard English, while others simply got lost in translation. The terms "finna" and "fitta," for example, no doubt derive from "fixing to," but they now have taken on linguistic lives of their own. In the end, we decided to use dialect on a case-by-case basis, but only sparingly and always with the dignity of the speaker in mind.

Once the narratives were close to completion, we sent them to the respective interviewees for fact-checking and review. I confess that this part of our plan did not sit well with me in the beginning. Years of training and experience as a journalist had taught me that allowing a source to see a story in advance was questionable on an ethical level and often unwise on a practical one. But the students convinced me that we had a special obligation to the people who had opened their lives and hearts to us. If we were planning to present these narratives as *their* stories, told in *their* words, didn't they deserve to have creative control over the material?

It took weeks—and in some cases, months—to track down all the people whose stories appear on these pages. Nonetheless, this book is deeper and richer as a result of that final round of give-and-take with participants, many of whom supplied vivid new details that helped make the material come alive on the page. And it's a tribute to their courage and honesty that relatively few of them ended up asking to remove, alter or otherwise sanitize things they had said, no matter how sensitive or controversial.

This book contains crude language and graphic descriptions of violence—the result of our decision not to censor the narratives. There was only one exception to this rule: protecting the safety of our subjects. Toward that end, we have changed the names of several people who risk retaliation under "no snitch" codes or might otherwise be endangered by identifying themselves. In a couple of cases, other minor details have also been fudged to protect the security of certain participants. As with all of the narratives in *How Long Will I Cry?*, however, their stories remain faithful to the speakers' words and have been verified to the best of our abilities.

The title of this book (and the theater piece) comes from a conversation I had with the Rev. Corey Brooks, a South Side pastor who, in the winter of 2011 and 2012, spent 94 days camped out on the roof of an abandoned motel to draw attention to gun violence. When I asked Brooks what Bible story had been his biggest inspiration during the vigil, he pointed to the Book of Habakkuk from the Old Testament. Set in an age of bloodshed and injustice, Habakkuk tells the story of a prophet who goes up to a watchtower. There, the prophet speaks to God:

O Lord, how long will I cry, and you will not hear? I cry out to you "Violence!" and will you not save?[2]

Those words were written about events that transpired in 600 B.C.—but when I read them in 2012, I was struck by how they spoke to the frustration and rage that so many Chicagoans feel about the slaughter on our streets today—the same frustration and rage that had prompted Hallie Gordon and me to undertake this effort in the first place. I was also struck by how that passage touched upon the two goals Hallie and I had envisioned for this project from the start.

This book embodies both definitions of the word *cry*. On the one hand, it is intended as an expression of grief, a means of mourning the hundreds of young Chicagoans whose lives are lost every year. On the other, it is meant to be a howl of protest, a call to action, a cry for peace. But more than anything else, it is an effort to *hear*. When we began this project, I told my students that we live in a world where everybody's talking—blogging, texting, tweeting, Friending, shouting each other down—but nobody's really listening. So that was their assignment: just go out and listen.

No book, of course, will stop the violence. But I believe in the transformative power of telling stories. I believe that stories connect us with other people and open us to new worlds, that they help us discover ourselves and show us ways to change, that they have the power to heal. And I believe this, too—that stories can save lives.

The people in this book regularly find themselves in difficult and dangerous situations, the kind where one choice seems worse than the next. What's amazing is how often they respond with grace, resourcefulness and bravery. My hope is that *How Long Will I Cry?* might inspire readers to act with similar courage. For young people in violent neighborhoods, that may mean the courage not to give in to the perverse logic of gangs, not to reach for a gun, not to lose sight of your own humanity and potential. For the rest of us, those lucky enough to live in places where our children don't have to risk their lives every time they step out the door, it means the courage not to turn away. These stories belong to us all.

ENDNOTES

1 These results are from a January 2012 census data study conducted by the Manhattan Institute. See Edward Glaeser and Jacob Vigdor, "The End of the Segregated Century," *Civic Report*, No. 66. http://www.manhattan-institute.org/html/cr_66.htm

2 This version of Habakkuk 1:2 is from the World Bible translation, with one minor change. I have substituted "O Lord" for "Yahweh," as is often done in other translations.

By Alex Kotlowitz

The numbers are unimaginable. During this century's first decade in Chicago, 5,352 people were killed and, according to the University of Chicago Crime Lab, another 24,392 shot. So many that the violence has necessitated its own language: "To change" someone is to kill them; "a black cat" refers to a woman who has children fathered by at least two men who have been murdered. So many that funeral homes have rules about burying the murdered: Only during the day. No hats. Police present. So many that during the spring and summer, makeshift street side memorials—consisting of balloons and flowers and liquor bottles—pop up like perennials in full bloom. So many that people arm themselves in self-defense, and so the police pull anywhere from 7,000 to 8,000 guns off the street each year. So many that "R.I.P." has become so commonplace it's scrawled on walls, embroidered on shirts and hats, and tattooed on bodies. So many that should you walk into a classroom in any of these communities virtually every child will tell you they've seen someone shot. Indeed, the vast majority of murders—82 percent of them in 2011—occur in public places such as parks and streets and alleyways.

I recently met one high school student, Thomas, who rattled off for his social worker the people he's seen shot. The first was at a birthday party for a friend who was turning 11. She was shot and killed when a stray bullet struck her in the head. Then Thomas saw his brother shot, on two occasions, the second time paralyzing him. He saw a friend shot while waiting at the bus stop. And then in the summer of 2012, as Thomas chatted on a porch with a fellow student, a boy with a gun approached. Thomas begged him not to shoot, but he ignored those pleas, and shot the 16-year-old friend three times in her torso. She died on the porch. After this last incident ("incident" seems completely inadequate in referring to such bloodshed) Thomas retreated into himself, unwilling, unable to acknowledge his grief. He could only manage to tell his social worker, "I want to hurt someone. I want to hurt someone." It was the only way he could articulate the pain.

We think that somehow people get hardened to the violence, that they get accustomed to the shootings. I've made that mistake myself. When I first met Lafeyette, one of the two boys whose lives I chronicled in *There Are No Children Here,* he recounted the time a teenaged neighbor had been shot in a gang war and stumbled into the stairwell outside his apartment. There, the boy died. I remember that as Lafeyette recounted this moment, he showed virtually no emotion, and I thought to myself, he didn't care. Over time I came to realize that the problem wasn't that Lafeyette didn't have feelings, it's that he felt too much, and the one thing he could do to protect himself was to try to compartmentalize his life, to push the dark stuff into a corner where he hoped it wouldn't haunt him.

But the violence festers. It tears at one's soul. I've met kids who experience flashbacks, kids who have night terrors, kids—like Thomas—who become filled with rage, kids who self-medicate, kids who have physical ailments (Lafeyette would get stomachaches whenever there were shootings), kids whose very being is defined by the thunderous deaths around them. For many, it's a single act of violence around which the rest of a childhood will revolve. And then there are parents who must bury a child, who swim under a sea of what-ifs and regrets. One mother and father I knew visited their 15-year-old son's gravesite every day for nearly a year, including grilling meals there. A mother whose 14-year-old boy was executed by a gang member grieved so deeply that for a period of time she only had a taste for sand. Another mother so mourned the loss of her son she left his bedroom just as he'd left it as a kind of memorial: his slippers by the end of his bed, his basketball balanced precariously on his dresser and his collection of M&M dispensers lined up on a closet shelf. In this remarkable book, you'll meet a number of parents who have lost children to the city's violence. One of them, Pamela Hester-Jones, says of her son Lazarus, "He loved art and loved to dance. He liked jazz music, and he loved to draw. He loved to swim, he loved going to play golf, he loved going to the movies, he loved Hot Pockets and vanilla ice cream. … I let my son Lazarus go outside. I would never do it again." Is that what we've come to? That the world is such a threatening place that it's best not to let your children leave their house?

These are parents and communities who have lost loved ones. They've lost ground. They've lost hope. They've lost trust. They've lost a part of themselves. Drive through the city's West and South Sides, and you'll be greeted by an array of Block Club signs, and on each of them, neighbors have listed not what they celebrate, but rather what they dread: "No gambling (Penny pitching or dice playing.)" "No drug dealing." "No alcohol drinking." "No sitting in or on cars." They speak not to their dreams, but rather to their fears. These are communities, to borrow a term from the world of psychology, that are hyper-vigilant, that are back on their heels, trying, understandably, to keep the world at bay.

In *How Long Will I Cry?*, one former gang member told his interviewer, "We're telling each other, 'You're not alone in this.'" It's something many need to remind themselves of because more than anything the violence, the killings, push people away from each other like slivers of magnets of opposite poles. Neighbors come to distrust neighbors. Residents come to distrust the police, and the police come to distrust the residents. The police decry the no-snitching maxim, and think it's solely because residents don't respect the police. There is, indeed, a history there, most notably the torture committed by Commander Jon Burge and his underlings—though what really had people incensed was not so much that it had occurred but that for so many years those in positions of power, from Mayor Daley on down, refused to concede that it ever happened. But people also don't snitch because they don't trust each other, because they no longer feel a part of something, because they no longer feel safe.

Which brings us to the blunt, discomforting truth about the violence. Most of it occurs in deeply impoverished African-American and Latino neighborhoods, places where aspiration and ambition has withered and shrunk like, well, a raisin in the sun. Look at a map of the murders and shootings, and it creates a swath through the South and West Sides, like a thunderstorm barreling through the city. How can there not be a link between a loss of hope and the ease with which spats explode into something more? There's a moment when we were filming *The Interrupters*, and Ameena Matthews, one of the three Violence Interrupters whose work we chronicled, reflected on what she calls "the 30 seconds of rage." She described it like this: "I didn't eat this morning. I'm wearing my niece's clothes. I just was violated by my mom's boyfriend. I go to school, and here comes someone that bumps into and don't say excuse me. You hit zero to rage within 30 seconds, and you act out." In other words, these are young men and women who are burdened by fractured families, by lack of money, by a closing window of opportunity, by a sense that they don't belong, by a feeling of low self-worth. And so when they feel disrespected or violated, they explode, often out of proportion with the moment, because so much other hurt has built up, like a surging river threatening to burst a dam.

Then there's the rest of us who reading the morning newspaper or watching the evening news hear of youngsters gunned down while riding their bike or walking down an alley or coming from a party, and think to ourselves, they must have done something to deserve it, they must have been up to no good. Virtually every teen and young man shot, the police tell us, belonged to a gang, as if that somehow suggests that "what goes around, comes around." But life in these communities is more tangled than that. You can't grow up in certain neighborhoods and not be affiliated, because of geography or lineage. (An administrator at one South Side high school estimates that 90 percent of the boys there are identified with one clique or another.) Moreover, it's often safer to belong than not to belong for you want someone watching your back. And honestly, as Ameena suggests, many if not most of the disputes stem not from gang conflicts but rather from seemingly petty matters like disrespecting someone's girlfriend, or cutting in line, or simply mean-mugging. This doesn't explain the madness. Not at all. It's just to suggest that it's more complicated and more profound than readings of a daily newspaper or viewings of the evening news would suggest.

Let's be frank, these neighborhoods are so physically and spiritually isolated from the rest of us that we might as well be living in different cities. When was the last time you had lunch in Englewood? Or tossed a football in Garfield Park? Or got your car repaired in Little Village? Or went for a stroll in the Back of the Yards? To understand—I mean really understand—what it's like to grow up in these communities requires a leap of faith—or maybe it's just a leap. For reasons that no one can really explain, Chicago has been the epicenter for very public and horrifying youth murders—Yummy Sandifer, Eric Morse, Ryan Harris, Derrion Albert and now Hadiya Pendleton. And each time public officials shout, "never again," and then do very little to strengthen these neighborhoods, do very little to ensure a sense of opportunity—real opportunity—for the kids. Let's be frank, we've abandoned these places, just walked away. We tore down the public housing high-rises, and in places like the State Street corridor have rebuilt just a little over half of what was promised. We talk of dismantling neighborhood schools in communities where the local school is the very fiber that holds things together.

A place like Englewood is pockmarked by boarded-up, abandoned homes, so many that on some blocks there are as many as every other structure. Where's the outcry? Sometimes it feels like even a nod of acknowledgement would do.

Yet in the midst of all this, people go about their lives. They hold down jobs. They raise families. They go to school. They play basketball and skip rope. They attend church and get their hair done. They shop and grill and mow their lawns (and the lawns of neighboring vacant lots). They tend their gardens and rake their yards. They gossip and share a beer. In other words, despite the five people each day (on average) who are shot, people still are immersed in the routine and banal. They seek some normalcy. So lest we forget, those in Englewood share more than you might think with those, say, in Lincoln Square. Maybe it's not a leap of faith that's required, but rather just simply a faith, that everyone wants the best for themselves and those around them.

It's the power of what follows here, the frank and often profound reflections of those who have been there, of those who have lost. In their words, often philosophical and poetic, they move us to see what they see and to hear what they hear. They make us all feel less alone.

LOVE WITHOUT CONDITION
T-AWANNDA PIPER

The beating death of 16-year-old Derrion Albert, near Fenger High School in 2009, focused worldwide attention on the horrors of street violence in Chicago. The video of that incident—which went viral on the Internet and received widespread airplay on TV—was a profound shock for many viewers. It shows young men bludgeoning Derrion Albert with scrap lumber, then continuing to beat and kick him as he crumples to the street. Off-screen, meanwhile, we hear someone—presumably the man holding the camera—laughing approvingly and, as if watching a prizefight, shouting "damn" when the attackers land new blows on the victim.

But if the video is a testament to the viciousness and callousness of urban violence, it also documents an act of great courage and humanity. Just before the film concludes, the blurry image of a woman rushing into the crowd appears in the frame. Along with other bystanders, she lifts the limp body of the boy and drags him into a nearby building, the Agape Community Center on 111th Street.

Her name is T-awannda Piper, a longtime community activist in the Far South Side neighborhood of Roseland, where the attack took place. A dignified and thoughtful woman of deep faith, Piper has not spoken publicly about the incident since immediately after it took place. The following narrative is based on her first in-depth interview on the attack and its aftermath—a conversation she agreed to only after careful consideration. "I want to make sure that, whatever comes from this project," she says, "it is going to benefit the people I love, the community I love, as well as the city at large."

I moved to this community in the summer of 1998. I am originally from Washington, D.C. I attended college in North Carolina, got involved with a ministry called Campus Crusade for Christ as a student. I grew up in an at-risk community and felt like the Lord was leading me to go back and work with young people who were considered at risk. One of the places Campus Crusade owned was in the city of Chicago. That ministry is called the Agape Community Center and it's on the Far South Side in Roseland.

Agape means God's unconditional love. Love without condition. Every Thursday night for many years, the Agape Center had what we call Teen Night. Teenagers from all over the Roseland neighborhood, from all different high schools, would come. We'd have snacks, we'd have games, and then we'd have some time centered around the Bible. And on a given night, we could have 60 to 80 kids there. And what I loved about that was there were some kids who were involved in gangs, but the Agape Center was neutral territory. They did not bring that to the center. They respected our rules: remove your hats, pull your pants up, take your earrings out. So just to see that kind of ministry happen with young people was amazing to me.

The attack on Derrion Albert took place as I was setting up for our Teen Night on a Thursday afternoon. There's a window at the receptionist's desk of our building. It's the only window we have on the first floor. For security reasons, all of the other windows are on top of the building. And the receptionist said to me, "T," she says, "there's a group of kids in front of the building looking like they're getting ready to fight." I ran over and said, "Call 911 and tell them 'mob action' on 111th." If there's a group of kids outside fighting and you say, "mob action," it gets the police there quicker. That's why I said it. I had no other reason.

But then, I looked out the window and I looked at the TV monitor for our security cameras. I was just immediately overwhelmed, because there were a lot of kids out there. And so I ran upstairs and I told the other staff in my building, "We need your help." I was just yelling out loud, "We need your help downstairs. There's a group of kids outside of our building fighting." I came back down to the front desk, and that's when I saw the attack on Derrion.

Almost immediately when I got to the window, I saw a young man take what looked like a two-by-four—it was a big piece of wood—and hit someone over the head with a board. And so, I saw the injured boy fall to the ground and try to get back up, and another young man came and punched him. They began to kick him, and the next thing I remember was the second hit with the board. I turned to my co-worker and said, "They're gonna kill him." And before I knew it, I was outside of the building.

There were a bunch of co-workers standing there at the time, and I don't know how much they saw or didn't see of the attack. But later, one of the women who works with me was like, "We're not surprised that it was you who ran out there."

See, I've always just really felt burdened to give back and work alongside young people who may not have had the exact experience as I had, but something very similar. I started out as a statistic with all of the odds against me, so to speak. I was born to a drug addict. My mother was addicted to heroin, and just about any drug that was out there, she used. I mean, she was full-blown out there, and is still struggling today.

I have a twin brother. My maternal grandfather took us in when we were born, and we lived with him until we were about 5 or 6 years old. Then, we relocated in Southeast D.C. with my mom. She had gone through a recovery program, and we went to live in public housing with her. And after about a year or so, my mom did not make it through her recovery—she became addicted again. And to get away from investigations with the Department of Children and Family Services, we moved to Harrisburg, Pennsylvania. She ran off with us with a boyfriend there. And her addiction did not stop, so eventually my grandparents got us back, and we moved back to the Washington area. I would say that half of my life was kind of lived in instability, because I was staying with a distant family member there, or a distant family member over here, and then we moved here, and then I was back with my mom here, and so there was a lot of moving around.

Chicago was the first place I ever lived where I didn't move around a lot. Really, to be honest, Chicago has been my first home. When I arrived in Roseland, I saw a community that was hurting. But I also saw people who were willing to do something about it, people who weren't accepting things as they were, people who were saying, "We've had enough."

So, I don't know that I felt scared when I walked out the door to try to help Derrion Albert. I felt like I was doing what I needed to do. And I did for him what I would have done for any kid in our neighborhood. And I did for him what I feel like I would have wanted someone to do for my child if that was my child out there. So, if there was any fear, the fear was of what would happen to him, not of what would happen to me.

It was chaotic out there. I mean, it was kids running in the street; it was just people everywhere. I don't remember seeing very much, because my focus was getting him out of there. I do remember a black SUV coming through the alley at the time, and I just kind of waved to the driver and said, "Please, get out. Help me. Help me get him." He got out of the car. But I have no idea who he was or where he went after that—never heard anything else from him.

My focus immediately became Derrion. All I know is I went over to the crowd and I remember saying, "Get away from him," you know, "leave him alone." And I just wrapped my arms around his chest and picked him up and carried him into the Agape Center. He felt as light as a feather at the time. I don't know if it was adrenaline; I believe it was the Lord that allowed me to lift him. I lifted him up off the ground. And someone—I think it was the man that got out of the black SUV—I think he had his feet, but I'm not sure. I took him inside.

We laid him on the floor of our receptionist area. I immediately got on my knee to check to see if he had a pulse, which he still did at the time. He had a lot of swelling in his face. There was blood coming from his nostrils, from his mouth. I could definitely tell that there was head trauma. He looked like he wasn't sure about where he was. He looked to me like he felt he was still outside, still vulnerable, about to get hit again. He looked very intense.

There was so many people around me at the time and I'm pretty sure someone said his name, but he also had on a school name tag. So, I looked at his name tag and immediately called Fenger High School and told them that I had a student named Derrion Albert. I said, "He's badly injured and we need to get in touch with his family, immediately."

One of the other staff members at our facility had already called an ambulance. I reached back down to check his pulse again. When I called his name, he did what I thought was him trying to answer me. But he took a deep breath and nothing. And so I called his name again and he took another deep breath, but then I called his name again—and after that, no more.

We waited for the ambulance. It took them a while to get there, which I was very angry about. And when they came, they were not prepared. They came in with a stethoscope. There was no defibrillator. I didn't see any type of equipment that would address what looked like a pretty traumatized kid, you know, in terms of injury. One ambulance guy did say, "We need to call for backup." And the other guy said, "No, we'll just put him up on the board." So he came in with the board, and they put him up on the board and took him out.

Roseland's always been kind of notorious for deaths associated with violence, but it has increased within that last five years or so, after they began to tear down the big housing projects of Robert Taylor Homes and Cabrini-Green.[3] The Roseland area got an influx of families that moved from those particular projects and, while there were some really beautiful families that moved to the area and wanted a chance to make it and do okay, there were some other families that brought on a lot of conflict to our community.

Gang activity increased, territorial wars began to take place, and we began to start losing a lot of our kids to gang violence. It's because of money, to be honest. People want money from the drug trafficking and with that comes a cost, so they fight over it.

In the last five years or so, it also became more evident that our kids were coming from families that were in distress. There's a different kind of poor taking place right now. And what do I mean by that? I'll give an example. Though my mother put me at a high risk in terms of her lifestyle, there was still the expectation that I would do better than she did. My mom would always say, "Don't end up like me." And my grandmother had a sixth-grade education, but she expected me to not come home with less than a B on my report card. The expectation was that I would not back-talk to teachers; the expectation was that I would respect adults.

But with the new poor, it feels like the family is in such distress that the expectation to do well in school, to have respect for adults, has gone down tremendously. Not even grandparents are stepping up the way they did when I was growing up. We have a lot of grandparents my age—and I'm only 39—so for multi-generational households, things have really gone down in terms of people feeling responsible for the young people in our community. I'm not against public aid, but in some ways it has handicapped some of our family dynamics, because it's taken away the ownership that poor families once had with their children. Don't get me wrong, I support Section 8 home vouchers, for example. But the way the program is structured, it is taking away the dignity and the responsibility of those who are receiving it. So our people have been given and given and given and given to, and because of that, parents don't have that sense of responsibility anymore. And so, the kids are kind of left to their own devices.

A lot of the time, kids I work with don't even want to go home. And this is why they end up doing some of the things they end up doing out on the streets. It opens up the door for them to get involved in what we in our community call "traps." A trap house is an abandoned building that has been overrun by gangs in the neighborhood—they do drugs there, they sell drugs there, a lot of times there's sex involved there—and they do what people do on the streets. And so our kids are hanging out at the trap instead of going straight home.

Then you have a situation where some kids are actually growing up in the trap. Can I just keep it real with you? Their situation is that everybody in their family gangbangs. That's all they know, that's all they do, that's what they're about. It's their lifestyle. It's what is considered *the norm* in their home.

I knew that this was a community that was at risk when I moved here. I knew full-fledge what I was getting into. I was not going in blind. So while one event in my life, the killing of this young man, took me aback—yeah, it did—it's a kind of event that has long been known to happen in Roseland. Until Derrion's death, it just wasn't publicized.

I knew about the video even before it hit TV and the Internet. There was some police officers at the Agape Center right after Derrion was loaded onto the ambulance. They asked if they could view our video footage. We have a control room where you can play back all of the video and all that, and they asked if they could go up. And one of the staff members there said, "There's another video. There's a guy with a video camera."

It was not a cell phone as the media has often reported—so let's just correct that. It was one of those small video cameras—handheld. She said the guy doing the filming tried to enter the Agape Center to follow me in when I was bringing Derrion into the building. She shoved him out of the building and told him that he could not come in.

I turned to the police officer, and I said, "YouTube. They're going to post it on YouTube."

He said, "What do you mean?"

I said, "Sometimes they do that if there's a fight or something like that. They'll record it and then upload it to YouTube."

And then, a few days later, one of the kids said, "We saw you on TV." I thought that they were talking about seeing me on TV from the initial interview that I'd done with the media about the incident. But they said, "No, we saw you on the video. It's on the Internet."

So that's when I discovered that Fox News had the breaking story, you know: Derrion Albert, teen boy beaten on the South Side, and this, that, whatever—and you see the whole clip of video. And at the time, I knew it would probably go viral, but I didn't know it would go viral like *that*.

The publicity surrounding the case has been very hard for our community. I'll give an example. The year that Derrion was killed, I had a group of seniors from Fenger High School that I was working with at the time—they've since gone on to college. It was a group of five girls, and they were sending in their college applications and trying to pull themselves together from everything that happened, being surrounded by the media. Some of my girls went to college fairs, and I remember a specific instance where one of them had given her transcript and her résumé to a particular school, and they asked her what school she was from.

And she said, "Aw, I'm from Fenger High School."

And the person said, "We're not accepting applications from there."

And I had kids looking for jobs—you know, trying to make a little change to have something to contribute towards expenses your senior year. And some employers literally tore up the applications in their faces because they were from Fenger High School. Whenever they would go somewhere for a school activity or for a basketball game or volleyball game, schools would beef up their security, because Fenger students were coming. Or schools would say, "Well, can you all come here, because we're afraid to come there." Like all of our kids were animals.

That did something to the hope of our kids. Their whole thing was, "It's not all of us. We didn't do it. I wasn't there. Why are they treating us like this?" And so I feel like our kids and our families have been boxed into this stigma. They have been portrayed negatively by the media as unpromising, as a breed of animals, as a menace.

What I would say to those outside looking in is to expect from our kids what you expect from your kids wherever you are, and to give our kids an opportunity. I want you to know that there are future doctors, there are future lawyers, there are future advocates, there are future actors, there are future environmentalists, there are future scientists, there are future mathematicians coming out of Fenger High School and coming out of Roseland. These are kids that need our support and encouragement. And the media has taken that opportunity from them.

But we have people just like myself, from Roseland, who are still pushing our kids. We tell them, "Despite the odds, despite the disadvantages, you still need to do what needs to be done, because the world is not going to be accepting excuses. They're not going to accept that you grew up in a hard neighborhood and you had it difficult and you didn't have the same education—they're not going to go buy that story. They're going to be looking to you to produce."

So the airing of the video had its negative side, but it definitely had its benefits, too. I think a lot of people who saw what happened, it opened their eyes, not just about what's going on in Roseland, but what was going on across the city with our youth. People who didn't have any idea that things like this could happen—who were just kind of removed from these problems—it was a wake-up call to them, and now they're just trying to figure out what it looks like for them to be involved. I mean, look at yourself. Would you be interested in Roseland, had not Derrion's death gone the way it did?

I have never gone back and watched the video. Every time I saw it in court, I broke down, and probably if I saw it this moment, I would still break down. But, honestly, I didn't really need to see a video. I saw what the video didn't show.

I'm pretty sure that Derrion was pretty near death when I was with him. I'm convinced that I am probably the person that he had his final moments with. I really do believe—and this is why it's taken me two years to even openly share what my experience was that day—I really do believe that God placed me there for those moments to make sure that, if the Agape Center was in fact the place where Derrion died, he died with some dignity and he had some people around him that truly cared. We tried to give him what his mom or any of his other family members would have wanted him to have—some comfort.

And that is a very sacred moment when someone is transitioning from this life to the next. I don't want to defile the experience. So I would just ask that, whatever you take from this interview, you would honor and respect that the dignity of his family be preserved and that Derrion's dignity be preserved. Though he died a very violent death, he had purpose, he had life, and we need to honor that. So whatever happens with this project, my expectation would be for it to be used as a vehicle for exposing young people to the idea that they can make a choice. No matter what your circumstances are, you don't have to allow someone else to write your story. It's not how you start; it's how you finish.

—*Interviewed by Miles Harvey*

ENDNOTES

3 Spread out along two miles of State Street from 39th to 54th Streets, Robert Taylor Homes was once the largest public-housing project in the United States. In the early part of this century, its high-rise towers were torn down as part of a community redevelopment scheme, displacing thousands of residents. The Cabrini-Green public housing project on the Near North Side was razed around the same time, as was the Stateway Gardens project in Bronzeville.

MY LIFE WAS ONLY WORTH A FEW GUNS

JAIME MIRANDA

Jaime Miranda—not his real name—is a 17-year-old high-school student who lives on the West Side of Chicago. Because he recently quit his gang, Jaime fears for his life and wants to keep many details of his past confidential. He's hiding from his former associates, whom he tricked into believing he was moving out of town.

During his time in the gang, Jaime witnessed, and took part in, "terrifying things that still give me nightmares." These acts of violence have traumatized him—but he can't confide in his parents because he's never told them about joining the gang. Jaime is a short, intense young man with close-set eyes that tend to dart around the room. When he describes his fear, he looks down and speaks in a somewhat shaky tone.

The first time I fell in love I was on vacation with my family in Mexico. I was 11. I met this girl and, as soon as I seen her, I was like, "Man, she's the one." I bought her flowers the second day. I was there for about three months and every day we would be together, we would spend time together. We still stay in touch. We still have a connection from our childhood—knowing that I was her first boyfriend, she was my first girlfriend. We talk, Facebook and everything. I can't recall anything else in my childhood that made a good memory for me.

I have older brothers, but I never grew up with them. I have no idea where they are. I've never seen one of them. So to me, the members of the gang were like my brothers. I just seen these guys as my family. The first day that I joined, my friend told me, "I'm not going to look at you as my friend anymore. I'm looking at you as my brother." If I needed something, the gang would get it for me. If I was hungry, they'd go get me something. They'd buy me clothes. They'd look out for me; I'd look out for them.

Even before I joined, they used to do a lot of things for me. One day they told me, "Hey, would you like to join with us?"

I said, "Fuck it, let's do it. Let's go." And that's how, pretty much, my life started going down as soon as I said, "Let's go. Let's do it."

At first, I'm thinking it's fun. You know, I'm enjoying myself, being with my friends on a daily basis. What I used to like about being with them was that, on the weekends we'd have cookouts. You know, all of us just drink—you know, have our own fun. Those are things that I used to like.

There was only about five of us from the gang in the school, but we would still keep our reputation up. If we see one of the other gang members throwing the gang signs up, and if we see them throwing ours down,[4] then we'll go confront them. We'll fight them wherever it's at. In front of the office, in front of the principal, it doesn't matter. If we show fear, our own friends would deal with us, because that's not what they want in a gang. They want people that are willing to do whatever it takes to protect—and just do what's needed.

Once you're a gangbanger, the only thing going through your head is, "Fight. Do what you've got to do." The one thing that gangbangers like is that fear. Personally, I used to walk through the blocks around the school being feared. When people used to look at me, they used to hide behind cars, go back to their homes or whatever. I wouldn't even have a knife or a gun on me. No, they were just afraid of me. 'Cause they know if they do something to me, then everybody's gonna be involved.

Every Friday, it was mandatory, we have to be at the block. We'll all pack up in a car; we'll go to the block; we'll do, you know, our routine. Just walk around, two, three, four blocks, make sure nobody's tagging where they're not supposed to. If we see anybody that doesn't belong, we'll deal with him. One thing that I was told was, "Don't mess with people that live in the 'hood." If we see a kid walking around and we know he lives around here, we're not able to touch him. But there's days where, if we don't see nothing going on, then we'll start the trouble.

There was times when we'd go with a bunch of people to a different block and try to take over. A lot of times we'd succeed and sometimes we'd fail. It pretty much came down to whether they could outgun us. It was like 40 to 43 of us around there at one point. We went with that perspective that, "We're going to make our point be noticed." You know? At first, it was…I found it fun. I found it, like, "Man, I have all these people with me. There's no way I'm gonna get hurt."

But once a person becomes a gang member, he's easily targeted by everyone. There was a few times where I would come close to being abducted by other gang members. I didn't know if they had a gun. It was last year, during the middle of my sophomore year, when it first happened. It was on California, about to hit Division. I was coming out of school. Both of my friends that were usually there with me went to a gang meeting that I chose not to attend.

Apparently, these two rival gang members knew that I didn't go and, as soon as I was going to step into my car, they slammed the door and they hit me in the head. I fell. They picked me up, put me in the backseat of their car. It got me dazed. As I gained my consciousness back and noticed that the car was moving, I panicked and I started hitting them both. They stopped the car and both came out. They started beating me.

Something in me told me, "Don't give up. You need to survive. Do what you've got to do." I got up and I fought them both. By luck, I got a few good hits in on them and, as soon as they both fell to the floor, I ran. The guy in the passenger side chased me for about a block and a half.

I went back to the school. As soon as I got into my car, I called my mom and told her, "Mom, I'm gonna be late. I'm gonna be doing some after-school activities." Then, I went back to the block to tell them what had happened. They gave me a gun and three of us went driving around their 'hood. Whoever we found would have been an S.O.S.—shoot on sight. Luckily, we didn't find anybody out there.

I'd carry a gun most of the time. The first time I got my gun, I—I was terrified. I didn't know even how to use it, you know? That's what always kept going through my head, like, "Man, if I get caught with this…what's gonna happen to me?" But if I said no—well, there's punishments for us as gangbangers, even with our own brothers. There's a lot of things that I would like to say, but I can't. Um, the hardest moment that I've gone through was shoot or be shot.

My parents never knew what I was doing. I really wish I could tell them—but at the same time, that would freak them out about being with me. Them trying to go with me to go see a movie or something, they'll be afraid. I decided never to fight in my own neighborhood 'cause that could bring trouble to my house, that could bring trouble to my family, to myself. That's just too much, too much to be going through.

I messed up once by coming to the house stoned. I came home way out of my mind. I'm thinking, "My parents are sleeping. It's 1 a.m. They're sleeping." I just got dropped off at home. I stumbled going to the bathroom and that's when my parents came out and: "Oh my God, look at your eyes; they're ruby red!"

I had to sit down with them: "Mom, I smoke. I'm sorry."

She had, like, a nervous breakdown. My dad wanted to kick me out the house for that. Imagine if I would have told them what I used to do? My mistake was that I didn't show my parents the same amount of love that they showed me before I joined a gang.

I was involved for about two and a half years, starting freshman year. It got to where I didn't like being on the block. I preferred to be in school than to be at home. The only place where I'm able to be free is in school. I get along with all my security guards and all the school faculty so, you know, if they see me doing something wrong, they'll come and talk with me. A security guard at my school was the one who told me I was pretty much throwing my life away.

I told myself, "You know what? I can't be a part of this. This is pretty much me living life through hell." Being in the gang was very scary to me: knowing that four out of seven days of the week I have to be in the block. I have to risk my life those four out of seven days, and there's times where I had to stay weeks at a time. I couldn't go home. I couldn't do nothing, 'cause I had to stay in the block.

I got arrested about six times for having drugs on me or for robberies— just little things. But if you tell cops information about the gang, if you snitch, you're pretty much signing your death waiver right there. That's one of the things that a gang member has to live with.

I would never be able to bring my fellow gang members home to my house because they'll have tattoos of the gang, or tattoos on their face, and my parents don't like that. Before I left the gang, they wanted me to get my back tattooed with the initials of the gang. I refused. They wanted to threaten me by giving me a beating, and I told them, "If you guys are going to do that for me not wanting to get a tattoo, then go ahead. Beat me then. It's okay. I'm not getting a tattoo."

They were telling me, "Why? Are you planning on leaving the gang?" And in my head, I don't want to let them know that.

It's hard to be in a gang and to try to leave. It's really hard. When I started wanting to leave, there wouldn't be a day where I could go to school and not be afraid. Every day I was afraid for my life; every day that I didn't hang out with my friends was a day that I would get a beating for not being with them. That drove away a few of my girlfriends. If I told the guys, "Hey, is it okay if I hang out with my girlfriend today?" They'd say, "Nah, nah, we need you here, man."

There was times where I couldn't even walk with my mom to get groceries, because I was afraid of them doing something to me or to my mom.

She'll tell me, "Let's go through here," and I'll be like, "Let's go around." 'Cause if I go through there, I'm pretty much risking my life and my mom's life. My mom asked me plenty of times if I gangbang. There were a few times where my mom would pick me up from school and there would be bottles thrown at the car and my mom would be like, "What's going on?" I'd tell her that I just have problems at school with people that didn't like me.

I got cut in a knife fight about two weeks before I left the gang. It was my final march around the enemy 'hood. I used to love to fight. No matter who it was, how big he was, how old he was, I would fight. But after me getting cut, that's when something in my head said, "I can't do this." I have a scar about five inches long, by my stomach. It scared me. It scared me to know that somebody would always be better, somebody would always be stronger, somebody would just not care. That's what freaks me out.

In the end, my chief told me, "In order for you to leave the gang, you have to get a violation—a beating for a certain amount of time." But I didn't choose that way. I told him, "You know what? Fuck it, I'll stay."

So I stayed for a while, about another month, and I told him, "Is there any other way, instead of me getting a violation out that I could do?"

And he said, "You could pay a fine, about $600." Or I could just give them my personal weapon and four to five other weapons that I had to go purchase. That kind of made me feel useless to know my life was only worth a few guns to them. It made me feel like I was just being used. It made me feel bad about myself.

Around that time, one of my old friends came by the school and he told me that he was personally coming after me. And I thought, "Man, my own brother's trying to kill me now? My own family, the ones that I would take a bullet for, they are trying to do this?" But in the end, if you try to leave, all that was just for nothing. According to them, I wasn't a man for not letting them beat me. They were calling me a wuss, because I preferred to choose a different way. It's all or nothing with them.

Since I left the gang, my life has been so much better. I began to dress nicer—more appropriate. I don't sag my pants anymore. I don't have them below my waist anymore. I would like to go to college: DeKalb, Northern Illinois University. Get an apartment over there, something like that. I haven't took my ACT yet. I'm nervous about it.

I'm more involved with my family now. I love to hang out with my cousins. They look up to me; I'm pretty much like a role model to them now. When I used to be in my gang life, they used to hate hanging out with me. They used to be like, "No, man, I'm afraid. I'm literally afraid." Ever since I took that step to leave, I told my cousins, "I don't gangbang anymore. Let's go hang out."

My cousins are not the type to be involved in gangs. They're mostly about living their own lives under their own rules. If somebody tells them to do something other than their parents, they gonna look at you and say, "Who the hell are you?" And I'm the type that, if I go out to parties with my cousins and I know that something's gonna happen, I tell them, "Let's leave." I'm willing to do anything for my family.

I've been able to walk with my mom. I don't have to keep looking behind me every 5, 10 seconds, making sure nobody's behind me. Nobody's running up or anything. Now I'm able to walk through any—well, not through *any* 'hood, but mostly everywhere. There is certain spots where people know that I left the gang life, but they still want to get at me for fighting one of their members, beating them, or stabbing somebody, or just basically shooting at them.

It's hard to know that you have to do what you have to do in order to stay alive. It's terrifying. But when you join a gang, it's necessary for you to fight with other gang members, no matter what the cause is. I'm happy that I've been able to change my own life around. But to tell you the truth, I don't think the violence will ever stop.

—*Interviewed by Alexis Wigodsky*

ENDNOTES

4 To throw down a gang sign means to do a hand signal with the opposing gang's sign upside down in a show of disrespect.

WHY SHOULD I HARASS PEOPLE FOR STANDING ON THE CORNER?

HARLON KEITH MOSS JR.

Critics claim that street violence in Chicago has been made worse in recent years by an inadequate number of police officers on the street. A 2009 analysis by the Chicago Sun-Times, *for example, showed that once various factors were taken into account, the Chicago Police Department was nearly 2,000 officers short of its authorized strength of 13,500.[5] The city planned to hire 500 new officers in 2013, but Fraternal Order of Police President Mike Shields insisted that number was far short of what was needed to keep the neighborhoods safe. "If Chicago wants to lose the title 'homicide capital of the nation,'" he said, "it's time to get serious about increasing the number of patrolmen and detectives on the street. We at least need to hire 1,400 officers. That's at a minimum."[6]*

One man who knows the effects of this manpower shortage all too well is Harlon Keith Moss Jr. Born in the city, he was a Chicago police officer for more than 20 years until leaving the force in 2010. He has spent his retirement resting, spending time with family and traveling with the Buffalo Troopers, an African-American motorcycle club.

At the time of the interview, he sits in the comfort of his house, wearing a black jogging suit and still sporting his Chicago Police Department ring. He eagerly waits to start the discussion, ready to offer candid views on the lack of officers on the street and other challenges facing the force—including infiltration of gang members into the ranks.

When I first started on the job, I trained in Englewood, which is one of the most dangerous areas in the city of Chicago and, I believe, the most dangerous area on the South Side of Chicago. But there's just more gun violence now. These kids, they pick up a gun and they're more apt to shoot you and try to kill you. And it's not only other gangbangers they target. They have no regard for regular civilian life—and it's gotten to the point where they have no regard for the police out there anymore.

Over the years, a lot of people have lost respect for the police because of the way police deal with them. Who wants to be walking down the street, minding their own business, and the police pull up and grab them and throw them up against the car? You have the right to walk down the street and not be bothered just because the police pull up, especially in black and Hispanic neighborhoods, which is where you're going to see a lot of this happen.

Why should I harass some people for standing on the corner? Now I'm just making you mad at the police. Now I'm making you ready to do something. So, if I see a group standing on the corner, there are different ways to come up to them. For example, I might pull up and say, "Yo, listen, fellas, you know that there's this lady somewhere on this block and she's watching this corner. And, you know, as soon as we pull off, she's going to call the police saying that you guys are standing here. But if you go in your backyard, you can sit there and sit and talk all night. You can drink all night. Unless you all get loud, we won't know about it."

Instead, the police pull up and automatically think you're a gang member, and you may not be a gang member. Once the police actually start treating people with respect, then some of the respect, if not all of the respect, will come back to the police. Because, as things stand, the police disrespect pretty much everybody.

I always wanted to be a cop, from the time I first saw Dick Tracy on TV as a 5- or 6-year-old. When I first started on the force, it was very exciting and I didn't have any regrets. But, as I progressed in years on the police department, I could see things really starting to make subtle, then more drastic, changes. One of the drawbacks was that the city stopped hiring as many police officers. Now there's a shortage of police officers. I don't care what the new superintendent says.[7] He's trying, in my opinion, to do more with less people, and you can ask other police officers that are actually out in the field and they will agree with me. With a shortage of police officers, you're putting the regular beat officers in more danger. And you're shortchanging the citizens of Chicago because you don't have the adequate patrols that are necessary in order to stop crime.

But the police need to actually get out there and do their job a bit different than they do. One thing my partners and I did was, when I worked the 6th District[8] and when I worked the 22nd District,[9] was that we patrolled our beat—constantly. You never could tell where on our beat we would pop up, but we were always there. If they wanted to give out a job on our beat, we would answer up on the radio and say, "We're here on the beat; we'll take that," because we were there. We got to know the kids on the beat. We got to know the parents on the beat. We went to the beat meetings. By being in and out of the alleys, up and down different streets at any given time, it makes it harder for perpetrators to do something, because you never know when we were going to pop up. But if you have an approach that you take your job assignment and then you go someplace else where you meet up for coffee, or meet up with your buddies or you do whatever else is on your agenda, and you're not on your beat, then people get used to the fact that, "I never see the police."

Unfortunately, the only time I see the police in my own South Side neighborhood is if something happens. But by then, it's too late. Prior police administrations, under Jody Weis[10] and some of the other superintendents, what they wanted to do was they wanted to have the gang unit. They wanted to have the mobile strike force. They wanted to have a gun task force and any of these other units swoop into an area, let's say like Englewood, after a shooting occurs. That's a reaction. That's not pro-action.

And, unfortunately, you have a lot of police officers that come on this job just so they can have the opportunity to go into minority communities and assert themselves as supposedly superior. I've seen Caucasian officers fight black males only when they have handcuffs on them. I had one Caucasian officer that got dispatched to the 7th District[11] with me, and the first thing out of his mouth was: "I can't wait till I get into a shootout." We hadn't been in the district for two or three days, and he couldn't wait to get into a fight. Unfortunately, less than a year later, he got shot.

Most of the gun violence now is done by kids under the age of 25. They get involved at a much younger age. The gangs seek them out—and, in a lot of respects, they seek the gangs out as a means of belonging to something. Sometimes it's environmental: "I'm hanging out with Jim over here. And if Jim is a member of a gang, and a rival gang member comes by and shoots at Jim, he is going to shoot at me, too. It's guilt by association. So, I might as well join this gang so I have some type of way of being protected."

Another reason could be the fact that the work ethic is a whole lot different now than it used to be. If we look back at history, black people came up here from the South, and they were some of the most impoverished immigrants of all. But they still survived. They still made it, and they tried to do everything they could to make sure that their families made it—get an education, work hard. Even when I was little, the thing I wanted most to do was to get a job and be able to make my own money—honest money. Nowadays, these kids see the gangbangers and the dope dealers riding around in these nice cars, and they don't think about the fact that this guy's retirement plan doesn't go past a certain age. They see the glamour in it, and that's what they want. So what do they do? They go out and they start slinging drugs. They start gangbanging.

But a lot of people consider the Chicago Police to be a gang. And the truth is that you're going to always have some gang members or former gang members that are on the police department. Some join because they quit the gang and they want to try and stop other people from joining the gang. But some gangs actually encourage their members to join the police department. They want you to go to school. They want you to get into a high-ranking position on the force. Even if they don't exploit you, now they have an "in," so that other gang members can join.

I do know some police officers that were gang members, and some of them actually became very good cops because they knew the ins and outs of the particular gangs they patrolled around. One of the best ways to catch a dope dealer is to get somebody that used to be a dope dealer to tell you how this guy operates.

Now, the negative aspect of the police department having gang members is 'cause now you don't know who to trust. You don't know who to talk to. You don't know what high-ranking members are either current or former gang members. So you don't know who has your back out there on the streets. For instance, you could go into a situation where there's a man with a gun, and you jump out of the car, and it's a gang member, and you don't know if your partner is a member of that gang. You draw down and get ready to take this guy out and your partner might pop you. And that is very scary. But just being a police officer is scary.

These younger gangbangers are quick to pick up a gun and they're more apt to shoot you and try to kill you. I can remember one instance where there was a shooting on 75th at about Evans, and, after my partner and I arrived, a gangbanger drove down Cottage Grove and opened up with a TEC-9 semi-automatic pistol towards the police. Fortunately, nobody was injured. The police all ran to their cars in order to chase this idiot that was driving down the street. Unfortunately, he got away from us, but police are the type of persons that, instead of running from gunfire, they run to it.

But I don't believe tighter gun-control legislation would help. For instance, there's a law that states that a guy that has been convicted of a felony cannot own a gun. But you have convicted felons that keep getting guns. Now, if you cannot buy a gun, how are you getting a gun? Somebody else is either buying the guns for you or you're stealing the guns. My opinion is that guns don't kill people, people kill people. And when you take guns out of the hands of the citizens that need them to protect their own selves, then what you're doing is outfitting the criminal element to take advantage of the citizen.

In order to stop the violence, there needs to be more funding for the police. And until the police and the community and the school system all get together and decide we're going to work together to provide programs, to try and provide jobs and to provide ways for these students to have some hope for the future, we will never get anywhere.

Someone once asked me if I would be a cop again. My answer to that question would be, "No way in the world, because you're going to have more police officers getting shot and more police officers getting killed."

Right before I retired in 2010, you had three police officers get killed. One police officer was leaving his father's house to get on his new motorcycle and some gangbangers—who didn't even live on the South Side of Chicago—wanted to relieve him of his motorcycle. And they killed the young man over there on King Drive—right off of 84th or 85th and King Drive.

Another black police officer got shot wiping his car off in front of his house. He bought the car, a Buick, as a retirement present to himself and was going to retire a month later and got shot in an apparent stickup. Last night, I talked to one of my friends that's a police officer in the 22nd District now, where I was a police officer at one time. He told me a police officer got shot last night. Did it make the news? I watched the 6 o'clock news and it wasn't on there. You know, there are so many instances where police officers get assaulted, get shot at or get shot that never make the news. So no, not in the city of Chicago.

—*Interviewed by Adrienne Moss*

ENDNOTES

5 Fran Spielman, "Police Shortage a Growing Problem," *Chicago Sun-Times*, Oct. 29, 2009.

6 Quoted in Fran Spielman, "Hiring 500 Cops in 2013 Not Enough, Aldermen Say," *Chicago Sun-Times*, Oct. 10, 2012.

7 Garry F. McCarthy has been the police superintendent since 2011. He was formerly the police director in Newark, New Jersey.

8 The 6th District covers the Gresham neighborhood on the Far South Side.

9 The 22nd District covers the Morgan Park community on the Far South Side.

10 Weis served as Chicago's top cop from 2008 to early 2011.

11 The 7th District covers the Englewood neighborhood on the South Side.

FOUR BULLETS

JOHN McCULLOUGH

In 2012, Chicago's homicide rate rose for the first time in four years—an increase that experts attribute in part to the breakdown of larger street gangs into feuding factions. According to a Chicago Tribune *investigation,[12] roughly one in four of the city's 506 slaying victims in 2012 was affiliated with the Gangster Disciples (GDs), a powerful South Side gang that, in recent years, has splintered into at least 250 smaller, younger groups—sometimes referred to as "cliques" or "sects"—which now battle over turf older gang members once shared.*

One person who has experienced this bloody infighting firsthand is John McCullough. Born and raised in the Englewood neighborhood, he has been shot and incarcerated on numerous occasions. At age 25, McCullough says he is no longer involved in gang activity and is attempting to stay out of trouble.

In my neighborhood, it's shootings everywhere. There are a lot of vacant lots, abandoned cribs boarded up. Some kids aren't going to school or anything. Six guys got killed between 2009 and the end of 2010. Terrible as usual.

Ain't no activities, I mean *positive* activities. They got playgrounds, but then in the playgrounds you see the teenagers. The teenagers, they gangbang and all that, and the kids in the park see this. They're just gonna copy that. So they need some recreational centers or something. In the '70s and '80s, they had game rooms. As times went by, everything that was around our area got burned down or abandoned. The government could put a little recreational center up for these kids so they could see something different, besides being out there in the streets.

The key thing is, kids gotta have things to do besides sitting around on the block. The kids that are growing up right now, they're paying attention to us. They're following our footsteps.

See, I had a beautiful childhood in my eyes. I stayed around my family and didn't need for anything. I remember playing with cousins, climbing trees, playing cops and robbers and making guns out of wood, just doing what kids usually do.

I went to Harper High School.[13] Freshman, sophomore, junior year, I was an A, B and C student. I stayed busy, stayed working. I loved high school. I got kicked out my senior year, acting a fool. The guys who I hung out with, man, we just wanted to run the whole school. We was just having a ball in school. We just got super reckless and started pulling fire alarms, like eight times a day, just to get outside. They kicked us out. They kicked us all out.

My senior year, I think I had like 20 ½ credits when they kicked me out. I could have enrolled in another school, but I wanted to have fun and hang around in the streets. I could have put a stop to it. I could have just singled myself out and did the right thing, but instead I wanted to be bad. I wanted to have fun.

I remember it was the summertime that my dad got shot and killed. I don't really know the reason. He was in Michigan. I don't know why he was out there. I think it was one of them white girls he was messing with that stayed out there.

My mama told me to come into the crib. I was, like, 13. She told me and my sister that my dad had just got killed. Everything went blank. I remember that day like yesterday. Everything went blank and I couldn't cry. I didn't know what to do. It was hard to take it all in. I just remember thinking, like, "He's gone."

I think my mama took it worse than me. Even though they weren't together for a while, she took it harder. While she was telling me, she was crying. My grandma was crying. My sister started crying and I'm just sitting there, the only one not crying. Just sitting there, like I'm retarded, puzzled. The day of the funeral, my little brothers see my daddy in the casket. They was saying, "Daddy, Daddy, Daddy." They was crying for their daddy. That's all I could hear.

My Uncle Delvin, he took care of us when my father got killed. He made sure I was straight and didn't need nothing. He would go to my football games and all that. He took care of his family; he took care of everybody. He was about the only male influence that I was getting. He was a Chicago police officer. He was there for me, so I'll say he was my biggest role model.

He killed himself.[14] I don't know why, but he killed himself. I think he shot his wife, like, seven times, then killed himself. Somehow he snapped, because that wasn't him. He wasn't a killer and wasn't the type of person to harm a female. He just lost it.

When he was alive, I was on football teams, basketball teams and softball teams. I stayed in school. All that went down the drain when he left. I was

15, and I wasn't getting that extra push or that guidance anymore. So, it went from kicking it with family to kicking it with the guys.

I'm soft. People who know me know that I am a sweetheart. But people who don't know me, just based on how I look, they would think I'm a hard-ass, super tough. I'm hard on the outside and mushy on the inside. I'm the type of person that's not gonna bother anybody, you feel me? But if somebody bothers me, I step up and give them what they're looking for. Other than that, I'm a good person.

As a whole, it's just me and my guys. We ain't no big gang, not like how it was back in the day, like a big nation and all that. When you go to high school, you link with a lot of guys. So we started meeting with other guys in the neighborhood, which made us bigger and bigger. These are my close guys. We don't hang in the area where all this gangbanging is happening. I mean, when we go out, we have fun, we party and we get out of the neighborhood so we don't have to look over our shoulder and stuff. We'll probably go downtown to restaurants or something, like to Dave and Buster's or the Cheesecake Factory. We don't go looking for trouble.

The most recent time I was shot, it was gang affiliation. Over the years, we never liked each other. The guys that shot me, we went to high school together. Ever since then, it just escalated, bigger and bigger. I got locked up and everything came right back and haunted me. It beat me in the ass. It built up over the years. The beefing, all that, and not liking each other. We all Gangster Disciples, but they call they self something else, and we call ourselves something else. It's not a big organization. So when people say gangs, it's not no gangs out here. It's just individuals who claiming something. We're Creep Town Gangstas. I don't know what they call themselves. Everybody got their own little cliques and their own little names, but at the end of the day, they all Gangstas, GDs.

Nov. 4, 2008. That's the day I got locked up for selling drugs. I was 20, locked in Pinckneyville Correctional Center.[15] At the time, I was working, but I didn't have a high school diploma, so I didn't have a decent job. There's a lot of stuff I like, and there's a lot of stuff I be needing, and my people and my family be needing. It's not going to come to us, you know. So I was working in a furniture store, delivering furniture, and selling drugs at the same time. I ain't going to say I had to, but I wanted that little extra money. That's one thing I hate, is to struggle. I hate struggling.

Jail is what you make it. I mean, it's going to have some challenges, and there's going to be some guys that are going to try and test you. But at the same time, to me, jail is like college, like going away to college somewhere. The only thing on your mind is your people, or what's going on outside of the jail walls.

I came home Jan. 4, 2010. I was supposed to have come home earlier, but I messed up in jail. I was fighting my cellmate and I put him in the hospital. They took three months from me, so I had to stay. Finally, I came home. When I was in jail, I said I was going to change. I said I was going to do everything different. But I mean, that's just jail, period. It's going to change your mind state, because you're not going to like what you're seeing in there.

I was shot on two different occasions. The first time, I was on 79th and just got off the bus. I'm walking to my grandma's crib and, as soon as I get up the alleyway, two guys come up. I had a pocketful of money and these guys tried to rob me. All I could do was run, because they weren't about to take my money. So that was probably why they shot at me.

I got shot in the back of my leg. I didn't know I was shot at first until I got like two blocks away, and my leg went out. I couldn't even walk no more. I was scared. I went to the hospital the next day. It wasn't internal bleeding or none of that. I could see the bullet in my leg. It was throbbing, but that's about it. When I got to the hospital, the nurse told me that it would come out on its own. So, I just signed myself out and left. I took that one out myself.

That was in November 2007, and then I got out of jail in 2010. The summer of 2010, I got shot again, three times. I had just come from my grandma's house. The guys who I was into it with, they were close by, on 69th and Ashland. Me being me, I get off the bus at 69th and Ashland. I always look around. You know, just the neighborhood that we stay in, you gotta look around and pay attention to your surroundings. That's what I was doing, and at the same time, somebody was sitting there watching me. As soon as I get to my grandma's crib, somebody popped up from behind and shot me.

Man, I was scared that time. When he shot me in my chest, I seen my blood splash in my face. I turned around and I ran and he kept on shooting. He shot me in my back; that's when I felt everything get numb. My back, my side and my chest, everything got numb. I jumped my grandma's gate, then I went in my neighbor's backyard. I was scared, super scared, because I didn't know how many times I got shot. I couldn't breathe, so that really made me panic. The bullet that went in my chest came out my back. The bullet that went in my back got stuck in my lungs; it messed my lungs up. When I got shot in my butt, it came out my hip. So two of them came in and went out, but one of them was stuck.

The first week, I don't remember nothing. I don't remember talking to nobody because I was so drugged up. When everything started calming down, though, I couldn't think about nothing. My mind was just going everywhere. I didn't know who shot me; I didn't know what was coming up next. I was just glad I was here, though. That first shot was supposed to kill me. It was like literally two inches away from my heart. I just gave thanks every morning. I did that anyway, every morning I wake up. I made it my business to acknowledge God. He was most definitely with me that whole time. It slowed me down, gave me an eye-opener.

The police tried to find the guys that shot me, but they couldn't, as usual. There was a police camera right there where I got shot and the police say they don't know who shot me. Basically, I say them cameras up there are for nothing, because there was no footage of what happened to me. So, we take all that up in our own actions. We protect ourselves instead of being quick to call the police. They come on their time; they gonna do the job on their time.

It's a lot of police out here that's dirty. I'll say they're the biggest gang out here, the Chicago police officers. They can do whatever they want to do. If you don't have nothing on you and they don't like you, they're going to put something on you and send you to jail. They can beat you and leave you right there. Or they can beat you, and then take you to jail and say you swung on them.

You got some that do their job. Some police officers got a lot of respect out here, because they respect the guys on these streets. We got a lot of people out here, like myself, that don't be looking for no trouble, but we try to get some money to try and better ourselves and our family. Some of these police out here see that and won't bother us, and some of them out here just want to make our lives miserable. Make our lives worse than what it already is.

My proudest achievement: I've been out of jail for a whole year! And, I mean, it's shocking. Since I was 17, I've been going back and forth to jail every year; every year, I was in jail at least once. But I just broke my record. I went a whole year without getting locked up. I'm proud of myself. Mainly, I'm just sitting back right now. I ain't got to sell drugs because my people don't want me to go back to jail, so they're going to make sure I don't need for nothing.

What motivates me? Today? To get up? My family motivates me—my Granny Bertha, my mom, my sisters and brothers. I just want to do something better for them. Because, since I turned 17, everything started going downhill. I want to show them that I ain't just a bad person.

I wouldn't want to be in a new environment because I would have to start all over again. This is where I feel comfortable. I know everybody around here. I can't go nowhere yet anyway, until I get off parole.

Violence has affected me mentally, though. You gonna always have to look over your shoulder. Violence, that's every day. We see that every day. It's gonna be something petty, and it's gonna end in violence. But we adapt to our environments, we're just so used to it. You'll hear some gunshots, but all you gonna do is look around and see if they coming towards you. Unless it's right there, and you're in harm's way, you don't go in no house. It's just normal. It's normal. A lot of young males don't have any type of guidance, so we go by what we see every day and that's all we know. That's all we know.

My biggest fear is getting shot down and just being laid out in the middle of the street somewhere. I don't want to die like that: getting shot down, beaten to death or stabbed to death, just being laid out on the sidewalk, period. I want to die in my sleep, that's all.

Being stretched out in the street, you gotta wait for the police to come. You'll be out there for hours. Just out there. Too many of my guys got killed around us, so I see that. Too many times. I don't want to go out like that. Everybody standing around, looking at my dead body.

—*Interviewed by Stefanie Jackson-Haskin*

ENDNOTES

12 See Jeremy Gorner, "Gang Factions Fuel Violent Year," *Chicago Tribune*, Oct. 3, 2012, and Jeremy Gorner, "A City Battered by Killings Struggles to Find Answers," *Chicago Tribune*, Dec. 30, 2012.

13 William R. Harper High School is at 6520 S. Wood St.

14 Officer Delvin Williams was 29 at the time of his death. See "City Officer Kills Self, Wounds Wife," *Chicago Tribune*, Dec. 30, 2001.

15 The Pinckneyville Correctional Center is a medium-security prison in downstate Illinois.

MY SON LAZARUS

PAMELA HESTER-JONES

The windows of Pamela Hester-Jones' North Side apartment are filled with pictures of a little boy with a gap-toothed smile. Inside, the door that leads to her office is draped with a black curtain, and the walls are covered with missing children fliers, funeral programs, newspaper articles and more photos of the boy whose face haunts the window.

His name was Lazarus. In 2007, the 13-year-old was beaten to death on a busy corner of Albany Park, a North Side neighborhood that several gangs call home. His murder remains unsolved—but that has not stopped Hester-Jones from honoring her late son with the Lazarus Jones Save Our Children Campaign, which hopes to keep children off the streets and get them involved in the performing arts. It also acts as a service center for families that have experienced trauma through violence.

Hester-Jones, 42, is a thin woman with olive skin and a reluctant smile. She is nervous at the start of our interview, and busily walks about watering plants and organizing her desk. She tries to make small talk but doesn't make eye contact; her hands anxiously tap the surface of her desk. Rarely does she talk about Lazarus' murder or her own childhood, but today is an exception.

I grew up in the West Side of Chicago. My dad put up a red, wooden fence. It was so high that we couldn't look over it. I think my dad was doing the right thing for his children, because he didn't want us to get in harm's way or get into trouble. He kind of isolated us. We couldn't go off of the block; we could only play in the yard and in front of the house. Back then, the crime wasn't as bad as it is now. You can't have your children outside anymore.

I let my son Lazarus go outside. I would never do it again.

My mom and dad met at Marshall High School. It was very interracial back in the late 1950s and early 1960s.[16] My mom is Greek and German. My dad was African-American, from the South. They married and had seven Hesters. I was 11 years old when he passed away. He had the worst heart attack you can have. He left seven of us for my mom. She remarried and had my little sister and my little brother.

When I was 16, I had a baby. I never told my mother that I was pregnant. I was very small and super thin. They used to call me "Olive Oil," like the cartoon. I had a basketball in my stomach; it was shaped just like it, a perfect, little basketball. My mom couldn't notice because I wore this purple and maroon jacket all the time.

My girlfriend, Regina, she told my mom when I was eight months pregnant, and my mother called my older sister who lives in California. My sister flew in. I was sleeping in my bed, and they raised my shirt. I woke up and everyone was staring at my belly.

My mom said, "Oh, Pamela, you should have told me. You could have got an abortion." I think she said that because I was young and maybe she didn't know what else to do. Everybody was really supportive, but it was me doing all of the work. My days were over from playing outside or doing anything. Back then, I think I didn't know what I was missing in my life, but my son Jasper was like my shelter. I'm so glad that I didn't tell my mom and I'm so happy Jasper is here today. He's a fine young man and I'm so proud of him.

Jasper's father died in high school. He was playing Russian roulette with his friends and he got shot in the head. I went to the funeral, and that was my first experience with someone dying from an injury or being killed. I went to prom with his friends. They said, "No, you're not going to miss your prom. Come with us." I'm so glad I didn't miss it. I was nominated for prom queen. But it was sad. We had our prom on a boat on Lake Michigan, and I remember going to the bathroom and crying. I was thinking about him. We would have gone together.

After graduation, I worked at Bennigan's as a food-runner, and went to school for a nursing assistant certificate. I received two: one for advanced nursing and a regular one. Later, I went back to school to become a cardiologist technician. It was a great experience and I met a lot of doctors working at Evanston Hospital.

My last year there was when it happened to Lazarus. That was my last year ever doing that type of work, because my life has changed.

Antonio Jones came into my life when Jasper was 4 years old. We married and I had Lazarus. Antonio had gone to college and worked as a designer. He made the beautiful carpets and the clothes. He was a great father, a great provider. Lazarus and his dad did a lot of things together, like roller-skating and golfing.

Lazarus was 10 when Antonio went to jail. It was drugs. Attempt to deliver drugs, I guess that's how they say it. His friends were doing it and he wanted to make more money. From my understanding, the police were building a case on him for two or three years. They finally arrested him and they gave him 20 years and he has to do 10. Never been in jail for nothing. I just couldn't believe he got that much time. We got a divorce in 2009. We're still the best of friends. He really didn't do anything to me; you choose your own paths in life.

In 2007, Jasper, Lazarus and I were living near the corner of Foster and Lincoln Avenues in Lincoln Square. I wanted to be on the North Side, by my mom's house, and I always lived where there were different cultures and different nationalities. I never wanted to live in an area where there was just one side, so my children always went to school where there were interracial children. Lazarus' school was Budlong Elementary. There were Greeks, Asians and Latinos. It was a whole variety of cultures. Lazarus' assistant principal was Greek and she used to call him "Black Greek."

I wasn't surprised that the day after he was killed, all of the children were at my apartment. The principal called and said, "Mrs. Jones, I heard that all of the students are at your apartment and I understand, but you let them know that they have to get back to the school." So many children came to Lazarus' funeral. He was so popular, even at such a young age—13. He had a lot of friends that loved him.

He loved art and loved to dance. He liked jazz music and he loved to draw. He loved to swim, he loved going to play golf, he loved going to the movies, he loved Hot Pockets and vanilla ice cream and those toy boxcars. He liked writing in journals that teachers gave him. The last entry he wrote in his journal was called "Where I Want to Be When I Get Older." I recited some of his entries at the funeral, but I couldn't finish reading the last one. I broke down. My oldest brother came up and read it for me.

Lazarus wanted to be the president.

On the corner near Budlong Elementary is Swedish Covenant Hospital.[17] When the kids go that way, they can make a left and go over to the Albany Park neighborhood. That's where Lazarus was on the day the tragedy happened.

I never knew about gangs being over in Albany Park. I didn't realize that until the night of the incident. Some of Lazarus' friends said that Lazarus met some little boy and he started playing with him. I guess the boy lived over in Albany Park and I guess that's how Lazarus ended up going there.

He had a 10 o'clock curfew. He always went to the CVS next door. He'd buy candy and chips and sell them to the classmates at lunchtime. That's how he'd make extra money for his pockets. But he didn't come home that night.

I was on the recliner asleep when I got the knock on the door. My bell didn't ring, so I was like, "What's going on?" I opened the door and the police officer said, "Are you Lazarus' mom? I need you to come with me."

I said, "What happened?"

"Your son has been in an accident."

I told him that I didn't have a ride and that I was on bed rest because I was pregnant. "Can you please take me?" I said. And he did, but he didn't tell me anything. The car was really quiet. No one said anything.

When I got to Children's Memorial Hospital, they put me in a wheel-chair and pushed me into a family room. I knew it was serious when they put me in there. It was a nice little room. Private. No TV, just chairs.

The nurse told me to call my immediate family, and I knew something was wrong. The detectives and the nurse came in and everybody was talking to me. The nurse said, "You want to go see how he's doing?"

I said, "No." I couldn't go in there. All I was thinking was this: I was in a wheelchair, I was pregnant, I did not want to go into the room by myself because I did not feel like I could handle whatever I had to look at. I was horrified. I felt numb. I was thinking I was in a dream.

I called Antonio's mom, my sister, my best friend and my brothers. I still didn't want to go into the room first, so they went in and they said, "Pam, it looks really bad." I was just crying all over the place. But then I said, "Okay, take me in. I have to go in."

What happened was his injuries were so bad that he actually died on Lawrence Avenue and Troy Street in Albany Park. They found Lazarus in the fetal position. At the hospital, his blood was coming out of his ears and his rectum, and he was brain dead.

I had just lost a sister a year-and-a-half earlier to breast cancer and her face was so swollen. You know, like a Cabbage Patch Doll. I saw my son like that. I was like, "No, stop! This is not how Lazarus looks." All of his injuries were on the left side. He had a black eye, because they kicked and beat him with a hammer.

I was holding Lazarus' feet and they were so cold. I was telling him that everything would be all right.

The nurse came in and said, "We're going to stop the machine." I said, "No! No, absolutely not! I want Lazarus' heart to stop on his own."

So we waited. And he had a strong heart, because I always said he had my heart and my hair and my eyes.

It had to be three or four in the morning. His heart finally stopped and his spirit went away.

There were actually three killers. The night of the incident, Lazarus was out with two of his friends. The detectives said that Lazarus didn't run, because he had no reason to. But Lazarus' friend recognized the men. He said one of the men said, "We're going to fuck him up."

So his friends ran. I'm not mad at them. They were little kids; they were just scared. Those guys had weapons. They came out of a van with no windows. After it happened, one of Lazarus' friends went into the Jerusalem Food and Liquor Store and told the owner to call the police. The owner had seen everything. After the murder, I actually was trying to get his liquor store closed down. That's how furious and angry I was.

There is a bus stop there right where it happened. A bus came back and forth. Right across the street, there is a diner and a big old grocery store where they sell fresh fruits and meats. And all of this stuff was open. Right at that busy intersection, where everybody just looked like it was a parade when they saw a child getting beat like that.

Nobody did anything. No one called for help. They could have saved his life.

Those killers are still out there. There's a $10,000 reward and no one has come forth. If the reward was $100,000, they wouldn't come forth. You can't put a price on someone who wants to keep silent.

But God sees everything. The detectives are on the case. I will be getting a phone call one day. I will be going to court like all of the other parents who have lost their children to gun violence.

On my wall I have a list. The year that Lazarus died, 2007, there were 32 children. That's how many children followed *after* Lazarus. I keep track every time the news comes on of how many kids there are. It's devastating.

I've been focusing on what we can do about the murderers walking on our streets. I worry about other people's lives and their children. When someone hurts someone, whether they're an adult or a child, why can't they get caught? They've probably committed more crimes. I always ask myself, "How does the person sleep at night?"

The very next day after Lazarus left, every news channel was at my apartment. Every news channel you can think of, even the Latino news channel. I was like, "Open the door. Let them in."

I was there, bad breath and all. I got up out of my bed and sat on my sofa. My little sister, Susie, she talked when I couldn't talk.

I really wanted to die. I didn't want to be here anymore. But because I was pregnant, I said, "This is for me to still be here." I couldn't harm a child.

When my water broke, I was like, "Oh, my baby is coming." I don't even think I was in the right state of mind to think that he wasn't even due yet. I was 32 weeks when it happened. The doctors said the baby couldn't come until I was 38 weeks, so it was six more weeks in order for him to be a full, developed child.

I couldn't believe it. I said, "No way. You're kidding me, right? No one stays in the hospital this long." I stayed at the hospital where I worked. My room was nice and my co-workers would come and visit me.

It was a miracle delivery. Israel came the day that he was supposed to come out. He was four pounds. He didn't have any eyebrows when he came out.

I'm a single parent right now. Israel's father wasn't ready for marriage, so I couldn't be with him. I know I had a baby out of wedlock, but what can I say? I'm not perfect.

I'm happy to have Israel. I think God was preparing me because of the loss of Lazarus. Israel gives me hugs and kisses out of the blue. Like in the middle of the day he'll just be sitting there and come and say, "I love you, Mommy. Hug me back."

I've never had any of my children give me so many hugs and kisses. But he will never take the place of Lazarus.

I let Lazarus go outside. He had a key. I figured since he was 13, he was getting big. Israel can never go outside. I will not allow it.

I want to have a safe haven for the children. I was a parent that was working and I really thought it was okay to let Lazarus go outside. But it's not okay. They need to be somewhere where there is an adult.

Because of my hours at the hospital I couldn't just say, "Okay, doctor. I have to take off these scrubs and I'm going to leave you in surgery by yourself." I didn't have someone to look after Lazarus. So I left Lazarus to be an adult at the age of 13.

We need programs; we need safe havens. There's not really a safe haven in the North Side. The streets of Chicago are not safe, and parents need to be more aware. It's up to us parents to stand together and take charge of our children. We need to stand together and let the gangs know that we're not afraid of them. I think each area of Chicago should really do that. Even if the crime is not bad here, where I live, it could get bad.

The night after Lazarus died, I had a vision. I was sleeping in my bed. Lazarus' room was right across the hall from mine. I could see the inside of his room from my bed.

I saw him. He came past and he threw his shirt over the door and grabbed his book bag. Then he smiled and walked out.

Sometimes, I don't think I was asleep.

—*Interviewed by Jacob Sabolo*

ENDNOTES

16 A 1958 article in *The Crisis*, the official magazine of the National Association for the Advancement of Colored People (NAACP), estimated that Marshall's "student body is about 50 percent Negro now." See "De Facto Segregation in Chicago Public Schools: A Report from the Chicago Branch of the NAACP," *The Crisis*, February 1958, 87-93, 126-127.

17 Budlong Elementary School is at 2701 W. Foster Ave.

WHAT THE WATCHMAN SAW

COREY BROOKS

On Nov. 22, 2011, Pastor Corey Brooks climbed onto a rented construction lift and took it to the roof of a vacant two-story motel across the street from his New Beginnings Church in the 6600 block of South Martin Luther King Jr. Drive. Then he set up a tent, climbed inside, and began a vigil against gun violence.

No one paid much attention to Brooks at first, but as he continued to camp out during a Chicago winter, his rooftop vigil became national news. By the time he came down 94 days later—on Feb. 24, 2012—he had raised $450,000 to purchase and demolish the dilapidated motel, a longtime haven for drugs and prostitution. The last $100,000 of that money came from movie mogul Tyler Perry, who heard about Brooks on a radio program and wrote a check the very same day.

We visited Brooks twice in his tent, a cozy space into which he had packed an impressive array of furniture, space heaters, computer equipment and books. A steady stream of advisors and well-wishers kept stopping by to see the 42-year-old pastor, who greeted them in a track suit and work boots, his hair and beard growing a little nappy but his energy and spirits undiminished by the long odyssey.

We spoke with him a final time after he had left the roof and begun work on his next project: finding funds to build a community center where the motel once stood.

This started with a shooting. Actually, it started with ten shootings.

In 2011, I did ten funerals of young black men between the ages of 13 and 25 and none of those young men were covered in the press or anything like that. And then the 11th funeral was a young man by the name of Carlton Archer, 17 years old. And right before the service began, some of the children coming into our neighborhood for the funeral, they started being shot at by another group of kids.

I was upstairs, getting prepared, so I just ran downstairs and I saw all these kids running into the church. I saw kids underneath cars. I saw adults under cars. Everybody was trying to hide. And it was just, it was chaotic—it was, it was really scary. I've never experienced anything like that in my life.

Something drastic needed to be done. Something radical.

I used to be pastor of the West Point Missionary Baptist Church[18] in Bronzeville,[19] on 35th and Cottage Grove. It was real traditional, real conservative, with an upwardly mobile-type congregation. So it wasn't a good fit, because I was young and progressive and wanted to do radical stuff. And so the more radical stuff I would do, the angrier the leadership would get—even though a lot of the church members loved it, because their sons and daughters were coming back to the church. But a lot of ex-cons, a lot of gangbangers, a lot of people who hadn't been in church before started coming, too.

The leadership didn't like that, and so I decided that instead of trying to fight them for their church, I'd just start what I felt led to create. And so that's how New Beginnings was birthed. We call it New Beginnings because it *was* a new beginning—I wanted to do something fresh and creative and contemporary. We started the church in November 2000, and we've been in this neighborhood for the last six years.

The church building used to be a nationally famous nightclub. In the 1950s and early 1960s, jazz entertainers from all over would come to the city and perform at a place called the Roberts Show Lounge. All the great entertainers played there—Count Basie, Duke Ellington, Sarah Vaughan. Muhammad Ali used to frequent the club. Everybody who was somebody, they came to this location.

The club was owned by a man named Herman Roberts, an entrepreneur way before his time. He was one of the first black hotel owners in the Midwest, and he decided to build this motel across the street from the Roberts Show Lounge, because, back in the early 1960s, blacks did not feel comfortable going downtown to stay. So he built this motel and a few others in predominately black areas and became a very successful businessman.

See, back when everything was segregated, people had no choices but to live in this area, take care of this area. You had upper income, middle income, lower income living together, and as a consequence those at lower income had people who they could look to and say, "That's Doctor Johnson or that's Attorney So-and-So, or that's Mr. So-And-So who owns the store." They had living examples that education works and hard work pays off and determination goes a long way. But as integration came,[20] black people who had middle income and upper income started moving out and going on with their lives. And so what we're left with is a neighborhood where people have been far removed from the American Dream.

Over time, Mr. Roberts started losing business, so he sold the motel. And from that point on, it started going down and down and down. If you wanted a prostitute you could get one here any time of the night. If you wanted any drugs—heroin, crack, weed, whatever—you could easily get that at this motel. That's the type of people that this motel did business with: bottom-feeders who prey on people in poverty. And that's what we experience all over America in inner cities. There it goes. The cookie starts to crumble.

And so, as I was coming out the door of that funeral—the one with all the gunfire—I was thinking I had to do something. And I looked at the motel, and instantly the thought came to my mind: "We need to get that motel. We need to get it now. And we need to turn it into a community development center."

And then right after that thought was: "How?"

Then right after that thought was: "I'm gonna put a tent on the roof of the motel. I'm gonna hold a vigil up there. I'm gonna raise the money and bring attention to the gun violence and to the deaths."

And I laughed, you know, and said, "I'd never do that."

And the next day, that thought would not leave me.

What does it feel like to be called by God? Wow. I think if I had to describe it, I'd say it's a prompting, an urge to do something that does not go away. And you can try to get rid of that urge, but it just maddens you. It haunts you.

I imagine for some people it may be different. Maybe they have a Moses-type of encounter where God speaks in the burning bush and all of a sudden they get this revelatory thought. But for me it has always been more like an ongoing, haunting thing that was prompting me to do better, to excel and not settle for less. It just kept pulling on me.

I was born in Union City, Tennessee, and I lived in a little town called Kenton, population of about 2,000. I stayed there until I was 8 with my grandmother and my grandfather. My mother left me with them so she could go off to pursue a job in Muncie, Indiana. And later on I found out the real reason she left was because she had a boyfriend and she was gonna get married and they wanted to go and get things set up before I came. But I didn't find that out for a long time. Being left behind, that hurt. Me and my mom were really tight; we still are to this day. So being left with my grandparents—even though they were wonderful—was traumatic.

And when I moved to Muncie, it was a very violent household. My stepfather was abusive. He was crazy. He's cool now, but he was crazy then. And when I was about 12 or 13, he got addicted to drugs. And that even made it worse.

I used to get in trouble at school all the time. It wasn't that I fought every day, but I had a reputation of: "Don't, don't mess with him." I've always had that attitude: "If you hit me, I'm gonna hit you. Don't go to sleep around me, 'cause if you hit me, somehow, some way, there will be payback."

I was just a real bad kid. But in fifth grade, I got a new teacher. His name was Joe Stokes. He was white, by the way. Red hair. Very white. And he just stayed on me. Every day. I mean *every* day. And if that had not happened, who knows? I probably would be doing something illegal. But Joe Stokes, he made me believe in myself.

I stayed in Muncie until I was 18. I played basketball at Muncie Central High School and ended up getting the basketball scholarship to Armstrong State, in Savannah, Georgia. I stayed there for a year, and then I quit playing basketball and moved back to Muncie to go to Ball State. And in around the time I moved back, I had a call to ministry—to want to preach.

It was a gut feeling. I'm just now, in my latter years, understanding it, and learning how to listen to it. So when I had this idea about doing a vigil on the roof, I kind of pitched it to God that if I found one person who agreed with me that it was a good plan, I would do it. But everybody thought it was stupid. My staff members all laughed and joked and begged me not to do it. Then I told my wife, and she begged me not to do it. But there was one last staff member I hadn't told about it—and he's not a "yes" guy. When I mentioned it in the staff meeting the next day, he said without hesitation: "Pastor, I think that's the best idea in the world."

So that very moment, I stopped the meeting and said: "I'm going to get a tent."

The first night it was raining. The second night the wind was just blowing so hard, and the third night I think it was raining again. So the first three nights were kinda like: "Oh my God, what have I gotten myself into?" And for the first three weeks I was upset, because I felt like: Man, people ought to get this, you know? Young kids are dying and no one is doing nothing.

But then I came to recognize that you can't get mad at everyone because they don't see what you see. I take inspiration from the Book of Habakkuk in the Old Testament. The prophet goes up on the watchtower to hear from God. And God speaks to him and gives him a vision and tells him to write it, to make it plain, so the people can run and see it. So I just kind of feel like that's my job. For whatever reason, I'm the watchman.

Being on this roof has brought me isolation, but it's also given me perception. The number-one thing I hear are the sirens. Until I came up here, I never realized how many sirens actually go off on a consistent basis and you pay no attention to them. But now I can even distinguish the different types of sirens. Is that an ambulance? A fire truck siren? A police siren? Because if it's the ambulance and the fire truck siren you know: "Wow, somebody probably got shot."

I hear gunshots all the time. Even the gunshots that happen ten blocks away sound like they're next door. I don't know why, but it's like sounds are magnified. And unfortunately, I have learned to tell the different types of guns apart from each other. A .25, that sounds more like a large firecracker. A .45 has a ferocious volume to it. Semi-automatics are repetitive: *pow-pow-pow-pow-pow.*

New Year's Eve—that was frightening. In this community, it's a ritual to shoot off guns on that holiday. So what happened was around 11 p.m., I began to hear sporadic gunfire, gun here, gun there. But at 12 o'clock, there was nothing but guns—small guns, large guns, automatic guns, shotguns. And it can be horrific if you're in a close proximity of where these guns are being shot. Because at any time a stray bullet could come from anywhere and take you out.

So what I did was, I pulled the futon over me, 'cause I figured if a bullet came through it wouldn't hit me because the futon is so padded. I just stayed underneath the futon and slept as best I could. And it really, really sounded like a war zone. There's no way that a person could have heard all this gunfire and not start to think differently about guns.

In January of 2012, I came down to do two funerals. One was the young man that was killed in Church's Chicken[21] and another was a young man that was killed at Marquette Park.[22]

It was bittersweet to be back on the ground. I was glad to be down off the roof and to be able to walk around and socialize with people. But the bitter part was to come down for funerals and to see so many young people who looked so hopeless. I think that a lot of kids in this neighborhood feel like they don't have anything to live for. They don't have any education, they don't have any jobs, they don't have any family, so what's the point? They're just like: "whatever." Whatever happens today, it happens. *Whatever.* And when you start having that approach toward your own life, you begin to have it toward other people's lives, as well. And I think that's where a lot of kids are. Life means nothing. Life has been devalued.

Being up on this roof has made me more compassionate, because it's made me more keenly aware of things that are going on around me. Every day I ask God to forgive me for not paying attention to people who were hurting. Especially when gun violence is involved. Because I think for a long time I just really did not think about the fact that so many young black men were dying. And it almost seems as if these kids don't understand the magnitude of what's going on. For them, it's almost as if this is *normal.*

When you turn the light off at nighttime, this tent is really dark. There's that eerie feeling, that sense of nothingness. And I know this is going to sound strange, but sometimes when it's dark like that, I think about people who don't have electricity, and I think about when I grew up, how my mom couldn't afford things. So that's what I think about at night: "Man, this is lonely; it is cold; it's dark. How many people have to live this way?"

If you look north from here at night, you see the lights of the Loop. And there's been nights that I've been on the roof and all the street lights on King Drive have been turned off. And you think, here you have the bright lights downtown, with all the resources and all the things that make it beautiful and you're in the same city and it's almost, kinda like, in a different world—the haves and the have-nots.

I mean, everything in Chicago is divided. The educational resources are divided; that's the reason why you see the schools in one area better than the schools in another area. The police resources are divided; that's why you see higher crime in one area than you do in other areas. The economic resources are divided; that's the reason why you have an unemployment rate double in one area what it is in another area.[23] Obviously, there is still systemic racism. I don't think we can argue against it.

But before I came up here, I used to be really dogmatic about how government ought to do something. You know? Government, government, government. I still think government ought to do its part. But after getting away and thinking and reading, I realize that government can change laws, but they can't change hearts. It's always easier to change a law, but as we see even when they change the laws, nothing really changes around here. So changing hearts takes longer; it's harder work; it's a tougher task; it's more daunting. But when you change a heart, it lasts for eternity. So my thing now is to help change people's hearts.

There have been times when I get depressed, and I feel like it's taking too long to raise the money. I don't know if I blame it on God or on people or on circumstances. This is probably the first time I've ever said how I feel about it, but I sometimes think that if I were on the North Side and if I weren't black, I would have been on this roof a night at the most before somebody would have rushed to my aid.

But if I didn't have hope, I would not still be on this roof, that's for sure. Not after 87 days up here. If I didn't believe that things could get better, and if I didn't believe that I could help them to be better, I would definitely be on a beach in Miami or Jamaica or somewhere, enjoying myself. I hope and pray that I never get to a point to where I have a sense of hopelessness— because I think when you reach a sense of hopelessness, the next step is destruction, is doom.

A lot of times, people say they're gonna do things to make our community better, and they never end up doing it. And as a consequence, people lose a lot of hope. They get frustrated and disappointed and have broken dreams. That's why I want this place to be the Taj Mahal of community centers. I dream about it all the time. I dream about what I want it to look like. I dream about the programs we'll have there. I dream about the people that are gonna be there.

I see a facility that is cutting-edge, that is state-of-the-art and that is the prettiest building on the South Side of Chicago. I see a community and economic development center with entrepreneurial spaces for businesses to help create jobs so that people can sustain their families and take care of their children. I see a full recreation facility, a full theatrical facility and a full technology center. I see facilities where people can get counseling, do conflict resolution, develop life skills.

This motel—it was all about taking people's lives and destroying them. But the building that we're going to construct in its place is all about giving people life.

There's certain laws in the universe that apply to everybody: When you try to do good, you get good back. And in the end, I think that's what really happened, you know? I spent 94 days on the roof, and I then one morning I got a $100,000 gift from Tyler Perry.[24] I came off the roof that same day. It just happened so quick. There were so many emotions going on, it's hard to describe.

When I came off the roof that night, it was just people everywhere. Cameras, people, screaming, hollering. It was amazing. It was almost like a ghetto-MTV-type thing. I don't know what you call it. It was like an awards show, only we weren't in L.A. We weren't in Beverly Hills. We were on the South Side; we were in the 'hood. To be a part of something that had so much energy and excitement, and to see all the people in the streets, all different races, was amazing.

And when I got on the lift, I turned around and said, "Goodbye, tent."

And then we started going down.

It was a celebrative moment, but it was also a preparation moment, a check for myself to let me know: This is awesome, but this is not it; this is not the end.

It's not over.

Epilogue: After buying and tearing down the old motel, Pastor Brooks still needed another $15 million to build the community center. So in the summer of 2012, he walked all the way across the U.S. from New York to Los Angeles. He raised almost $500,000 on the trip, but as he puts it, "We still have a long way to go."

—*Interviewed by Miles Harvey*

ENDNOTES

18 West Point Missionary Baptist Church was founded in 1917. Brooks was pastor there from 1997 until 2000. See http://www.wpmbc.org/church-history/.

19 Bronzeville was a cultural hub for African-Americans who came to the South Side of Chicago during the Great Migration in the early 20th century.

20 The motel sits in what was once an overcrowded area known as the Black Belt. Most African-Americans in Chicago lived in this area until the mid-20th century, when legal restrictions that had kept them from moving to other neighborhoods were lifted.

21 On Dec. 27, 2011, Jawan Ross, 16, was shot and killed at a Church's Chicken on 66th and Halsted in the Englewood neighborhood. Dantril Brown, 17, was also killed in the shooting. Five others were wounded. See Tina Sfondeles, "Charges in Deadly Church's Shooting," *Chicago Sun-Times*, Dec. 31, 2011.

22 The second funeral was for Deontae Malone, 15, who was found shot to death just three blocks from his home in Marquette Park on the Southwest Side. See Brian Slodysko, "Boy's Fatal Shooting Called Part of 'Crisis': Student is Second from Same School Killed This Year," *Chicago Tribune*, Dec. 30, 2011.

23 In 2011, unemployment among African-Americans in Chicago was 21.4 percent. The city's average was 8.6 percent. See Mary Mitchell, "The Making of the 'Other' Chicago," online site of *The American Prospect*, March 18, 2013, http://prospect.org/article/making-other-chicago.

24 See Ryan Haggerty and Cynthia Dizikes, "Rooftop Vigil 'a Victory': 3-Month Stay Raises Nearly $500,000 to Buy Old Motel," *Chicago Tribune*, Feb. 25, 2012.

DON'T TRUST NOBODY

ORA THOMPSON

Ora Thompson—who requested a pseudonym—is a 17-year-old high school se-
nior from North Lawndale. Once prosperous, North Lawndale boasted over
140,000 residents in the 1960s. Its population drastically declined soon after,
however, when its primarily white residents fled from an influx of black new-
comers from Southern states and other parts of Chicago. Local industries even-
tually moved elsewhere, resulting in unemployment and poverty that still haunt
the area today.

As Ora talks, her expressive eyes dart around, conspicuous behind
thick-framed glasses. A textured bob frames her heart-shaped face. She shares
stories with ease, gesturing frequently and fully with her head, hands and long,
thin arms. Shifting in her chair often, she speaks quickly and uses emphatic
repetition.

Months from graduation from North Lawndale Preparatory Charter School,
Ora plans to study dance and theater at Illinois College in the small town of
Jacksonville, Illinois.[25] *In her free time, she participates in the Steppenwolf The-*
atre Young Adult Council, a selective, yearlong after-school program introducing
teens to professional theater. She is the only council member from North Lawn-
dale. Ora lives there with her mother and her three sisters.

North Lawndale. Something good? I've been living over there for 16 years,
and I really can't say something good about it. It's mostly apartment buildings. There's not really a lot of houses. Most of the buildings are abandoned.
You can tell a lot of people moved out of that area. It's a lot of vacant lots.
Three or four buildings on the block just got rebuilt. They tore them down
and rebuilt them again; I guess trying to attract new people to the neighborhood. If they're there for long, they're not gonna like it. They're not gonna
like it. You don't want to live somewhere where there's drug dealers selling
drugs right outside your house.

The route I take to school, there's drug dealers and crackheads on the
block. I leave out the back door, and it leads straight to my gate and then the
alley. There's garbage dumpsters right there, and I always see poor people—I
don't know if they're crackheads or not—but poor people digging in the
garbage, looking for food, clothes or whatever. And when I start turning the
corner, the same drug dealers are right there, early in the *morning*. Like, I be

going to school at seven, and they be out there, standing there. I just don't understand that. Then there's crackheads and hypes[25] walking past, getting the drugs from them. I just look and keep walking. I usually see people I went to grammar school with selling drugs too. I just don't understand that. Half of them were smart as ever. But down the block, it's basically that. Just drug dealers. And when I turn, it's my school right there.

There's a lot of drugs floating around North Lawndale. It's getting *bad*. There's so many crackheads on the block. I don't know if that's the right term I should use, but that's the only term I use when I'm in my community. I *hate* crackheads. I feel so much hatred towards them because I don't feel there's anything in life that can get you as low as starting crack. There's nothing. I mean, people gonna die regardless, you gonna lose your job, your house may go in foreclosure, but nothing can get as low as, "Yeah, I'm gonna start crack because of this. I'm gonna start crack because I'm depressed." Maybe I take that personally and I have anger towards them, 'cause once you start crack, you *end* your life to me. You end your life.

I know they would do anything for money, so I protect myself. When I go to and from school, I always carry a pocketknife because I don't feel *safe* around there. It don't matter where I'm at, but mainly around my area where I live, I'm always on guard. I carry a knife with me, even if I'm just going to the store. It's not sharp or nothing, and it's small enough, so if I pull it out, people wouldn't be like, "Oh my gosh, she got a knife!" They wouldn't see it until it's close up on them. I'm so serious! I carry it in my hand sometimes, and I put it in my sleeve so I'll be ready. If somebody's walking behind me, I reach in my pocket and hold it.

I will never forget the day I started carrying knives. I was still in grammar school. I think I was in eighth grade, and my sister was in fourth. We were walking to the store, and there was this man. He looked like he was in his late 30s. And he looked drunk. You know how people wear old clothes and stink? He looked like he was in that category. Out of nowhere, he just ran up to my little sister, grabbed her and picked her up. Then he was like, "I'm taking you home with me." I was *so* scared. I didn't know what to do. You don't joke with no kids like that, especially kids you don't know. And I just went up to him and started hitting him. I was like, "Put her down! Put her down!" When she got down, she was still shocked. She didn't know what was going on. So we didn't even go to the store; we just ran back to the house. I was scared to come out. For some weeks, I didn't even come out of the house.

Even though I know people in North Lawndale, and my mother knows people, I don't trust nobody in that community. There's been so many times where on the news the people that you're closest to hurt you, and I just don't trust nobody. I might laugh and talk to you, but I don't trust you.

I stay isolated because I don't like violence. It's to the point where people in my neighborhood fight over anything: boys, clothes, a seat, if you look at them a certain way. Our last house was right next to the projects, and there were these ladies—all of them were grown, and they got into it over a piece of gum. They actually fought over a piece of gum.

Certain people, they get excited off of violence. Fighting makes them happy. They fight just 'cause it's like a *game* to them. They fight just for more violence. I don't understand that. I think it's probably about personal problems—problems back at home that can't even be solved or anger that they can't take out on the people they wanna take it out on, so they just do little stuff to get into a fight.

I had a couple fights in my life, but I didn't do it for fun; I did it because I had to. I don't like fighting. I cry every time, every time I fight. I cry every time I fight. Even if I do win, I still cry. I don't know why. I get sensitive when that goes on. Maybe 'cause I'm scared because all through your life you're gonna have to fight people, no matter if it's over something major or something stupid, because people feel like they gotta prove themselves all the time. That pride comes before anything. I hate that. If you gotta prove yourself by fighting, then there's something wrong with you mentally. Really there is.

Recently I broke up a fight at my school between these two girls. I think they were juniors, and the problem wasn't between them. It was their two older sisters' brawls, and they brought the garbage to the school. They actually fought each other just because their big sisters told them to. Like, one sister probably said, "If you don't beat her butt, I'm beating your butt." It's crazy.

It was the quietest fight I ever seen. My locker is there, and I walked right into the fight. I'm so serious. I walked right into it. I didn't even know they were gonna fight 'cause I was switching classes, and people were just walking through the halls. Then it got real quiet. You know how everybody talks, and out of nowhere it just gets quiet for that two seconds? That's how it was. One girl was standing here, and the other one was right here. They were just staring at each other. All you heard was one girl say, "I'm finna zone-six this bitch"—basically beat her up. Then she just ran up and started hitting the other girl. They were fighting for like three minutes. People's hair got pulled out and everything. Everybody was shouting, "Beat that bitch ass!" Just everybody saying little stuff. That's all it takes to get loud in our school. They pull out their cameras. They be so thirsty to put it on Facebook and YouTube.

The thing is, they were fighting right in front of the counselor's office. That's an automatic three-day suspension. Why would you fight in front of the counselor's office? Crazy. And in the end, when one of the girls' mothers came up to the school, she didn't even say nothing. All she asked the girl was, "Did you win?" That's all she asked her. Wow, your mother condones you fighting, too?

I actually saw my mother fight once. I was *real* young, like 6 or 7. It was summertime, day, and my mama was coming to pick me up from my dad's house. My daddy's girlfriend was there with me. Truthfully, I loved my daddy's girlfriend as much as I loved my mother. I know it was wrong maybe because, I don't know, it seemed wrong to my mother. But I was young, and both of them cared for me and showed me love or whatever. Actually, there was one point where I thought both of them was my mama. I'm so serious. When I was young, I used to call both of them mama. But they didn't get along at all. At all!

So when my mama got there, she and my daddy's girlfriend started arguing. I don't know what the argument was about, but I knew it was over something stupid. Out of nowhere they just started fighting. Then glass was everywhere and I saw a lot of blood. It was on my dad's girlfriend's face and it was on my mother's back. I was just sitting right there watching. I just remember sitting on a little log, crying so hard. I was crying so hard because two people I loved were actually trying to kill each other—over what, though?

My dad came over and he started breaking it up. And I remember my grandma, she was there, too. She wasn't down there; she was at the window. Then she came downstairs. I remember little stuff. Little stuff. Maybe because I was crying. That's the stuff I remember. I remember my mom having glass in her back because there was an ambulance. She went to the hospital.

And when she went home, some days after that, she had this scar on her back. She still got this long scar on her back.

I brought it up a while ago to my mama, and she was like, "I can't believe you still remember that." Whatever, but I hate that day. If I was older, I know I would have tried to jump in and stop it. I was so scared. I was so scared. But now, they cool. They're friends. It's crazy, though, 'cause you go through all that and you could have just resolved it. If you knew in the future that y'all was gonna be friends, then what happened in the past was uncalled for. It really was.

My mother is not my role model. I don't think of her as that. I don't look up to my mother because she has her hand out way too much. It's to the point where she wants other people to do stuff for her, but she knows she wouldn't do it for herself. I don't understand that at all. If you want something, you gotta get it yourself. Don't depend on others. And that's all she does. I hate asking people for money. What's the point of that? You had your whole life to make your *own* money, start a career, do anything you wanted, and instead you just wasted it.

I don't really talk to nobody in my household. My mother turned into nothing, and my one older sister is slowly turning into nothing. I see my sister as a failure. For some reason she just can't get her life on track. She has so many opportunities, but she just don't take them. She just don't take them. She was a straight-A student, like she had good grades, everything, the whole ten. As she got older, she got more interested in boys and less in school, so in high school she continued to get F's. I still remember her coming home with F's on her progress report. I was still in grammar school, so she had me thinking, "When I get in high school, I'm gonna get F's too. The work is gonna be so hard." So, when I first went to high school, I thought the work was gonna be hard, but I saw it was easy. I just don't understand how she got F's. Whatever, she wasn't paying attention. She wasn't doing the work.

She didn't graduate on time, but actually, it wasn't too late for her. This school accepted her. They had a scholarship for her; she even won a laptop. And instead of taking the opportunity, she got pregnant by this dude I really don't like who sells drugs. I was mad. Even though that's my big sister, I was disappointed in her because she had her whole life back on track, and then she failed again. It's like every time she gets back on track, she finds something to distract her from what she doing. I noticed that. Every once in a while, she sees other people's lives, and she be like, "Oh, that's how I could have been," so she starts back with the little educational route. And then when she gets on it, she gets bored, so she goes back to her regular life. When she was little, all she would talk about was being a lawyer. And now she don't talk about being nothing.

It fascinates me, though, because when people are young, they have a lot of dreams. All I hear is people saying, "I wanna be this. I wanna be that," but they never break it down and say, "Okay, how am I gonna get there to become this?" Maybe 'cause they're young, and they think, "Well, I won't take this opportunity. I'm gonna get another opportunity later in life for the same thing." You gotta start off when you're young. I don't know, maybe it's the way I think.

People my age, their mind-set is way different from mine. I heard so many little girls and dudes my age who say they don't care about college. So they don't care what they do in school or outside of school. They know it's not going to affect them because they don't have a life after they leave high school. I feel sorry for them, actually. I feel sorry for them, because you're failing in high school and you don't wanna go to college? You messing your life up. Then, half of the girls at my school have kids. So, what's really your point? You gonna be living with yo' mama all your life? But when people first get into high school, or when they in grammar school, they don't think, "Yeah, when I get into high school, I'm gonna drop out." I mean who actually does that? Wait to graduate and then fail? They don't think like that. They just probably stop thinking.

For example, there's this girl at my school. She's the same age; she's 17 years old. And she recently had a baby by this dude. *He* looks like he could be my father. No lie. It's terrible. There's girls that actually talk to older dudes, saying, "He buy me stuff." You stupid! You would actually talk to an older dude because he buys you stuff and treats you like he cares about you? These girls don't *think* first.

And there's so many teenagers my age that's out there selling drugs, robbing people, and their siblings do the same thing. There's this 13-year-old boy. He goes to school with my little sister, and he's out there selling drugs. He steals from his mama, and he tried to steal his sister's Xbox game, that she got for Christmas, and pawn it for some money. Yeah, that little boy got his nerve. His big brother, Darryl,[27] sells drugs, and I guess that what got him turned on to it.

Darryl and I have been friends since fifth grade. Through grammar school, it's like I already knew how his life was gonna be by the way he acted. But he's easy to talk to. That's probably why I was friends with him. As he got older, he still acted the same, but it's like he matured just a *little* bit, maybe just a drop. His mother is not his real mother. His real mother is on drugs, and his sister got killed three or four years ago in a car crash right outside their house. He was real messed up by that. He still be talking about her to this day every now and then. He always has this certain look on his face when he talks about his sister 'cause his sister was like a mother figure to him. Probably adds to why he act like that. But I feel he could change for his little brother.

The people around you—family, friends—if all of them bad, and you're around them 24/7, most likely you're going to engage in what they're doing. 'Cause "your chance of success depends on the five people you hang with," my counselor said to all the seniors in the school. So I don't hang with a lot of people. Instead, I just watch people a lot to learn stuff from them. You don't know—seems like I'm listening or watching? I am. 'Cause it's just the little things that people do that tell you a lot about themselves.

I don't do this in school, 'cause people would think I'm crazy, but when I'm in my room alone, I just sit and talk to myself about stuff, like, all the stuff I *know* I *could* be, and then start brainstorming. I always connect it back to school. Right now, I graduate in June, and all I'm really thinking about is leaving. I wanna do all the work I have to do in order to graduate. I *owe* it to myself. I deserve to graduate on time. Not with the rest of them kids. That can't be me. I'm trying to get up outta here.

—*Interviewed by Bethany Brownholtz*

ENDNOTES

25 In the fall of 2012, we contacted Ora to see how things were going at Illinois College. She reported that small-town life in Southern Illinois had proven to be something of a culture shock. "It's just cows and farms everywhere," she said with a laugh. "To be truthful, I thought I wasn't gonna like it. But I was so wrong. It's like a variety of different ethnicities there. It's like so many Africans, it's a lot of Latinos, whites, blacks. It's just like a mix of everybody and, at that school, everybody's so nice.

"The crazy part is that, as soon as I got out of Chicago, I stopped carrying that knife. I put it all inside this little red box where I keep my change. I don't carry it with me on campus at all, even when it's nighttime. My sister, she's a freshman at North Lawndale Prep and has to walk to school. She can have my knife. I'm serious."

Ora noted that although she received a large scholarship to attend college, her mother has never said she was proud of her daughter. "I don't like talking about her," she said. "She's the reason why I just want to go so far away from home. She's the main reason."

26 A hype is an addict.

27 Ora asked that we change her friend's name to protect his safety.

MEET THE JUJU-MAN

JULIAN

When we visit 9-year-old Julian at his house on the Northwest Side, he seems like any other kid with a passion for skateboarding. "I was going up the ramp, and I was like, 'Ahhh,'" he says, motioning with his hands to illustrate his adventures at a skate park. "I would be like this high in the air!"

But Julian's childhood has been anything but normal since Halloween night of 2009. That's when his brother Manuel "Manny" Roman was shot in Humboldt Park while driving with another brother, Damian. Twenty-three-year-old Manny was on life support for several weeks, until his parents decided to allow him to die. He left behind a wife, an unborn daughter and twin sons. Police—who say that the attack was unprovoked and that Manny and Damian were innocent victims—filed charges against Andrew Ruiz, a paraplegic gang member with a lengthy criminal record. As this book went to press, the case was still awaiting trial.

When Julian's mother, Myrna Roman, tells the story of the murder and its aftermath, tears fill her eyes as Julian jumps in to console her. Afterward, the energetic and articulate boy settles in the kitchen. Occasionally breaking his story to hum or draw or play with a tiny toy skateboard, Julian begins to discuss life without Manny.

Can I show you something? It's in my backpack. You'll probably think it is just a binder, but I will tell you the story. I know I kind of doodled on it, but I will always, always, always treasure this binder. This is the last thing Manny gave me on the day he died.

Manny was like "Hey Juj!"—he called me Juj that time—"Come here! Come here!" I said, "What's up?" And he was like, "Here."

"What's this?"

"You'll see."

I opened the binder. It had nine basketball cards inside. Ron Mercer, Magic Johnson… He gave them to me. It was the last thing he ever gave anybody. After we left, we started collecting candy. Then we went to dinner. He went out. He died. Simple as that. I treasure this binder like it is my brother.

My name is Julian, my nickname is Juju, my nickname for my nickname is Juju-man. And my nickname for my nickname for my nickname is Juj. I am 9. I am in fourth grade at a Montessori school. It is not like schools you watch on TV. I like it because it is a unique school, and I'd rather be unique than normal. Normal schools have desks and get tests every day. This school we get a table with chairs and a work plan.

I like the kids I go to school with, but not all of them. Some of them are bullies. One of them walks to the corner, right? My grandma and I passed by, and we saw him with a bunch of other kids, and their underwears were coming out. I could tell they were bad by the way they sag their pants and act like bullies. Becoming gangbangers, that scares kids.

One time I was at school, right? I saw these kids playing basketball or whatever. This one kid wanted to play, and they denied him. Simple as that. Like, "No!" Just because the way he was. No one really likes him, except for me. I didn't really do anything to stop it, but I helped him. I told him, "Hey, come here! Come play with us." That's what I did.

I know this for a *fact*. Bullying starts off with a push, then somebody gets addicted. Then it starts being a bunch of bullies and being a gang. A mini gang, then becoming a big gang. Then they get older and become real gangbangers. So it starts from something small to huge. Either way, if you become a part of a gang you are just kidding yourself.

I could explain the day Manny got shot like it was just a moment ago. It was Halloween, and I think I was The Scream. But I am not a hundred percent sure. That day, I was like, "Oh my God, it's Halloween! It's Halloween! It's Halloween!" Then we set sail. Me, my grandma, my mom, my dad and my two cousins went trick-or-treating, along with Manny and his two sons. Manny was nothing that year. One person thought he was, what do you call that? They thought his Halloween costume was a "cute guy." It was funny.

One of Manny's sons had a hole in his bag and candy would go right down to the sidewalk. Well, some of it stayed in the bag, but not all of it. It was our trail. We ate dinner. I don't remember where, but I remember it was Puerto Rican food. I had pork chops and stuff like that. We had extra time because the adults were eating slow, so we started eating some candy. Then we decided to go home.

My mom said, "Hey, Manny, would you like to hang out with your friends tonight?"

And Manny was like, "Yeah, sure."

Then he jerked back. Like, you know the dance "the jerk"? He went like that, and then he walked away, wearing blue stripes, black hoodie and a white T-shirt. We were just on the side of the houses. That was the last time I ever saw him normal.

We all went home, and we all went to bed: me, my mom and my dad. Manny went out, and they drove to the gas station, then *boom, boom*. I heard, *roo-daa-loo*; that was our old phone call. It just kept calling, calling, calling, calling, calling, calling.

Dad was like, "What the—" And then he went to pick it up, and he was like, "Hello?" It was my older brother on the phone. He was like, "Damian just got shot! Manny, too! Manny, too!"

Then my dad started yelling, "Tell me what happened." Sort of talking deep. I wasn't sleeping. I was in my room, lying down, and I heard a bunch of yelling. I started listening. They went to the hospital, and my uncle came over before they left. I just saw him looking at the TV. It was scary. And the next morning, I heard about it. I don't remember how…I don't remember when they told me. All I remember is thinking, "Manny got shot. … Manny got shot. … Manny got shot."

I was there the last day he was alive. Or the day he was going to die. I was there the day that they said they were going to unplug it. To let him go. It's sad, man. Just sad.

I heard my mom talking about Manny's shooter. The night he shot Manny, he had an argument with somebody; I think it was his girlfriend. And he said, "Someone is going to die tonight." He went in a car, and went around looking in windows of other cars that people were driving. He pulled out a gun at some people and they said, "No, no, no, it's me!" Because it was someone he knew, someone from the 'hood. He kept going. Then he saw Manny. Somebody was like, "Look, look, look!"—trying to point to the shooter. Manny was good-looking, so he thought it was a girl trying to say hi and stuff like that. He smiled at her. He got shot right there, in the back of the neck. *Pow*. Simple as that. Makes no sense. Anger, jealousy, greed and bullies. Doesn't make any sense. I mean, I don't understand why. You kill them, for what? You see them? They dress nice? You shoot them? Really? It is greed and jealously. A lot of people get greedy. You can't just shoot him because you *think* he's in a gang.

I really didn't know how bad it was until afterward. Before Manny got shot, I didn't really notice there was violence. I knew there was violence, but not bad like that. Then I started paying attention and I was like, "What?" I started reading articles because of my homework: *Forty-nine people got shot this weekend.*[28] I'm like, "Are you kidding me?" It gets me so pissed off. Violence is never the answer. If you want someone's territory, buy it. But, either way, you don't *need* anyone's territory. You don't need money to go into a neighborhood. Like, I could just drive into Indiana. Do we have to fight over the whole Indiana or can we just drive right into it? It's stupid stuff.

Everywhere I go, I always am a little bit of scared. I'm scared right now. Even when I'm in my own house. When I go to sleep, I'm scared. Whenever there is a moment of silence, I am scared. That reminds me. Like, a couple of times at my grandma's house, I heard *vroom-vroom*, and I heard yelling and people arguing. When there is people yelling at each other, that is when I'm most scared. And I always hear, like, an ambulance and cops going by non-stop. Like, really? Can there be a day when there is *no violence?* Why are you guys killing each other? It doesn't make sense. I mean are they just killing each other for fun? Go out and play video games about that stuff.

I'm not scared of ever joining a gang. I know I am smarter than others. I get straight A's all the time. Why would I join a gang if my brother died by a gang? I am smarter than that. I was never a bad person and I don't want to be a bad person. I don't ever want to become bad in any way. Why would you be bad just to become better than everyone? Kind of like a popularity contest type thing. I would rather be the most hated kid in America to stop violence.

I like to sing and dance. I got that from Manny. I think I'm better at dancing than singing. I'm like James Brown. I am not one of those people who just sings. I'm one of those people who *dances*.

I'd say I am creative, an epic, *epic* gamer and a big dreamer. I'm a big dreamer because every day I come up with something different. Like, if I'm thinking about Manny, which I do just about every day, I'm thinking… thinking…thinking…then *boom*, I think about becoming a doctor, because a doctor can always make a difference. I want to do whatever I can to make the world better. You know what? I think they should stop making guns in the first place. I mean, because without a gun, the guy can't shoot nobody. I mean there are people legally selling guns on the street, right?[29] If that is true, I'm not sure if it is, but if it's true, why would you give them a permit for it? Even if only one bad guy got the guns himself, and said, "I'll sell these guns…Here." *Pow, pow, pow, pow.* Like, really? I mean, I *have* to blame the bad guys, but I sometimes don't blame the bad guys. I mean, I don't 100 percent blame the bad kids. I blame them for shooting them in the first place, but I also blame a couple of other people for, like, giving them the guns and making the guns.

If I could make a law, it would be that everybody can go into anybody's neighborhood if they wanted to. They will have rights. Like, you can't just say you can't go in here because you don't live here. That's stupid, that's why. I mean, it just doesn't make sense. Why don't you stop the whining and just walk into the neighborhood and don't be all gangster? *Just walk.*

Do you see that picture right there wearing the Gap sweatshirt? That was me when I was a baby. Me on top of my brother Manny. You know how brothers are sometimes just brothers? We had a dream of becoming best friends, too. We were already friends, but we wanted to become best friends as brothers. One day, he was downstairs mixing music and I ran down there to tell him to lower it, because my dad told me to. I went downstairs, and he said, "We could mix some music, and we should play some Xbox, and just do it all day." And I said, "Cool." That dream never got to happen. I was crushed. That's why I say, "Killing *kills* dreams."

—Interviewed by Monica Schroeder

ENDNOTES

28 On the weekend of March 16-18, 2012, a total of 49 people were shot citywide, 10 fatally. See Ashley Rueff, Jeremy Gorner and Jason Meisner, "Shooting Death of Girl, 6, Marks Lethal Weekend," *Chicago Tribune,* March 20, 2012.

29 The city outlawed the sale and possession of handguns in 1982. In 2010, the U.S. Supreme Court threw out the handgun ban, saying it was in violation of the Second Amendment. In 2012, the city rewrote its firearms ordinance, but gun stores within city limits remain outlawed. This has not, of course, kept guns out of the city. Police confiscate an average of about 10,000 firearms each year. See Geoffrey Johnson, "Bullet Proof," *Chicago Magazine,* September 2012, 30.

LIKE WALKING THROUGH BAGHDAD

DESHON McKNIGHT

Marillac House—a social outreach center for the poor and the working poor—is located in East Garfield Park on an inconspicuous side street right off the Eisenhower Expressway. Established in 1947 by the Daughters of Charity, Marillac originally served a mostly white clientele. By 1960, however, the neighborhood had become mostly African-American. In the 1970s and 1980s, poverty and unemployment consumed the area, triggering a surge of drug and gang activity.

Nineteen-year-old Deshon McKnight, who grew up in the nearby neighborhood of Austin, sits on a sofa within the Marillac House waiting room. His mannerisms are polite and reserved; his tattooed arms seem at odds with his clean-cut style of dress. His face is young, but his expression is intently serious, his gaze straight and unwavering. Born into a gang-affiliated family, Deshon speaks about the dangers of his neighborhood with deep and mature insight. His words are unpolished, honest and poetic. Every syllable and inflection feels deliberate.

What I remember from being little is gunshots every night. Being in the house before the streetlights come on 'cause that's when all the action happens. Don't stray too far from the block. It was like my childhood was *contained*. The only time I would go out, the only time I would get a chance to go out—our parents had to take us out. Because, like, it wasn't that safe to go outside or ride the bikes, or go outside and play basketball, or play hide-and-go-seek. I never really got a chance to, like, hang out at the park, play at the park, with all the other kids. I couldn't do that. That's in the enemy's territory, and my mom didn't want anything happening to me. So basically, my life was playing video games.

When you hear gunshots, the first thing they tell you is get on the floor. And they cut all the lights off. I don't know why they cut all the lights off; I never got that point. But I understood why to get on the floor, in case a bullet came through the window. But, like, one day, when I was about 9 or 10, me and my mom was watching TV in the front room, and we heard gunshots. So she instantly pushes me on the floor and she runs to the back to make sure all the other kids on the floor. But while she was doing that, I creep to the window, and I peek out. And I just see, like, a guy on this side of the street, and a guy on the other side of the street, I just see them, like, shooting at each other. Shooting at each other.

Then I see more guys run out shooting, more guys from the other side, coming out shooting. Then the police came on the block—and I just see my older cousin, running. He running upstairs, and then he get in the hallway, and he fall—because he got shot in his leg, and he got shot in his ear, and there's just blood everywhere. So I'm like, I don't know what's going on, but that shocked me. You see all the blood, you see how much pain he in, and you like, "This a grown man. He's right here. He sounds like he's crying." So you don't want that. You scared. You don't know what'll happen to you if you go outside.

After that, I was just more cautious. I was suspicious of everybody. I was basically paranoid. I'm still like that now, but when I was little it was even worse. Because there's people that knew my name, that I didn't know. They know me because of my parents, so I don't know if... Is this the enemy talking or one of my dad's friends speaking to me? So I would just turn my head down and act like I don't hear them.

I got a gun when I was 13. The chiefs of the block, the upper generals of the block, they buy the guns. And as soon as you walk up there on the street, they gonna tell you that you going to need one. They say "You protected?" And you be like, "No" and they be like, "Hold up" and they give you their gun, and they'll go get another one. It's that simple.

I don't have a gun anymore, but I used to keep it in a shoebox. Or, then I had got me a tackle-box, like fish tackle-box, and I put a lock on it because I know my little brothers come in my room to play. And I would slide it under the far end of my bed, and I'd throw some dirty clothes on it or something, to make it look just like my room's junky.

I was basically dragged into gangbanging. Because if you related to this person, and they in a gang, their enemies are going to assume that you're in a gang, too. Like, so, you get forced into it. You have no choice. You got to protect yourself somehow. You gotta...if you out there by yourself, if you not claimed by a gang...basically, that gang is not going to help you. If this other gang attacks you, because they think you in a gang, you out there by yourself. You're out there alone.

The area I live in has always been rough. That violence—everything just got out of hand. The streets aren't really safe no more, like there's more gun violence, more gang violence, drug violence. People getting beaten half to death—or beaten to death. This side of the street don't like that side of the street. I don't know why, it's just been like that all this time.

When I walk at night, it's like walking through Baghdad or something. You don't know when somebody might pop out or shoot at you. I was standing, and the streetlights all got cut off for some reason—every now and then they get cut off. When that happens, that's when everybody starts shooting.

One time, somebody shot in my grandma's house and a bullet missed two inches from my head. Hit the couch pillow. Another time, when I was 19 years old, I was at my house, and my mom was around the corner at my grandmother's house. I was in the house playing a game. I heard the gunshots, but they sound far away, so I can't really tell where they coming from. So I'm thinking, they could probably be coming from over there by my grandma's block. So I'm like, "Nobody's really getting to it, so what could have happened?" As I'm walking up the street, I see one of my friends and I ask him, "Did you hear some gunshots coming from this direction?" He was like, "Yeah, they was shooting on your grandma's block." So as I was walking down there, I was thinking in my head, "Please, nobody hurt. Nobody shot."

But it was my mom. She was just sitting on the porch. They just came right through, shooting. At first we thought she was shot in her stomach—though later we realized she got shot in the hand. So everybody's mad and angry and upset. Then everybody just went looking for guns.

It escalated to a big, all-out war. They would come by and shoot inside my grandma's house. All the windows were shot out, with bullet holes in the walls. None of the kids could stay there because of what happened, so we had to get them out. But my grandma—they still stayed, I don't know why, but luckily nothing ever happened to them. They come, they shoot, and then we'll go back and shoot at them.

Nobody knows what the original argument is. It's been like that for years. Since my parents, it's been like that. Since my mom lived there, nobody on that side of the street likes this side. And my mom told everybody to leave it alone, let the police handle it. We were just leaving it alone because she said it. But they kept shooting at us.

It's basically all about territory. In this neighborhood, all the gangs be on the same block. There's Vice Lords on this block, Latin Kings on the other block—each block got their own gang. Whether you gangbang or not, if they see you on that block, they gonna assume you a Vice Lord or something, especially if you a male. They're just going to assume.

Because you can't really tell who's affiliated by looks alone. You can't do it. There's a lot of drug dealers that wear baggy clothes, like baggy jeans. Then you see these guys who are wearing skinny jeans. Some of the dudes in skinny jeans don't like the baggy clothes, and some of those guys wearing the baggy clothes styles don't like skinny jeans. Clothes don't matter. You gonna try to have something with your gang color in it. You could have on a whole green outfit and you gonna put on some red shoes because your gang color is red. That's how it goes. So it's like a fashion thing.

Police don't understand that. Just because you have your hat cocked a certain way, that don't necessarily mean that you're in a gang now—that's more of the style. Everybody cock their hat now, just to be doing it. Justin Bieber be cocking his hat, but the police aren't calling him a Vice Lord.

The police can only help so much, though. They can't catch every bad guy, every person with a gun, every person committing a crime—they can't catch everybody. It got to be an internal thing. There's got to be a person saying that they want to make a change. People know what they're doing is not right. They know deep inside it's not right. But still, that's the path they choose. It's got to be an internal thing for you to have your own change. Because if you don't change, who's going to change? You got to set an example for somebody.

I didn't have a lot of examples of my own. All the dads in my family are either dead, in jail or hang with gangs. It's like no real fathers around, just mostly stepfathers. We don't have a dad. All my cousins, brothers, friends— all of them, same thing. My dad's a deadbeat. My brother, his dad got killed. That was my stepfather—that was who I called my dad. He got killed. My little brother—my youngest brother—his dad is engaged to my mom, so he's around. My little sisters—one of my little sisters' dad, he's around. But my other little sister—we share the same dad—he's not around. One of my cousins, his daddy's in jail. His brother's dad lives in Atlanta. He's a dead-beat. His older brother, his dad's in jail. And my cousin, his dad's in jail. His dad's a deadbeat, just like mine. That's something all of us have in common. We joke about it, but it hurt us, you know what I mean? We joke, "Ah, our daddies ain't nothing." We laugh about it, but we not really laughing, we're just expressing ourselves to each other. We don't want to seem like a bunch of wimps. We're telling each other "You're not alone in this."

I don't want my daughter to feel like she's alone in the world. I want to be there when she needs me. I know how it felt to not have a father and my biggest fear is that I fail her. I don't want to become like my dad.

I made high school rough for myself because I stopped going and started getting in with a tough crowd. I'd be on my way to school, uniform on, everything, And I'd get a phone call, like, "Oh, you wanna go play ball?" Or, "Do you want to hang out?" And I'd just ditch school and go with them. That was their life, the streets. It was all they knew.

But I just decided to start over. I missed out on the last semester, so I had to do my senior year over. I told myself, "No matter what, I'm going to keep going." I got my diploma in 2010. I'm the older child, and I didn't want my little brothers to see me not graduating. I felt like I was letting them down by not going to school. And I didn't want them to go the same route I was heading.[30]

I hate when you see someone fighting for their goals, for what they want to be and then they die or something happens to them. Broken dreams. Like, their dreams was broken and other people see that, and they'll be like, "Don't let that happen to me." And I'm like, "What should I fight for? What goals should I set for myself, besides staying alive?"

Like, my cousin Danta. His goal wasn't to be someone big or whatever— he was a drug dealer, he always been a drug dealer, since he was like 10. His goal was to go back to school. He told me he wanted to go back to school. He was supposed to start on a Monday. But he was killed that Sunday.

I feel like I just got to take life day by day. How many days can I get out of it? Nowadays, people my age, they're not going to live that long. Every night, I just felt like I don't know when it's going to be my time to go. I hear about it on the news: A guy my age that lived down the street from me was killed. That could have been me.

People who aren't from here don't have no clue about how intense it is. They gonna go by what they see on TV or what they read on the paper. But to really understand how intense the violence is you got to be living in it. You got to be part of the danger.

—*Interviewed by Colleen Wick*

ENDNOTES

30 Deshon reports that he now works the overnight shift at Target.

GOD, ARE YOU TRYING TO GET MY ATTENTION?

JORGE ROQUE

Residents of Little Village sometimes refer to their Southwest Side neighborhood as the "Mexico of the Midwest." A tiled, terra-cotta gateway over 26th Street, adorned with the welcome-greeting "Bienvenidos," has served as the point of entry for generations of Chicano immigrants to the city.

Little Village has a rich cultural life, bustling business district and proud heritage, but like many inner-city neighborhoods, it is plagued by street gangs, with the Latin Kings and the Gangster Two-Six Nation locked in a bloody and long-running rivalry.

Now 36, former Two-Six member Jorge Roque barely survived his teen years in Little Village. These days, he devotes himself to getting other young people off the streets. When we interviewed him in 2011, he was working as program coordinator for the YMCA's Street Intervention Program, an anti-gang effort with a presence in 11 of Chicago's at-risk communities.[31] The barrel-chested Roque has the hard look of someone who has known more than his share of tough situations. But as he tells his story, there's calm in his voice and compassion in his eyes.

Everything behind the gang is fake. It's people wearing masks, guys wearing different masks because they have to cover the pain that they're going through, the pain that they have in their lives. And, for me, that was maybe a fake type of love and acceptance, but it was that camaraderie between street soldiers. I always tell people, "Do not judge if you've never been there. Or if you've never tasted from that." Because I've seen gangbanging and drug dealing. It's an adrenaline—it's a rush. It's like a drug. It's an addiction of feeling that you're someone. Because everyone's looking for that acknowledgement and acceptance. That was that one missing thing in our lives.

I was born in El Paso, Texas, and raised here. In 1977, when I was 1, my parents brought me here to Chicago. I guess my father had been coming back and forth to the States from Juarez. He ended up traveling from out of the West Coast and finally touching down here in Chicago and liking Chicago for whatever reason. Liking the snow, I guess. And the first community that they ended up in was Little Village. So they stayed there for at least seven years, renting an apartment there on 22nd and Albany.

My parents saved up some money and they were able to buy their first home, like in 1982 or 1983, in we call it the suburbs of Little Village, which is west of Pulaski. But growing up in Little Village, from 1983 on, by Komensky, that was my block. I had my grammar school there, at Whitney Elementary. We never really left Little Village. My parents love this neighborhood, this community. They still own that house.

But with the beauty of the neighborhood of Little Village, there was the other side. The dark side of Little Village, when it came to the gangs and drugs and just the violence, the youth violence, the street violence, kind of impacted my life as I was growing up there. There were not too many of the role models that I wanted to look up to. Because I believe it's a choice of who you choose to hang with, be around.

The guys that I was kind of looking up to in my teenage years were the guys on the street corner. Instead of looking up to the doctors and lawyers, and the young women and young men that were going to college or university, I kind of chose the fast lane, the fast lifestyle of just, you know, the drugs and the money. And just what it offers: that package of making it easier and living a lot faster, and growing up faster as you experience violence.

And so at one time in my life, I decided that I just didn't want to be an outsider. I made the choice myself, that I wanted to be part of a street organization in Little Village. Some people say, "Well, you can blame your parents." But I had both parents. I come from a strong family of hard workers. My father worked long hours to provide and purchase a home.

But it's also true that I saw a lot of violence within my home. I got to experience a lot of infidelity within my father, got to see a lot of domestic violence, got to see the alcohol problems that he had and just the mistreatment that my mom experienced. I remember, you know, my dad just coming home at just two or three in the morning and wanting my mom to cook for him. I remember going to the bars in the neighborhood, in Little Village, looking for my dad—me, personally, at the age of 6 or 7, telling Dad to come home. I got to meet a lot of his girlfriends as a young kid.

I'm not going to say I blame my parents' issues or problems at home on the way I turned out. But I know it did affect me. I started to build a lot of anger towards my father. When you're growing up as a Mexican father, parent, you're brought up thinking macho. You know? And you can't cry, you can't show emotions, and you can't hug your child or give him a kiss or give him words of affirmation and just say, "Man, I'm proud of you."

That's the environment that I was growing up in. And not knowing how to deal with that anger was just building and building inside of me to the point that, I just didn't care no more about my father. I didn't care for my dad. I hated my dad. There was a time in my life where I wanted to kill my dad, when I started hitting my teenage years. And I started standing up for my mom. One time, I went at him and I hit him with a bat and he hit me with a two-by-four. This is a kind of violence that we both experienced with each other. But that was the last time that he hit my mom, because I stood up for my mom. And so I went through a period in my life where I got involved with the street gang in Little Village. That's where I learned to let out a lot of my aggression and anger.

I did my thing. I wasn't really into the drug dealing. I'm not a good salesperson. I'm not a good marketer, and so I did other things to make money. I didn't steal. I didn't like stealing cars or car rims and stuff, but some other people make money stealing radios. I made some of the money dealing weaponry. Because, part of this lifestyle, there's weekly meetings you have to go. There's your weekly dues you have to pay, just like being part of the Rotary Club, you know? You have to pay your weekly dues when you're part of that.

What I don't want people to think is that gang members are just monsters and they're out to just get anyone or anybody. There are rules and regulations at each gang and bylaws that they have to abide by. And so some of these street gangs do not let you steal in your own neighborhood, do not let you tag or write in your own neighborhood. Of course, you've got some renegade youth out there that don't follow rules, but there are consequences for breaking some of those bylaws.

So I was lost for a while. I was blinded in believing that that was the right way in dealing with your personal issues or the way of coping with things in your life. But you know what? My mom wouldn't give up. I was out there on the street corner, and she would stand out there until I came home. So my friends didn't want me out there. They would say, "Leave already. You'd better run home. Your mom's coming. Your mom's going to stay out here on the street corner with us."

And my mom would be like, "Either you let him go, or I'm going to stand out here with you guys and not let you guys do your activities, whatever those were."

And they'd go, "Mrs. Roque, we promise you your son—we'll have him there in 30 minutes." They knew my mom by her name.

And she'd go, "Thirty minutes, guys. If he don't come home, I'm going to come right back!"

It was like my mom became one of the enforcers. She's one of the reasons I started getting away from gangbanging.

There's this one corner, I was out there one night and a rival gang member passed by. He saw me out there, me and my friend that were on that corner saw him coming, and we knew what gang they were from. They passed by and I threw a brick through their window and dented up their hood. And there's one individual who I did that to, he was known as a killer, as one of those crazy killers. And they chased me.

There's a thing called security out there, so supposedly we had security. We got individuals in gangways or on corners with guns protecting, making sure that any intruders don't come in, and then they react. And at that moment, our security supposedly was just on something different that night. I tell my friend, "Run, run, run!" And so he runs and he tries to jump the fence and I try to jump the fence, and I get caught up in the fence. My shoelaces get stuck on the fence.

And so this individual that I did the damage to his car, he looked at me, and he goes, "Man, you're just, you're just a kid." And his friends there were like, "Who cares? Who cares? Look at what he did to the car. Look at what he did!" He was in his 20s, I was in my teens. I was about 15 at the time. And he had the gun to my head. His guys were like, "Man, kill him. Man, look at what he did to your car!" And for whatever reason—you know, that's why I say God works in mysterious ways—one of my friends was passing by and he jumps out with a weapon. He's like, "Don't shoot him! Don't shoot him!" He was the brother of my friend that was with me on the corner running.

Earlier that day, that same day, I remember my mom and my dad telling me, "Don't go out." And so I thought of my mom's words, you know: "I dreamt you were in a coffin. I dreamt you were dead." Her words start, in my mind, and I'm like, "I'm going to die here."

And so while they're negotiating, I get away, I cut loose. And all my guys, the guys on security, came out and they're all trying to negotiate. We knew them from the neighborhood so we grew up around them, around this gang. And so they did not shoot, they did not kill me, thank God.

I ran home that night, telling my mom, "Mom, I almost got killed" with tears in my eyes, remembering her words. And she's like, "Don't worry, you're alive. But what about you taking some time off from the community, from the neighborhood? I talked to your uncle today. And I was telling him all the things you were going through." And he's in Kansas, but she's like, "Go for a month! Get away. Think about what you're doing to yourself. Think about getting some breathing space."

Liberal, Kansas. Small. Where they filmed *Wizard of Oz*. They have a museum of *Wizard of Oz* there. I arrive there, and I'm looking around, and you've got to understand, I know the city, the big city. But all I saw was nothing but wheat fields. Nothing but wheat fields.

Then my uncle tells me, "There's rules here. We don't have women here, so guess who's going to do the cooking, who's going to do the laundry? We go to church here at my house two times a week." I looked at him like, "Are you crazy?" I mean, I only went to church three times a year: Easter, Thanksgiving and Christmas. So I always say that I was in my uncle's boot camp. Because what my own father should have maybe taught me, he taught me. He became a very, very important person in my life.

My clothes—I was still in my street uniform. This was before hip-hop culture hit, so I was wearing long socks, cut-off baggies to my knees, and Chucks—Converse All-Stars. I went to my uncle's church dressed that way, but people accepted me the way I was, and they allowed me to be myself. I liked that. Because I was so used to so many churches in the city closing their doors on us—just because maybe them not understanding the young Latino culture, especially the street culture, the gang culture. And over there in Kansas, they treated me so different.

I spent close to a year there, and I learned a lot. They talked about a loving God, a God who doesn't judge, a God who's about equality and respect and justice. They showed it and that they practiced it. And they practiced it with me. Knowing where I was coming from, knowing my background, knowing how I looked on the outside shell, and they still didn't see me any different.

I felt this big load on me. I was at the church on New Year's. The preacher was preaching that we only go to God when we need Him. And he was saying, "Any one of you who is right now hurting and wants to experience that loving God, come to the altar. Who's tired of their way of living?" I didn't know that God. I wanted to feel that peace. I wanted to forgive my dad. I wanted to get rid of the anger towards him. And I wanted to even forgive myself because of what problems I might have caused to others, guys that were hurt, you know. I wanted to be forgiven from that, and I wanted to feel that peace and joy that they were talking about. I remember being at the altar for like three or four hours, crying and sobbing and just letting God know to forgive me. It was like a relief. It was like this thing came out of me, like a thousand pounds came off my shoulder.

I ended up coming back to Chicago in spring of 1993, when I was just turning 17, and I told my mom, "Ma, find a church, because we're going to church." I got to Chicago, and she found a church right around the corner, a Baptist church. I started going there and I started getting involved in the youth group. For six months, I was doing very well. I started going to GED classes, because they had kicked me out of Kelly High School for fighting.

I told my friends, "You know what, guys? I'm going to just focus on school, my education and church."

And a lot of them were like, "Man, why you want to get out when you recruited us? You got us into this." There was a lot of pressure. Then, my youth pastor at the time, he fell. The guy that I looked up to so much, he slipped. He was going to get divorced from his wife. And that discouraged me. I was a baby believer, you know, and so I was new to this stuff. I did not stop going to church, but I started slipping myself.

I caught myself holding guns again on the block with these guys. But I did not feel happy. It was hard because I had experienced that change. And so it was like me taking 10 steps back. I wasn't happy doing it. I didn't have peace. I couldn't sleep. But I never stopped going to church.

And then one night, something happened that made me say, "You know what? Somebody's trying to get my attention here." Four guys got shot right in front of my mother's house. Good friends of mine.

It was just part of the retaliation back and forth between the Two-Sixes and the Latin Kings that had been happening for decades. We're talking about a war that's been going on from the late '70s, the '80s, '90s, until the present. It's a war that's gone on for like four or five decades. And it's been retaliation after retaliation.

I was in my mom's house. I had just gotten in. It was about two or three in the morning, and these guys were all standing two houses away. It was real loud. A drive-by, a real crazy drive-by. Two cars. They unloaded like three or four guns on my friends. And then one of my friends ran, and just fell in front of my mom's house. And the other guy was in a gangway, shot up. They got hit with deer slugs. Like, the 30-30 bullets.

Everybody came out, my mom, everybody. She's like, "Don't go out, don't go out." But I came out because I seen my friend lying there. We were grabbing the guys who got shot and putting the bodies in cars and taking them to the hospital. You wait for the ambulance, and some of these guys are going to die.

One of them was very critical and it looked like he was going to lose his life. He's alive. He pulled through. But that was the night where I said, "Lookit, man—God, are you trying to get my attention?" And ever since then, I've come a long way.

Staying in Little Village after I left the gang was the hard part. Imagine, coming from church and my friends making fun of me with my Bible in my hand. "Ha ha ha! Look at you, church boy." Imagine the pressure. I used to make guys do things when I was in the gang, and now they're making fun of me! My old friends from the neighborhood, man. But guess what? I went through it. I went through the pressure and the temptations.

I get emotional after all these years because a lot of my friends are coming back around and now they're helping me, they're supporting me. The guys with influence are making my job a little easier. In 2010, we were able to detach 10 youths from the gang. And so it's like, yeah we work with 60-something youth, but people may say, 10 youth? Even if I have one youth leave the gang, that's something.

A lot of people get stuck in gang life. A lot of my friends are locked up and shot up. But I knew I was created for something better—to help people, not hurt people.

—Interviewed by Miles Harvey

ENDNOTES

31 Roque left the YMCA shortly before this book went to press. He now works for CeaseFire and for New Life Community Church in Little Village, where he mentors young people who are on probation.

A MESSAGE FOR STUPID PEOPLE

REGGIE

Reggie—not his real name—is a 19-year-old who grew up in Chicago's Back of the Yards neighborhood, which takes its name from its location east and west of the old Union Stockyards. Once the center of Chicago's meatpacking industry, this Southwest Side community is now filled with abandoned buildings and vacant lots. Reggie and his twin brother were raised by their maternal grand-mother in a household that included several cousins and uncles. More recently, it includes the boys' 2-year-old sister. They also have three siblings they do not know who grew up in foster care, as well as some half-sisters through their father.

    Reggie's interviews took place at the Precious Blood Community Center at South 51ˢᵗ and Elizabeth Streets, near Sherman Park. Housed in a former school building, only yards from the border separating one gang's territory from another, Precious Blood serves as a kind of peace zone—providing young people with a safe place to hang out, while offering them creative outlets in music, art, video and writing. The center also regularly conducts peacemaking circles—a practice of restorative justice that seeks to address and repair the harm that has been done to the victim and to the community, without giving up on the offender.

    Although he still frequents the center, Reggie no longer lives in the neigh-borhood. After he survived a gang-related shooting in 2010, his grandmother moved the family about 20 blocks south to keep the boys away from their former associates in the Black P Stone Rangers, an organization that controls Sherman Park and the surrounding blocks.

    When speaking, Reggie rarely opens his eyes all the way; most of the time, they are mere slits in his face. But when he laughs, they open wide and he sud-denly appears much younger.

All I got to say—you don't got nobody else but yourself. Even me. I'm a twin, but no matter what, you still by yourself.

I was born and raised in the neighborhood. It was tough, rough. I been shot, gangbanged, but I'm not in a gang no more. I ain't been in a gang—all right, you could say I'm affiliated, yeah, but I don't sit on the corner no more. I don't hang with the wrong crowd anymore.

I live with my grandma. She my guardian. Me and my brother had drugs in our system when we was born. That's why my grandma got custody of us. My parents, they on drugs, both of them. But my mama, she straightened out a little bit. She live a block away. She got a little job at a little junkyard. Today, she's going to give me some money. But I don't really see her that much.

When I was growing up, there was a lot of us in my grandma's house. Like, 10 or 11 peoples. And the sad thing is—three bedrooms. Me and my brother used to sleep on the let-out couch. Grandma used to sleep on another couch in the dining room. And my uncle and his friends, they used to smoke weed in the house. He would leave 10 of them in one room, playing games and shooting dice for money, so we'd just go outside and play basketball.

Me and my brother, we were just raw with basketball. We used to play ball in the cold. We used to bring shovels and just shovel the snow so we could play. We couldn't really bounce the ball, it was so wet and cold. And then, in summer, we used to play tag, throw water balloons, then we'd go back playing ball. Ball, ball, ball, basketball, basketball. We was just outside having fun. Then, that's when all the drugs, all the guns, came to the area. And that's when everybody just became bad. Became negative. It's just the hope, like, went away.

"Rough twins," they used to call us. Bad twins. Like, if anything would go wrong, they'd say, "They did it." But we ain't never used to do it! We would just steal bikes, but we were never going in people's houses. But the more we grew up, the more stuff we seen, and the more we wanted it. It's like, you see people with new shoes, so you want new shoes. You want this, that, that. We seen drug dealers; they had females and cars. So we just wanted to make a name for ourselves. That's how the bad stuff started.

There wasn't no joining no gang. It was just, you born in it. If you were around this neighborhood, that's what you going to be. Mexicans, we different from them. For a Mexican, you gotta beat up somebody to join a gang; you gotta kill somebody to join a gang. You gotta sell drugs, do all types of stuff to join a gang. It's about loyalty. Loyalty to your fellow gang members. For blacks, everybody now is just about the money. Black people don't care who you are. It's about the bread down here. About getting money, that's all it's about. Or family.

The guy that shot me, we used to be friends. I probably know him all my life. We used to be cool. One of my close friends be his cousin. Then, when my close friend moved out of town, that's when he stopped hanging with us.

He went back across the park. You know how it is. The gang split. Divided. And it was just them against us.

They hated us. I don't even know why. Me and my brother and my friends had summer jobs, and we had bought two cars. We used to just drive around there, everything looking good. We had new clothes, but we wasn't really stunting. We weren't showing out. We were just—us. We wasn't thinking about them. Them—they be thinking about *us*.

So it's like that. They can't go over here; we can't go over there. It's like a bridge. You got this side of the bridge; we got this side of the bridge. But instead of a bridge, it's the park: You got this side of the park; we got this side of the park. That's how it is. If they catch you, you finna get shot at—*boom, boom, boom, boom.*

June 16, 2010. It was daytime. Sherman Park, kids was out—it was hot. It was a sunny, sunny day. Everybody was out. So he approached us like, "Hey!" And he said something, so we got to chasing him. He just shot, like *bam*. I think he wanted to shoot one of us, but, like, he didn't care if it was me. He just finna to shoot. He shot like at least nine times. *Doon, doon, doon, doon. Doon, doon, doon, doon.*

I didn't know I was hit. I thought it was a paintball gun. I was laughing: "Take a look, they shooting paintball guns!" But then, I felt it. And I get to the alley, and I felt a burn, and it was hurting. And I just seen the blood: "Dang, I been shot. I been *shot*."

I remember everything. I thought I was going to die. I was like, "Yeah, this could really kill me right now." But I wasn't really panicking; I was just calm. I was walking slow. I walked two blocks. I sat down when I made it back on Bishop Street. And the ambulance people, the paramedics—they wasn't trying to help me. They was just, "Who did it?" That's all they wanted to know, the police and all of them.

I was in the hospital for a day and a half. They wanted to keep me for a week, but I didn't want to stay in. I knew I was in pain, but I just wanted to go back home. I was just bored at the hospital, you know? So I went home. And after that, when I tried to walk to the store, I'd just have to pause and stop for a minute or two, 'cause it would get to burning and stuff. So that feeling, it would sting my heart. Just that bullet. It hit my stomach, but it entered through my hand, right here. But I've still got the bullet in me. I'm going to get it out, probably.

After the shooting, that's when I started getting mature. I had a friend named Martez who got killed. A lot of people in the neighborhood were getting killed. Before that, we ain't killing anyone. We just thought it was fun, you know. Then, it went to killing people, so that's a big change. That's a big difference. People right now are still getting their friends killed, and still just wanting to do dumb things. Don't wanna make a change.

Sometimes I'll say, "Forget the community, man. Forget everybody. I just want to go away, be rich and never come back." I ain't racist and all, but I don't want my children growing up in a black community. And I don't want them to go to no CPS. No Chicago Public Schools. If I have kids, they will be successful if I raise them in a good neighborhood, like the suburbs or up north. 'Cause they wouldn't be around all this negativity, all the homicides. I want them to grow up in a good area, like, with white people. 'Cause growing up around a lot of black people is going to be tough. It's going to be rough. It's going to be really rough.

But then I got my other good side when I feel like I ain't going to give up on the community. I'm just going to go do good, and come back and help the community. I think about the time I get grown—like 25, 26—the violence will probably have died down. I don't think the violence is going to be here forever. It's going to be violence, but not like how it is now. There's a lot of violence, because it's the money, people broke, the poverty. It's like hot water. Steam. You know, when steam needs to just open up the cap and you just let it go, and you see the hot air and stuff. That's like people, and they just shoot you—*boom, boom, boom!*

From now on, I got my eye on the future. You shoot at me, I'm not finna come back and shoot at you. I'm telling you, you shoot me, I'm running; you ain't going to see me no more. You trying to make me get a felony. You trying to make me throw away my future. You just want me to fall for you. And I'm not going to fall for you. Stupid people, I'm wise.

I'm just going to focus on school, get my grades back up. I been trying to get in college. I think I'll study marketing. I could find myself doing business, record labels and stuff. I'm hoping to go to St. Joseph College in Indiana. I want to go to a private college. I been there three, four times. I love that it's laid-back; it's not a university. They'll help you out. They're going to really help you out and be like, "Man, come on. Take it step by step.

You're going to have your diploma. You'll have a degree, bachelor's degree, everything—probably a master's."

So it's up to me to be successful. I ain't depending on nobody but myself. I gotta make that change. You want the jewelry, you want the girls—but I want the future.

—Interviewed by Rachel Hauben Combs

DEFENDING THE GONERS

KULMEET GALHOTRA

Kulmeet Galhotra is an attorney supervisor for the Homicide Task Force for the Cook County Public Defender. He was born 7,741 miles from Chicago in Allahabad, India, in 1966. When he was 6 years old, his parents moved to the United States, inspired by the progressive images of the civil rights movement. During his childhood, the family moved into a two-flat house in the Austin neighborhood before settling in Bucktown on the Near West Side. Originally on the path to become an engineer, Galhotra graduated from Illinois Institute of Technology as an English major and went on to attend Chicago Kent College of Law. At age 24, he began his career at the Public Defender's office representing juveniles, before moving to the adult division after 5 ½ years.

At the Homicide Task Force, Galhotra and his fellow attorneys face an incredibly challenging workload, as 8 out of 10 people arrested for murder in Chicago are represented by public defenders.[32] Candid and quick with a wry observation or joke, Galhotra speaks with a nasally Chicago accent that would make any native of the city proud. Nonetheless, he believes his background as a member of a minority helps him identify with his clients.

To me, there is nothing more important than a person's liberty. So it was pretty easy to decide to become a public defender. I wanted to walk into court and do things that didn't have a price tag on them. It didn't seem meaningful enough to just do it for the money. I think I'd have a real conflict with representing people, especially in criminal law, if I had to wonder, where does a client's money come from? You know, if Grandma just had to put up her house, I kind of feel bad about that. I don't know if I want Grandma's money. If the client just sold four kilos of cocaine to come up with the retainer, I'm not so sure I feel good about that, either. So it's nice not to deal with that whole business end of being a criminal defense lawyer, and to just deal with the law.

It seemed like, okay, if I went through all this trouble to get a law degree, I want to do something really important. And I thought the job was interesting. There's sort of the cops-and-robbers aspect of it, which is pretty cool. I have this fascination with thinking about why people do things, what makes them tick. Then there's just the absolute love of walking into a courtroom and arguing in front of a jury or in front of a judge, and cross-examining police officers and witnesses. So that's why I became a public defender. I get a kick out of doing it. I still get a kick out of doing it.

My first case—I don't remember the name but I remember what happened. It was this little kid. At juvenile court you either get sentenced to the Temporary Detention Center for up to 30 days, you get put on probation in addition to that, or you go to the Department of Corrections. So the kid had pled in a juvenile court, and I think he got something like 10 days—and I was devastated. I wanted him to get nothing. Now, of course, it seems like kind of a joke—10 days. Now, my clients, most of them are looking at 45 years to life on shooting murders and 20 to 60 years for murders without a firearm.

The youngest person I ever defended was 9 years old. This was, of course, 15 to 20 years ago. This was from a south-suburban area. This 9-year-old was in the kitchen and his grandmother was, I don't know, I think she was cooking bacon or something like that, and somehow an apron string caught on fire. And the kid threw the apron string behind a couch and ran out of the house. And the house caught on fire, and Grandma succumbed to smoke inhalation, and she was in the ICU for months, and the whole place was destroyed, so they charged this young man with arson. Not really the brightest thing to do. And this kid had post-traumatic stress disorder. He couldn't even talk to me about what happened. So he was found unfit to stand trial. Eventually, I think he was found guilty of criminal damage or something like that. But it was just a very sad story all around.

The really young clients are fairly easy to deal with—when they're 12, 13, 14, they are kind of bewildered by what's going on. They're not very talkative; they're just trying to get out. But as they get older, as they've been through the system, they start becoming a little more skeptical. They start questioning you. If you're working with somebody who has got at least a reasonable amount of intelligence—can read and write—there's a lot of time that they're spending in the jail with nothing to do. So they start trying to bone up on legal matters. It's absurd to me how they don't go to school, but when it comes to their own case, they'll be happy to look up laws and try to understand them. And usually, they have no concept of what the hell they're talking about.

Typically, I would say that when I first meet them, my clients are at a very self-destructive phase—at a very defiant phase in their life. I work with individuals who have basically spent a whole life making poor decisions. When they meet me, they don't suddenly start making good ones. I mean, there was one client—I had to put Band-Aids on his face every day at trial because he had teardrop tattoos; and he got them while he was in the jail. It's like: "Oh God, why did you do that?" But a lot of these young people just have a track record of being unrealistic and making bad decisions. It's very frustrating as a lawyer to give advice to somebody and then watch them not follow it. That's their prerogative—you can't live their life; it's their decision.

And there are certain decisions that have to be made by your client. Whether they want to plead guilty or not guilty, whether they want to be tried in front of a judge or a jury, whether or not they would like to testify on their own behalf, whether they would like to be considered to be found guilty on lesser charges, or if they want to go for all or nothing. Those are their decisions. So, many times I've advised people to plead guilty to a reduced charge or to a lesser sentence. You know, you have a young man who's 15, 18, 19 years old, and you would think this is the guy you can sell something like 25 years to, because they're gonna get out when they're 40-something, and they'll still have a life. And they say, "Fuck it. That's like the rest of my life. I'll roll with it; let's go to trial."

I suppose there is a level of attention that they get by going to trial. There is this whole idea of: "Are these people actually going to come in and say this shit about me? Let's see what my brother really does. Let's see if he really comes in and testifies against me." Or: "Let's see if my fellow gang member will actually come in and testify against me." Or: "Let's see if these witnesses actually come in here and stare at me and say I did that." And it usually happens. And the poor guy winds up getting 75 years after turning down something like 20. But at that point it doesn't make any difference to them.

The kids that I grew up with—we didn't want to fight each other. We wanted to play baseball, and we wanted to play Frisbee football, and we wanted to ride our bikes. So it just wasn't normal for us to always be engaged in some kind of fight. But it almost seems like that is the norm on conflict resolution now. There's almost an expectation now that fighting is the way you deal with conflict.

I think the violence comes from a lack of social skills, it comes from the inability to deal with conflict, and it comes from learned behavior. Unless you've got people who are providing some sort of structure for children, some sort of model on how to deal with conflict, they're going to learn the wrong way to deal with it. I think that happens a lot. It is very intergenerational—learning the wrong ways to deal with conflicts.

I had a case a few years ago, from the West Side. One of the guys got his teeth knocked out—he got beat up, jumped by these guys, got his teeth knocked out. So four months later, his buddies see the guy who they think was responsible. So they chase him down, stop him, broad daylight, summer afternoon—4 o'clock in the afternoon. They beat him with tire irons and a baseball bat, until he's just lying there like mush. Six guys on one guy. You know, that kind of brutality, it's just…there's just too much rage.

And obviously there are a lot more guns out there. I mean, they're usually coming from other states and straw purchasers.[33] My clients don't tell me how they got their guns. I've got cases now where people were using AK-47s—allegedly. In the old days, I don't remember any cases with machine guns. My perception is that there are more guns now than there used to be. There are a lot of gang guns, secreted in various areas, and everybody has access to them. I would say 20 to 30 percent of the firearms that show up in my cases have the serial numbers etched off of them. You know, there are a lot of states in this country where you can buy a lot of guns whenever you feel like it and those get into the supply stream and they wind up in the wrong places.

I recently started working with some schoolchildren with the Constitutional Rights Foundation and the Lawyers in the Classroom Project. We did this exercise called "Martians from Space," or something like that. The scenario is that these Martians come in from space and basically tell you that you can only keep 5 of your 10 constitutional guarantees within the Bill of Rights. So which ones are you willing to give up? Of course, I explain what the rights are and try to make them relevant to the kids, and then the kids talked about which five constitutional rights they'd want to keep. They all kind of caucus with each other, and I was stunned to find out that they thought that the most important right was the Second Amendment: the right to bear arms. I couldn't believe it. I was speechless. I really was. The Second Amendment? I think it's because they don't feel safe.

A few years ago, I represented a young man who was charged with two homicides. One was the involuntary manslaughter of his brother—they were playing Russian roulette and the gun jammed, so he struck it down onto the table to unjam it and it fired and went through his brother's torso and severed a major artery. They lugged the kid in a car to the hospital and told the police that he'd been shot by rival gang members. Eventually the police investigated it and noticed the trail of blood coming from the house. They spoke to some of the other participants, who not only said that it was an accident but also implicated him in a shooting that had occurred five months before, of a rival gang member whom he had shot to avenge the death of one of his friends. So this poor kid, who was under 18 and basically raising himself on the streets and getting affirmation and reassurance and a sense of being from these gang members, gets charged with first-degree murder and also gets charged with involuntary manslaughter of his brother. At the sentencing hearing, the father of the victim—who had given a victim-impact statement aloud in court—shook my hand with this look of reassurance, like, "I'm not holding against you what you do for a living. I appreciate what you do for a living." There really wasn't a whole lot to say to him, you know? I said, "I'm sorry for your loss." As a parent myself, it doesn't matter if your son is a gang member who gets killed by another gang member. It's still the death of your loved one, and it's still a loss no matter how you look at it.

Being a parent gives me a lot more perspective on my clients. I've represented parents as well as children who were charged with crimes, and that shows you the full cycle of things and how people get to be where they are. Why did this person turn out to be this person who goes around strangling and murdering women? You know? What happened in his life to make him this way? Well, maybe it was because his mother was a prostitute and would put him in the hallway when he was 3 ½ years old while she turned tricks, and maybe it's because women never really paid attention to him and always neglected him, and maybe he's angry because he never had a mother.

There are a lot of aspects to how I do my parenting that have evolved after seeing what other kids have gone through. When I think about my own children, I think about some of the children that I've encountered during my years as a public defender and how they got to be my clients and what it was that was lacking in the parents who were supposed to be taking care to train, protect and discipline them.

My clients—as they get older, especially if they've had a checkered past—they've had their mother come to court for them so many times, it gets to be to the point where the mom just can't do it anymore. Or it becomes shameful—here is a grown man for whom a mother may have gone to juvenile court over and over, perhaps even sharing her frustration with the juvenile judge, saying: "I can't control him." A lot of parents will fess up to that: "I can't control him; he's supposed to be in bed at 11 o'clock, but at 2 o'clock in the morning, he's running the streets with his buddies, hiding guns under the bed, bringing drugs into the house." So parents get burned out, and a lot of parents stop coming to court. I mean, I can't tell you how many times it's almost like, friends of the bride, friends of the groom. On one side of the courtroom you'll have all the cops, and the victims' family, and the victim witness coordinator, holding the hands of the victim's loved ones. But oftentimes, the defense side of the courtroom is empty, except for maybe a couple of people.

The victims usually have a few more resources. If you're unfortunate enough to have a loved one who was murdered, the prosecutor's office has somebody who will inform you about the next court date. If you come to court, they will sit next to you in court and explain to you what's going on, provide you with a lunch, perhaps even provide you with transportation expenses, give you reassuring hugs and things like that. I don't really have anybody in my office that does that for the defendant's families. My office doesn't have any social workers that will sit with my clients' families and hold their hand.

Losing a loved one is very difficult. It's very easy to focus that anger on the person that's been charged. It's really difficult to try and overcome that—and I've seen it over and over again, where I've walked into the courtroom for trial and the friends of the victim—you're getting the dagger eyes from them because they're still not over it.

The most fulfilling aspect of what I do is hearing the words "not guilty" from a jury. Somehow, it's addictive, you know? Just hearing those words is intoxicating. I mean, that's what makes me keep doing this. Even though I know I'll hear "guilty" far more often. We're just fierce competitors. It sounds kind of cruel for me to say this: Everybody thinks the law is a search for the truth, but that's not what the law is. At some point, I don't really care what happened. It's about strategy, it's about tactics, and it's about skill and advocacy. Maybe the truth gets lost. I don't know. But it's not a search for the truth. As far as lawyers are concerned, it's about whether the prosecution can meet its burden of proof. That's what it's about.

There have been times when I wasn't feeling very good about being a lawyer, and it took me a long time to have some kind of faith in the system again—that there is some redemption out there. Maybe there is a way to right wrongs. But if I had stopped being a lawyer after nine or ten years I would have never found that out.

There have been a lot of people that have come in and out of my life. Right after my juvenile court years, I would sometimes walk into a grocery store and get: "Hey, you represented me," or something like that. Some of my clients I really, really like, and it's like: "Oh my God, how did we wind up here?" But others are just set in their ways, and they're just not going to change. They're just damaged. What I've realized—what I've come to learn—is that once someone is about 16 or 17 years old, it becomes really difficult to rehabilitate them. You really have to get them at a young age—to try and disabuse them from acting out. Because, after a certain age, they are basically goners.

—Interviewed by Emily Ce Anderson

ENDNOTES

32 See Kevin Davis, *Defending the Damned: Inside a Dark Corner of the Criminal Justice System* (New York: Atria Books, 2007), 34. This book offers a compelling and insightful look into the Cook County Public Defender's Office.

33 According to the Law Center to Prevent Gun Violence, a straw purchaser is an individual who buys guns for people who are legally prohibited from possessing a firearm or for individuals who do not want their name linked to the gun. Straw purchasing is an illegal firearm purchase and is a federal crime that can result in a felony conviction. People can serve up to 10 years in jail and incur fines of up to $250,000. For more information on Illinois gun laws, or gun laws in other states, see: http://smartgunlaws.org

THE WHOLE WORLD STOPPED

AUDREY WRIGHT

Audrey Wright is an unlikely—if forceful—advocate for violent ex-offenders. In 1998, she lost her 24-year-old son, Gordie, in a drive-by shooting. But instead of wallowing in hatred for young people who turn to violence, she decided to help them find better futures.

The result is Gordie's Foundation, a vocational-training program for ex-cons located in West Englewood, a South Side neighborhood where the rate of youth homicide is nearly five times higher than it is citywide.

As this interview begins, Wright indicates that she is not feeling well and almost canceled our meeting. She seems impatient to get through the conversation, and keeps her coat and hat on as she recounts the traumatic story of her son's death and the way she chose to deal with that loss.

You just don't give up on communities. You don't just give up on young kids. You know? I don't know what kind of heart people have when their kids get killed and they just go home and sit down. They don't do nothing. They got to get up and say, "Let's fight. Let's stop some of this."

I have a 12,000-square-foot building that I train people in. I have about nine things in my building that I teach. I have carpentry, with weatherization. I have janitorial. I have the barber school. I have industrial sewing. I have embroidery and screen-printing, so ex-felons can get a job or open their own business. I have a city inspector, who teaches heating for me on Saturdays. Did you know that a heating and air guy that's been taught by a city inspector can go out and start his own business in his own neighborhood? You see what I'm saying? He don't have to worry about looking for work at McDonald's and whether he got a record.

Those are things that I do to help the community. We have a counselor. We can recommend some place to go if you are homeless. I have a young lady that always tries to put aside 13 beds for me. These are things that are important to people on the street.

It was 1998 when my son got killed. When he walked out the door that night, he said, "Mama, I'm going to get me some cigarettes." And I begged him, "Please don't walk around that corner. You know how these people be."

He went out of my house at 15 minutes to 12. At 12:01, my son was shot. At 12:49, my son was dead. It was like the whole world stopped. And you know what he said to me before he walked out the door? He said, "Mama, you got to turn me loose because if God get ready for me, there ain't nothing you can do."

I remember that, just like he said it yesterday: "If God get ready for me, nothing nobody can do. It's my time to go." And that's what keeping me going. God was ready for him. And he had to go; I couldn't stop it.

No mother wants to lose a son by a stray bullet, by any kind of bullet. Twenty-four years old—your life is just beginning. That was the hardest thing for me to accept—his life was gone at 24. But when you sit back to look at it, he lived a life that a lot of young men didn't live. We went to Denver, Colorado, and he did a movie with John Ritter.[34] He did commercials with Gus, what's his name, little white boy, Gus, what is his name? Anyway, he did commercials with him. He did commercials for macaroni and cheese. He was in a movie with Cicely Tyson.[35] He did a lot of things in his life that a lot of children didn't get a chance to do. And I said to myself, God blessed him. God blessed him to do some of the things an average black kid couldn't do.

It is just so sad to lose a child. You look to your son or your daughter to bury you, not for you to bury your child. When you bury your child, a part of your whole life is gone. You cry; you're gonna cry. It's not going to ever go away. So you have to wipe the tears and keep going to accomplish something. That's the way I think.

The day my son got killed, two mothers lost, not one. I lost and the boy that killed my son, his mother lost. Okay? I don't have no hate in my heart. I just wanted that person that killed my son to be taken off the street and punished because he didn't need to be on the street where he would kill somebody else's child. Now my husband feels differently than I do, okay? But I'm my own person and I have to account to God.

That's why I put the school here in Englewood after he got killed. I decided to help stop some of the violence, to give young men, ex-felons, ex-drug addicts and handicapped people a trade. Take the guns out of their hands and put a trade into their hands.

I reach out to help regardless of what kind of crime you did. I have a young man who was in the penitentiary for 25 years. And he's working on a newspaper. I put my head out on the block for him. You know why? Because he was sincere.

The person that called me said, "Miss Wright, do you recommend him?"

I said, "Yes, I do recommend him. If he don't do what you say, give me a call." He's been there over two years now. Those are things that I'm proud of because I've helped somebody. They can come to me and ask for help. I'm their mother, I'm their father, their brother and their sister because I leave my door open for them to come in.

Everyone asks me, aren't you afraid to be around all them killers and rapists? No. They human just like I am. They did something wrong, okay? They realized they done wrong. They ready to change. How come I can't give them the chance to change? We have to give another human being a chance to change. And if you don't give them a chance to change, they back out there killing again.

And I got backup behind me. It's like a safe haven here. I've never been broken into. I've never had big problems. They know not to come down here and mess it up. Now who put it out there I don't know and don't care, but I appreciate that because they say that Miss Audrey is the only thing we got to help us. Some of those same guys, I can call them up right now, and they come to the rescue. You know why? Because I changed their life.

A lot of these young men, they keep me on my knees, praying all the time. Right now, when they come through my building, they say, "Miss Wright, I might not live to 25." That's sad. We as parents, we don't fight hard enough to keep our children here. Do you think if you had a son he would come and tell you that the gangs want him? Let me say this. Open up your eyes and listen to what I'm saying. Open up your ears. The gangbangers on the street tell a boy, "You gonna do what we say or we're gonna do something to you and your whole family." That young man be scared that something gonna happen to him and his whole family. It has happened. We're losing our babies now. The gangs don't care who they kill. They shooting up in the house, shooting up in the yard, shooting everywhere, they don't care.

I've seen so much, where they got empty houses behind the buildings. Tricks go down there, and the summertime I used to sit in my lot and I'd call the police because the little kids coming though there, walking through the alley going to school. They seeing this, they've been exposed to these things when they 5 and 6 and 7 years old. Then the gangs drive by, *boom,*

boom, boom. This is what needs to be stopped. And we got to come together. If you got a strong group, you can stop them. If we start weaving ourselves together like a basket, you can't get through it. You can stop them. You *can* stop them. We can help our own communities.

Where I live—the Beverly neighborhood—they say I'm crazy.[36] But let me say this to you: Not only my son, it could have been your son, anybody's son. I grieve every day. Some days I cry, some days I don't. But I grieve every day. I was married 10 years before I got pregnant with my son. Then boom, he gone. I don't hate. I can't hate. I can't hate the young man that killed my son because that person has to give an account to God for all his wrongdoings. I don't feel that I have to give up on nobody. I don't ever give up. I don't *ever* give up.

—Interviewed by Mariah Chitouras

ENDNOTES

34 The 1987 made-for-TV film *Prison for Children*. Interestingly, the film is about how incarceration and detention can actually breed more crime than they prevent.

35 The 1981 made-for-TV movie *The Marva Collins Story* portrays one Chicago woman's successful attempt to start her own school for inner-city youth.

36 Beverly, on the Far South Side, is an integrated, middle-class neighborhood.

DEATH IS CONTAGIOUS
MAX CERDA

The Jan. 10, 1984, edition of the Chicago Tribune[37] *contained a special full-page display of mug shots—the faces of gang members from all over the city who had recently been sentenced to prison for murder and other brutal crimes. One of the most menacing mug shots on that page belonged to a teenager with a childlike face, a muscular neck and a fiercely defiant scowl. His name was Max Cerda—and a few years earlier, he had been convicted of two murders and an attempted murder.*

Nearly three decades after that story appeared in the paper, Max Cerda stares at his old mug shot with a look of wonder and sadness. Sentenced to prison at age 16, he spent 18 years behind bars. Now he sits in the Humboldt Park office of the Latino Cultural Exchange Coalition, a group he co-founded in prison with Jose Pizarro, who was another one of the murderers pictured in that 1984 Tribune *story. In those days, the two men were members of enemy gangs. Today, they work together to help ex-offenders re-integrate into society and to encourage teens to stay out of gangs.*

On the day we visit, Cerda is holding an anger-management class for ex-offenders and at-risk youth. Although the young men tease him with greetings such as "Wassup, Old School?", he clearly has their respect. At 50 years old, Cerda still has the thick black hair of his youth, which he pulls back in a ponytail. His world-weary face is calm and gentle-looking—but when he talks about the past, his dark eyes can go dead.

When I look at the face in the newspaper, I see anger, hurt, fear—just a lost kid chasing an urban illusion. I thought that life was about killing and dying. Nothing else.

You know, there's a myth that kids who join gangs come from broken homes and stuff like that, and I'm sure that's true in a lot of cases. But in my case, it was not true. I came from a good family. My mother came from Mexico, and my father, he was a Tejano; he was from Texas, from Brownsville. A lot of my uncles and my grandfather—I was named after him, Don Maximo—moved up to Aurora, Illinois. Then they just eventually moved into the city, perhaps just like most Mexicans and immigrants at that time, just trying to find opportunity.[38]

Where I lived in Little Italy—Taylor Street and Loomis—it was a beautiful neighborhood. I'll never forget it. I still go there today when I have problems in my mind and I gotta clear it out. There's a park there, and I can still see me and my father having a race on the sidewalk.

My father was a foreman for Acme Supply. He always had his shirt pocket full of pens. And it's funny, because today I've always got my own shirt pocket full of pens, and every time I reach for them, I'm always thinking about my old man. He used to come from work to take me to the park. We'd get some ice cream or buy some peanuts from the Sicilians who used to push the peanut carts on our streets. It was nice, man. It was my father. He passed away while I was in the joint at Menard.[39]

I was an altar boy when I was young. But one day, a friend and me got kicked out of there because we saw the Communion wine and we drunk that wine up, and we was eating the holy bread like potato chips, man. I was just restless back then. I didn't want to pay attention. I was a smart-ass. Every elementary school that I ever went to, I got kicked out of. I mean every one: Notre Dame, McLaren, every one, even Montefiore, which was a reformatory school.

I didn't take nothing seriously. Didn't care. The only time I cared was when they said they was gonna tell my father, 'cause my father played no games, man. He put it on me. I used to get whooped hard. I used to get welts on my back that'd be there for days, man. I couldn't lay on that side.

Fifth, sixth grade—that's when things took a turn. This was by McLaren Elementary School, in Little Italy. This was outside on the playground. I remember this one kid, I don't know if he was Italian or not, but he was white. And he said something to me, something racial, and I don't know why it bothered me because I never thought about, you know, being Mexican or nothing like that. But I was seeing people fight all the time, and I guess I was just waiting for somebody to say something to me. And this kid did. And I beat him down. I stomped him like he was on fire. I just couldn't stop. I felt empowered, man. I felt like, "Damn, I'm not taking shit from nobody. I've been whooped so much at home, I ain't taking shit from nobody on the streets." I didn't know it then, but I know it now. I know it now. It was exciting. It was contagious. It was like finding a gun.

When I was about 11 years old, my father bought a house up here on the North Side, by Avers and Iowa. I didn't wanna leave Little Italy. I kept taking the bus back to the old neighborhood to see my friends, but like a year or so later, I got to know young kids, Mexican kids in Humboldt Park. They was in gangs, so I fell into a Mexican gang called the Latin Diablos, and we were fighting the Puerto Ricans. But eventually, I ended up becoming part of that same Puerto Rican gang[40] we used to fight.

See, back in the day when I was gangbanging, we had what we would call our yo-yos, our peewees, our juniors, our seniors. I was a peewee, and we did something wrong. So one day, the juniors and the seniors called a meeting in the garage and we all got whooped bad by these older guys. That made us mad, so we made peace with the Puerto Ricans. We became one gang. We kicked the older guys out of the neighborhood and that's where it began. When we were able to overcome these older guys, I realized, "Damn, we really do got power." It was an illusion, but I believed it.

It wasn't about the girls; for me, at least, it wasn't about the girls. It wasn't about money or fancy cars. We didn't have none of that. Hell, we all had bikes. Regular bikes. Schwinns. It was about the camaraderie, man. We looked out for each other. And we protected the neighborhood. There was no burglaries in our neighborhood. There was no purses being snatched.

But when the gunplay got involved, that changed everything, man. Everything changed. People started getting shot. You know, nothing serious at first. The leg or the back or something like that, but then this one guy got killed, and we realized that this is life and death. It just escalated from there. It just didn't stop.

Raymond, Raymond Cruz, was the brother who died in my arms. The first time I ever saw him was when I was still a Latin Diablo. You know, Raymond's Puerto Rican, and I remember they sneaked up on us, and he threw a brick at me. I said, "Man, I'm gonna get this punk, whoever he is." But then, after my gang and his gang united, we became real cool, man. He got me into salsa—the Fania All-Stars, Willie Colón, Héctor Lavoe, all of those guys. He turned me on to a new world of music.

His mother used to live right behind our house, and that's how we got close to him. My ma loved him. He used to come to the house beat up, cut up. My mother would sew him up, take care of him. My mother was like his personal doctor. So yeah, we got close like that, man. We just ended up getting real close.

He was two years older than me. He was 18, going on 19. He decided to leave the neighborhood and move to Maywood and get a job at Zenith.[41] He was so happy he had just got that job.

I was always telling him, "Man, come back to the 'hood. We need you, man. You know, shit is happening over here. We need you."

And he kept saying, "Man, you need to give that shit up. There's too much stuff going on right now. A lot of people getting shot at, people getting killed.[42] Why don't you come hang out a couple weeks by me in Maywood, man? Let this shit blow over."

Finally, after like a month or two, I was able to talk him into coming back to pick me up, just to spend some time with me—and we ended up getting ambushed. We got ambushed. This happened April 18th of 1979.

It was on a one-way street. There was a car, an LTD Ford, parked in front of us. And they threw up gang signs. I threw up gang signs. I was the passenger and, when I opened my door, I heard another car come right behind us. And by the time I looked back in front of me, the guys that were in the first car came out firing.

I dove under the dashboard. I do not understand to this day why I did not even get wounded. Both them guys put their guns in the car, and I did not get hit one time. But they ended up shooting Ray. They shot him 13 times.

I remember hearing him gargling for air, and when I heard the other cars take off, I stuck my head up and I looked up at my brother, and I seen he was full of blood. This was in the afternoon, about 2:30. The kids were coming out of school. There was a candy store right on the corner and I ran to tell the lady at the store to call the ambulance. When I got back to the car, there was an old Puerto Rican lady holding his body. Half of his body was in the car and his head was hanging out. I put my arms under his head. When I did that, a big…a big thing of blood…could've been his brains, I don't know…came down. He was squeezing my left thumb. He had a bullet hole underneath one eye and his other eye was looking straight to the sky. He took his last breath. When that happened, I went straight to the dark side.

The night we buried him, it was like five of us walking around, trying to find the enemy. We were hurt. Full of anger. Full of pain. I didn't worry about getting locked up. I didn't worry about dying. I was looking for death, bro. I was running right into it, head on. The next day, I was arrested for murder.[43]

I was 16 years old, but I was tried as an adult. I fought my case for a year and a half or two years. In 1981, I got found guilty and sent to Joliet.[44] From Joliet, I went to Menard. And then from Menard, I went to Stateville.[45] And then from Stateville, I went to medium-minimum joints. You know, getting transferred from hole to hole to hole. I was incarcerated from the age of 16 till the age of 35. It was something else, man. It was something else. Prison was something else.

I did a total of five and a half years in solitary confinement. I would do 18 months one time, one year another time, six months one other time. A lot of people go to the hole and they find the end of the world. For me, I found a new world. I found a world of self. That's where I learned how to think. It's where I learned how to read. It's where I learned how to cry. I needed that so much.

Once, I was in the hole at Menard. And this brother next door to me, his name was Pops. He was from the Hells Angels, he was a biker. He looked like those bikers from the movies, man. Long hair, short, ugly, mean-looking. You know, for real. But he was a beautiful, beautiful brother, man. A beautiful brother.

When I first got there, he goes, "Hey little brother, how you doing? I'm a biker." He was trying to help me out, but I was so ignorant I thought he was representing.

"Biker? I don't give a fuck about a biker. I'll chop your ass up."

And he just says, "You know what, brother? I'll talk to you another time."

So then, like a few weeks later, he asks me, "What are you in solitary for, man?" And I started telling him, kinda explaining to him, but he goes, "What does your ticket say?"

I go, "My ticket?"

He goes, "Yeah, that yellow paper that they give you—your disciplinary report."

I said, "Oh, I…I…don't know what the fuck this says."

And now he's got this little mirror he's sticking through the bars of his cell so that he can see me. Now we're looking at each other in the mirror.

He goes, "I don't mean no disrespect, but do you know how to read and write?"

I go, "But I ain't stupid."

And he says, "Little brother, I'll work with you, man." And, I mean, he taught me. At night, he would write the vowels—you know: a, e, i, o, u. For a rugged-looking dude, he was smart, man. He was fucking smart. I mean, he got me to start to read, and I was a straight knucklehead. I was in 10 or 12 schools and none of them could do it. But he did it.

Acquiring the ability to read, it transformed me, man. Like we say it in Spanish, *la cultura cura*. Culture heals. And that's what healed me was culture. It made me positive. One thing for sure it did, it helped me to stop seeing my so-called enemy as my enemy and to start seeing him as my brother. Before that, man, I was so into gangbanging, I was in a trance—a trance of hate and confusion. You know, like a terrorist. To me, I was a soldier. I didn't see myself as a criminal. I wasn't a dope-dealer. I seen myself as a soldier.

I hit Stateville in 1984. That's where I met Jose Pizarro, the guy I work with now. But back then, I was still banging against his group. I was People, and he was Folks;[46] he was the enemy. The first time I saw him was on the gallery, the walkway in front of the cells. Stateville is a roundhouse. It's like a big-ass birdcage, and you can see everything. And they would be over there, and we would be over here, sizing each other up. Jose was his chief of security—personal security for the leader of his gang. And I was a security guy for my guys, so I knew that if we was ever gonna hit his chief, we had to hit Jose first.

We had this one brother in Stateville, Luis Rosa.[47] He was a beautiful, intelligent brother. He preached to us about Latino awareness and Latino unity. But I wasn't educated then. I couldn't understand. That shit sounded like Chinese to me. I thought it was too late for peace, 'cause too many brothers had died.

But after I went to solitary a few more times, I really got an understanding of myself and what it means to be Latino and everything. I started reading the history of Mexicans, what we went through with my father, what my grandfathers and them went through. I kinda started feeling what Luis Rosa was talking about then. I had an awareness, an awakening. And when I came out of solitary, I got involved in what Luis and these other guys were doing.

I guess that's what really got me and Jose Pizarro close to one another; we both started preaching Latin unity, you know. We didn't say to each other,

"Hey, you go talk to your guys; I'll talk to my guys." We didn't have that agreement. It just happened like that.

I had to explain to my guys, "This is what I feel, bro. I feel we're wasting our lives. We're killing ourselves for no fucking reason. This is crazy. This shit's gotta stop."

In fact, I even had to kind of manipulate the situation a bit to make it seem as if this unity was a good criminal enterprise for us. For me, it was all about Latino unity *for real.* But to have them understand it and accept it, I had to present it in a way where, you know, this would expand the criminal concept of what we're doing as an organization: As a united mob, we can do more shit.

When we had our first meeting between the two sides in the chapel at Stateville, nobody sat down. Everybody was standing up. Everybody had their knives on them, pipes. Everybody had vests in case we got stabbed so it wouldn't penetrate. It was hilarious. It was serious as hell, but it was hilarious. It was funny and scary at the same time, man. Nobody sat down, but we talked. We presented our case. Jose did it for his group, I did it for mine. That night, I figured one of two things was gonna happen: If I live to the morning, this is gonna work and, if not, I'm gonna get hit tonight. But it did work. This was in the early 1980s. We're out here now in 2012, incorporated and in the heart of Humboldt Park.

Death is contagious. It is, man. Especially when you're lost and you're confused and you got everybody around you telling you this is what you're supposed to be doing. It's so contagious, it becomes part of you. If you ain't hit somebody in one night—jump them, beat them up, shoot them, whatever—you can't even sleep well. I couldn't sleep well till I knew I hit somebody that night.

Yes, I was part of that stupidity and that madness. I believed in that crazy shit. Just like these kids from Afghanistan who come from a war-torn state, I was coming from a war-torn state of mind. But when I look at that mug shot of myself at age 16, it also reaffirms who and what I am today. It tells me that, no matter how bad our past was, it's not how the story begins. It's where it leads to and what kind of legacy we leave behind. That people can change.

I'm proud of who I am today and what I've done and what I'm trying to accomplish. Getting kids out of gangs, helping parolees prepare for reintigration into society and working with mothers who lost kids—it's a form of redemption. But all that stuff that happened with me years ago when I was younger, it don't go away. You know, man? It just really don't go away. Guilt, remorse—you're like, damn, man. Especially when I see a mother on TV crying that one of her kids got killed. There's times when I think about the moms I may have made cry. And it, it just, it really just fucks with me. It don't go nowhere. The more humble you become, the more remorseful you become. You know?

—Interviewed by Miles Harvey

ENDNOTES

37 William Recktenwald, "On the Wall," *Chicago Tribune*, Jan. 10, 1984.

38 In recent years, Cerda has returned to Mexico several times to conduct anti-violence workshops. These trips were sponsored by the U.S. State Department.

39 Menard Correctional Center is a state prison in downstate Illinois.

40 *The Chicago Crime Commission Gang Book,* published in 2012, still lists Cerda as an active gang leader. He vehemently denies this and has filed a complaint against the Crime Commission for false depiction. See James D. Hubbard and Katherine Wyman, eds., *The Chicago Crime Commission Gang Book: A Detailed Overview of Street Gangs in the Chicago Metropolitan Area* (Chicago: Chicago Crime Commission, 2012), 78-79.

41 Zenith was a radio and television manufacturer. It had a factory in Melrose Park, a western suburb adjacent to Maywood.

42 Cerda is referring to a deadly war that broke out between the Insane Unknowns and the Spanish Cobras.

43 See Bonita Brodt, "2 Slain in New Gang Terror: Shooting Linked to Street War," *Chicago Tribune*, April 23, 1979.

44 Joliet Correctional Center opened in 1858 and closed in 2002. After closing, it was used as a set for the *Prison Break* TV series.

45 Stateville Correctional Center is a maximum-security state prison for men in Crest Hill, Illinois.

46 People and Folks are the two major gang alliances. They were formed in the penitentiary system during the mid-1970s by incarcerated gang members seeking safety in numbers.

47 Luis Rosa is a Puerto Rican nationalist. In 1981, he was sentenced to 75 years in prison for his illegal activities with the FALN, the Spanish-language acronym for the Armed Forces of National Liberation. He was released from prison in 1999 after President Clinton gave him and other members of the group clemency.

UNANSWERED PRAYERS
PAMELA MONTGOMERY-BOSLEY

Pamela Montgomery-Bosley is an energetic, 40-something South Side resident who is not fond of sharing her real age. In 2006, her 18-year-old son, Terrell Bosley, an aspiring gospel musician, was gunned down in the parking lot of the Lights of Zion church on the city's Far South Side. In 2008, a 27-year-old man named David Stanley was acquitted of murder. Despite extensive publicity surrounding the case, and a $5,000 reward, Terrell's killing remains unsolved.

While she spent more than 20 years in the banking industry, Montgomery-Bosley now devotes her considerable talents to ending youth violence. In addition to her full-time job with a community youth center at St. Sabina Church in the Auburn Gresham neighborhood, she is the co-founder of Purpose Over Pain, an advocacy group started in 2007 by parents who lost their children to gun violence.

My greatest wish is to get my baby back. When I go to visit my son in the cemetery, I say to God, "I won't tell nobody; just give Terrell back to me." And I know that God can do this. I'm lacking in a lot of other ways, but I believe He can do it. My faith is *that* strong. I know He can do it, but He won't.

Even so, I still have Terrell's stuff down in my basement like I'm waiting for him to come back. My husband and I are waiting for him to come and ring the doorbell. We wait for him to call. This is something that you cannot accept as a parent; no mother or father should bury their child.

I grew up in K-Town, on Kedvale Street in North Lawndale on the West Side. Violence wasn't what it is now. We had people on the West Side just hanging out. Everyone liked to stay outside and enjoy the weather. I would ride my bike to downtown. We'd walk to school and feel safe.

My son Terrell grew up in the Rosemoor neighborhood, which is right next to Roseland, on the Far South Side. My husband, Tom, grew up in that area, which is why we purchased a home there in 1991. It was okay when we first moved there, and then as the years progressed, it started changing. Once the city started tearing down public housing projects in the 1990s, people started renting out homes to different individuals, and that changed our neighborhood. We didn't hear guns on my block, not till the later years.

Now, I can be in my house and hear *pow, pow, pow, pow!* And everyone just walks around desensitized.

Terrell had freedom, to a certain degree, but not a lot. My boys now—I have a 17-year-old and I don't even want him to walk around the corner; I drive him around the corner. I know that I am sheltering him too much. He even says that he feels like he lives in a bubble. It's overbearing for him and his brother. I'm not letting them grow up. I'm not letting them feel like teenagers.

But that's my biggest fear—to lose another child. If I lose another child, I probably will lose my mind. People seem to think that I am doing good, but I'm not. I'm horrible. I can put on my "front face" the majority of time, but my heart is broken; it's torn apart. To this day, I don't understand why God allowed me to be in this situation, because I was an excellent mom.

My goal was to protect Terrell as much as possible—from the gangs, the drugs. I didn't want him to be connected to nothing negative in the neighborhood. When Terrell met friends, I made sure I met their mother and father. That was something that he said parents don't do anymore, but I did it. I wanted to know whose house he was going to, and a little bit about their families. Is the father living in the home? I just needed to know some information. And then I *monitored* his friends. They would bring their book bags in the house and leave them lying around and, at times, I would peek in their book bags to make sure that their bags were okay, because I needed to know who my children were around.

Terrell had always been an advanced student. He started speaking and walking earlier than a lot of children, and he skipped a year ahead in grammar school. He was outgoing, outspoken, had to get the last word in. At school, his principal and teachers used to tell him he was a leader and to remain positive because other young people followed after him.

He started playing the bass guitar in his freshman year. The bass was his passion. He played for a lot of gospel artists—he played for a quartet group called The Victory Travelers. He actually got a chance to play on the Main Stage at the Gospel Fest with The Victory Travelers and some great choirs.[48] Terrell was doing everything that I always wanted to do. I sang, too, and was in the choir, but Terrell was making it and accomplishing everything in the gospel music world that I wanted to do. So I enjoyed supporting him and cheering him on from the audience. I was known in the music world as

Terrell's mom. It was just awesome to see him on the stage playing. His goal was to travel around the world and play the gospel music with his six-string bass guitar. But this did not happen.

My husband and I taught Terrell right from wrong, just like any parents who love their children. I'd stay up and watch him come home, just to make sure his eyes were clear. If I'd smell cigarettes, I would say, "You know what we studied about the lungs?" I'd grab this lung picture and show him everything. So my husband and I stayed on him, building him up to be the great young man that he was.

The day before everything happened, I had cooked a pot roast and meatloaf. I had made pot roast for that Monday night and meatloaf for that Tuesday. So that Monday night, he was talking to his girlfriend on the phone and he was like, "You gotta come over here—my mom, she threw down! She cooked some pot roast today." The next day was the meatloaf day and, when I came home from work and the meatloaf had been eaten off of, I called him to ask, "Why did you eat the meatloaf before I got home?" The moment I left the message was probably when everything was happening because he didn't pick up his phone.

At 6 o'clock that evening, Terrell took his girlfriend to church for her praise-dance rehearsal. While she was practicing, he was in the church playing his music. His friend, Darren, had drums in the car, so he put his bass down and went outside to help Darren, because he was helpful. That was something that he did. Then, this other car pulled up with some more musicians in it. They were out there talking for a moment at this car on church grounds, and somebody came by shooting.

Somebody said that the person was on foot, somebody said he was in the car. I don't know. I don't know. I just know that somebody came by shooting. My baby, after he was shot in the shoulder, he struggled back to the church for help, but they didn't know he was shot. They thought that he was just panicking or something. He started shaking, and they just kinda stepped over him.

That made me mad, because my baby got shot, and nobody even knew it. They were so busy running outside the door of the church, and everybody was stepping over my baby. So he stumbled to church, the place where you're supposed to get help, and they finally realized he got shot. He told one guy that he think he got shot. Those were his last words.

Me and my husband and my other two children was doing homework and preparing dinner. As soon as we got the call, we all ran out and went to the church on 116th and Halsted. They were bringing Terrell out to the ambulance. He was still breathing then. My regret is that I got back into my car, 'cause that's what they told me to do instead of getting in the ambulance. I wish I would've gotten into the ambulance. I wasn't thinking. I was just trying to get to the hospital as soon as possible. I never thought I was going to lose my son. He'd been hit by a car before—and he made it. And I thought that must be because of my prayers. So I never would have thought...

It was an eternity driving to the hospital. On the way there, I was calling friends and family and I said, "Praaaaaay and meet us at Christ Hospital—praaaaaay!" I'm calling everybody and telling them to just pray for Terrell and meet us. And my husband kept saying, while he was driving, "Breathe, Terrell, breathe!"

So when we got to the hospital, we were waiting, and I was wondering when they were gonna let me back there with my baby. The doctor came out to talk to us, and I wasn't really comprehending what he was saying to us, until my husband said, "Are you talking...you're talking in the past. Are you saying my son didn't *make* it?"

And that's when we found out that—and I lost it from there. This devastated my entire family. The first year without Terrell was horrible for my entire family.

When we got to the first-year anniversary of his death, I tried to take my life. And, you know, I'm a Christian, God-fearing woman, but I couldn't take the pain of him not being with me anymore. I took a whole bottle—a bottle of pills—and went to sleep. And then I woke up the next morning—I didn't wake up, God woke me up—and I saw the sun and I was mad. I was like, "Come on, God, you left me here again?"

I believe that if all of the kids got the love and attention they needed, we wouldn't be in this situation. True, you have parents out there who want to help their children but don't know how. But there are some parents not trying to raise their kids, not putting forth the effort. Like the ones who don't have nothing to do with their kids, but when they go to court, they say, "Johnny, he was a real good child." They need to be held accountable. Parents must raise their children, make sure that they get a decent education and do their homework. You need to be a parent and not be your child's friend, hanging and kicking it with them. It starts in the home.

I used to think that, as long as I raised my children right, as long as I kept them in order, then my boys would be safe. But now I know differently. If I don't take care of my neighbor's kids, if I don't take care of other youth, my own children aren't safe. So my goal is to work with the high-risk children and be proactive.

Everything that our youth have to look forward to is violence—it's the games, the videos with shooting at the police, the songs. There's a whole lot of pieces to this puzzle. Gun legislation, it's a big one. There are so many guns in our community that I don't know if they are dropping them out of cargo trains. Our youth can go get guns for $25; some can get them for free. I asked a group of young people, eighth grade and under, "So if you need a gun, where can you go get one?" And one of the boys was like, "I can go to my friend's house and get a gun." And I said, "Are you're serious?" He said, "I can get one. They sell them out of their car trunks."

People sell guns like it's candy.

We shouldn't have to live in fear. We shouldn't have to be afraid to let our kids walk to the store. We do not have to live this way. When we can get the people in our community to realize this, then we'll be okay. We don't need any more mothers in my situation.

We need to speak out. If we don't speak out, the black community is going to end up being in the museum. We are going to end up there, and people are going to say, "This is where black people used to live. This is how they used to look." At the rate that we are going now, we're going to have more black men incarcerated or murdered. And the generation is going to become extinct. So we have to speak out.

—*Interviewed by Ann Szekely*

ENDNOTES

48 The Chicago Gospel Music Festival is an annual city-sponsored event. The Victory Travelers are an acclaimed vocal quartet based in Chicago.

A TWIG IN A TORNADO

TIMOTHY CLARK

Timothy Clark—not his real name—is a 19-year-old who lives in Washington Heights, an overwhelmingly African-American neighborhood on the Far South Side, near Beverly and Roseland. He lives with his mother and two maternal siblings. He has eight siblings on his paternal side, although he doesn't have a relationship with his father or his paternal siblings.

Timothy is tall with a husky build. He is casually dressed for the interview, wearing jeans and a hoodie. He mentions that the hoodie once belonged to his best friend, who was shot to death on Timothy's birthday in 2009. Timothy's mother has repeatedly asked him to discard the hoodie because it is so old and dirty. But Timothy cannot bear the thought of throwing out this reminder of his friend, whose name is tattooed on Timothy's arm.

Timothy attends Community Youth Development Institute (CYDI), a small alternative school on the South Side that has approximately 200 students. He transferred to CYDI in September of 2010 after being expelled from two public high schools, Hyde Park Academy and Julian, because of poor academic performance and repeated fights. He credits the mentor in an after-school program for being instrumental in his determination to "turn a new leaf." Timothy is proud of his recent academic performance. He rarely misses school and hasn't had a fight in four months.

I've been fighting since I was 8 years old. When I was in preschool and kindergarten, I would come home crying, beating my head on the wall. People used to talk about me; they called me slow and stuff and I didn't have any friends. But one day, when I was in third grade, I fought somebody who was 14. He was messing with my little brother. I told him to leave my brother alone, but then he started talking about me, so I just hit him. He got to hitting me back, so I got scared and balled up. But then I thought about my big cousin Dee who used to tell me, "Ain't no losing a fight; you have to win or you have to fight me." I knew he was serious. The fight led from the alley to my backyard to my gangway to my front. I whupped him in the end, because I didn't want to fight my cousin Dee. Ever since then, I would tell people, "You ain't going to do too much talking."

I joined a gang in fifth grade. I thought it was cool. Everybody I knew was in a gang, even one of my friends. He was like a celebrity. Every girl in the school wanted to go with him. He used to have money. I wanted to be like that. I wanted to be in the spotlight.

The process was kinda sweet for me, because my uncles were big-time gang members when I was a shorty. I stayed in their old neighborhood, near 69th and Elizabeth in Englewood, so the gang members already knew me. There was really nothing to becoming a Gangster Disciple, or GDs as they call them now. I just had to learn some rules and I was basically in. When I first joined, they just told me to look out for the police and let them know when they were coming. Later on, I started selling weed.

It wasn't long before my friends started coming to me when they were getting into it with folks. One time, my friend was into it with a dude, and he came and got me. I told the dude he had to leave my friend alone. He was still woofing at my friend, so I jumped him. Another time, my friend smacked my brother. He was our family friend; his mama and my mama had been friends a long time. He hit my brother and tried to run, but my cousin caught him and punched him. I came over and kicked him and we stomped him out. We used to play football and basketball with him every day, but that day we had to beat him up.

When I think about it, I've been in quite a few fights. A couple of them were bad, but there was one time when I hurt someone really badly. Dude was short and I was kicking him in his face and stomping him with my boots. They told me he went to the hospital and I was scared that he might be in intensive care. Afterwards, I felt bad for doing him like that. I was like, "Man, I hope he is alive." Luckily, he was all right. I don't know why I didn't stop before it got that far. Sometimes, there is something that just comes over me when I fight; sometimes, I just black out.

Because of my actions, there are a few areas where I gotta look over my shoulder. Like, I work for the Chicago Park District at Fernwood Park. There's a dude that I got into it with who is always over there. When he sees me, or me and my friends, it's either going straight to shots or straight to fighting.

I ain't gon' say I've never been shot at; I've been shot at before, but I've never been hit. I've never shot anybody, either, but I have owned a gun. I bought it for crunch times, like when my community is in war. That's when there is so much fighting and gunshots that you can hardly go outside. I bought the gun from somebody I knew. I told him I wanted a gun, he told me what type he had, and I bought it. The gun was $280. Me and my mans bought it together; I put in $100 and he put in $180. I got my portion from my mom when she got her tax return. I told her that I was going to buy some clothes, but I used some of the money to get the gun. Me and my mans realized that we didn't really need the gun, so we sold it.

My childhood was crazy. I went to six different grammar schools and stayed in a lot of different places. I don't know why we moved so much. I guess my mother didn't get along with the landlord. I had a lot of time when I was young when I was without adult supervision. My mama had to work. My grandma was always kinda sick and kinda old. My sister was either working her candy store job or gone with her friends. So I just had the opportunity to do what I wanted to do. Who was there to tell me I couldn't do it? I just had too much freedom.

My father is a clown. I don't even call him Daddy. I call him by his name, Donnie. I got hate for the dude because he wasn't there. I have only seen him three times out of my whole life. When I was 6, I saw him at a family party. I didn't hop on his lap, though. He was like, "Yeah, you know who I is?"

I'm like, "Naw, I don't know you."

He was like, "I'm your daddy."

I looked at him and told him, "I don't got no daddy."

He was like, "You don't?"

I told him, "I don't got no daddy. I only got my mama and my grandma."

I seen him again when I was 10. We were staying with his cousin and he stopped by. He said to me, "What do you want? I am going to buy you anything you want."

My little brother was like, "Ask for a game."

I was like, "Naw, I gon' ask for some clothes."

I needed some clothes because my mama was trying to save to get us a crib. He never got me the clothes. The last time I saw him, I was outside when my mama was bringing in groceries. My mama asked him to help her carry in the groceries and he said, "For what? That ain't for me. I ain't fitta eat."

I was like, "But they are for your shorties though—me and my little brother." Ever since then, I ain't never seen the dude. I told him don't even call me. When I see him, I gon' knock him out. If he was in the hospital, I would walk in, spit on him and leave.

Dude don't care. Dude don't care. He probably is a drunk now because, from what I hear, all he does is hang out in front of liquor stores like Rothschild or Four Brothers. Or, maybe he's a crackhead. All drunks turn into something.

If I could, I would move out of the neighborhood. I'm tired of fighting. I'm tired of worrying about people coming after me. I'm tired of having to worry about my loyalty to my friends. I tell people all the time, my loyalty is a curse and a blessing at the same time. It's like a job. It's a 9-5. You can't tell your friend you're not going to help him fight. But sometimes I feel caught up, like a twig in a tornado.

I am still in a gang, but I don't gangbang anymore. If a fight broke out and my mans called me, I would help him fight, but I don't pick on people anymore. For now, I just keep myself busy and stay away from my neighborhood. Instead, I hang out at school, go to basketball practice, or I'm with my mentor. I really try not to be in the neighborhood like that anymore. By the time I go home, I've missed all the trouble.

It's been four months since I've had a fight. I'm trying to learn from my previous mistakes of not going to school and being in fights. So now I go to school, I don't fight, and I do something productive when I get out of school. Like, recently, my mentor took me on a college tour. Before that experience, I wasn't thinking about going to college, but now I am. During the college tour, one of the presenters compared the kids who don't go to college to kids who go to college. It made me think.

I am determined to turn my life around. I am now in it to win it. I can tell that I am changing. I was asked recently, if someone walked up and stole my cell phone, what would I do? In the past, I would have whupped that person. Now, I would talk to the person. I would let him know that I knew he had my cell phone and that I wanted it back. If he didn't give it back, I would try to talk and resolve the situation. If he still didn't give it back, I would be mad, really mad, but I would walk away to avoid further confrontation. I'm proud of what I'm becoming.

In five years, I see myself going to college and graduating. I also see myself getting my own crib, probably married with two shorties and working or owning my own business. I also see myself being a different father than my father; I am going to be there for my kids. For now, I am going to keep going to school and keep doing my work. I am going to keep myself busy so I can continue on this path.

I told myself that I can't be 25, out here still trying to hustle, and still talking about how I need to go back to school. I know somebody who is 40 and still on the block. Nigga, you 40 years old! When you gon' quit?

—*Interviewed by LaDawn Norwood*

EVERYTHING ABOUT ME IS TAINTED

MARIA HERNANDEZ

Maria Hernandez, who asked that her real name not be used, grew up in street-gang royalty. The man she believed to be her father, "Beto," was a leader of the Latin Kings in Humboldt Park, a Puerto Rican neighborhood on the Near West Side where the powerful gang was formed.

Two events transformed Maria's life when she was 11 years old. First came the revelation that Beto was not her biological father. Then came Beto's arrest and eventual imprisonment on drug-trafficking charges.

Despite her childhood struggles, Maria graduated from college and plans to pursue a master's degree. Although she still keeps in touch with Beto, she has not followed his path into the criminal underworld. Instead, she works in his old territory as a youth coordinator for an organization attempting to keep young people away from gangs. She frequently uses the word "crazy" to describe her life.

It's an incredible story, but it's a sad story.

I grew up in Humboldt Park, born and raised—story of a typical Puerto Rican, I guess. My mom was 17 years old when she was pregnant with me; she had my brother two years later. So we were raised by my mom who was a welfare baby, so they call it. It was a way of life. I grew up thinking, "Well, everybody's on food stamps. Everybody has cousins that are gang members, fathers that are gang- and drug-affiliated."

We grew up in a community where kids were having kids, so there were a lot of kids. Summer days were long. Back then, it was a popular thing to be outside. We spent all of our time outside, just being outside roller-skating, riding bikes, playing freeze tag, eating freeze pops. We would walk to the corner store about four times a day, I'm convinced of it.

Our father was an original Latin King.[49] It made me feel safe, because people were scared of him and everybody knew who he was. He was a great guy. His lifestyle was horrible, but for the most part I respected him as a man.

I remember one time I cried, because I was in grammar school and the kids were like, "You don't have a father, you don't have a father." So I went home crying and told my mom how they said I didn't have a father, and I guess she told him. My kindergarten teacher put together a little play—and in walks my dad. I'm like, "Yes!" He walks in so ghetto with all these gold chains, a wifebeater T-shirt and saggy jeans. And it was just like, "That's my dad!"

Everybody was saying, "He's so cool."

And I'm like, "I know."

There was an international drug bust and my father was one of those incarcerated. They didn't know that the FBI was in on anything and when they take you, they take all of your possessions, too. The cars, the house, the property—it's going with the FBI. Period. I was about 11, and I knew this is it. He's gone for good.

You got these fathers that are drug dealers and gang-affiliated and you start feeling like you're on top of the world. Then it's all wiped away, just like that. You never know when it's coming, but when it does, it hits you and you're stuck. Nowhere to go. It's like starting from scratch. That's why I kinda wish we never had anything. It was hard. You go from having money with this baller drug dealer to having nothing.

Right before he got incarcerated, my mom took me to McDonald's, sat me down, and told me that my brother's father wasn't mine.

She was the typical Puerto Rican mom that cooked every day, so if we went to a restaurant, we knew it was a good occasion. So she sent my brother to play in the play place, and she was like, "I have something to tell you. Beto's not your father."

And I was like, "What?"

"Yeah, Beto's not your father." And deep down inside, I felt it. I have older cousins and, when they would describe me, they would say, "He's his, but she's not."

I didn't know how to feel. I was young and I didn't understand it, but the more I grew up, the easier it was for me to just stick to myself. It's like you paint an image and you imagine your life as a kid and it never dawns on you that things are never going to turn out that way.

Beto's out of jail now. He was released a year ago. It's funny because he was released right before I graduated college, so he was able to come to my graduation. You would think you spend that much time in jail and you would learn—but no. He wasn't supposed to come back to Chicago; the authorities told him not to come back. He came back. It is what it is. Supposedly, he's back to the drug thing. You know, I see him when I see him, and we talk every now and then. But my brother and I had more contact with him when he was incarcerated.

The end of my freshman year in high school, I met my real father on accident. I was in the car with my mom. We were driving down Belmont and we were in the turning lane going left and there was a truck across from us going the opposite way in the turning lane.

I don't even know why I said something, and to this day I regret saying anything. But I'm like, "I feel like I know this man."

And she's like, "Who?"

I said, "The guy driving that truck."

She looks, and she was like, "You definitely know him. That's your father."

My stomach hit the ground. I didn't even know what to think. My mom, being the person she was, pulls through, goes around, follows the truck and is beeping, beeping, beeping till he pulls over. He pulls over. They get out of the car. She's having a conversation with him and she's like, "You need to help take care of her. I've been looking for you."

I just felt bad for her because she's seeking sympathy from somebody that doesn't care. I kinda wanted to be like, "Screw him, and let's go." Nonetheless, she talked and every month after that he sent me a check for $300. Didn't really get to know him much. I graduated from high school and invited him, but he had a daughter the same age as me and she graduated as well, so he said he couldn't come.

I went away to college for two years at Northern Illinois University (NIU) and I was having issues paying my tuition. My real father was frustrated. He was like, "I just can't do this anymore." So I could feel the tension building up and then, that was it; my sophomore year in college we had a dispute over money. He was like, "I don't want to have to do anything for you anymore." I could understand that if he didn't start doing stuff for me when I was 14, but he was off to a late start. Here I am trying to get my degree and he bails out.

It just got to the point where he was like, "This isn't my fault, anyway. You should've stayed here and went to school somewhere in the city or somewhere cheaper where I wouldn't have to help you. I told your mother not to keep you anyway."

And I told him, "My mom raised me. She did a good job, and guess what? I'm gonna make it with or without you. I don't expect you to be there. I don't even care that you don't want to be here. But when you're old and gray and the rest of your children abandon you, don't come looking for me." I haven't heard from him since. That was four years ago.

You come out of these situations and people don't realize the damage that is done to you psychologically. I wear a smile, but people don't see past that. I have a hard time crying and I think I love differently. I love to a certain point, but I can't love past a certain point. I feel like it will make me vulnerable and it will open me up to get hurt. I've been proposed to twice, and they don't know my story. I don't like sharing it; this is stuff that people don't know.

I used to have a horrible temper; it was just bad. Anything would just provoke a fight. And my mom was like, "I don't know what to do with you anymore."

I was still fighting in college. I felt unprepared for NIU. I wound up on probation and was about to get kicked out of my dorm room for fighting. So I had to leave. I was like, "You came here to do something, and you're not doing it."

I think when I got to UIC is when I realized just how different I actually was. You can't really hang with the people you grew up with too much. I love them, and I still talk to them. We have history together, and it's like, "You're always gonna be a part of me and, when you need me, I'm here for you. But right now, I got other stuff to take care of."

It's crazy, 'cause I met people at UIC and we would all walk to the Blue Line and they're like, "Oh, you're going the ghetto way. Catching the Blue Line west, that's to the *'hood-*'hood." They used to joke about it, and I joked with them too. But I took those thoughts home with me: "There's no way they'll ever be able to understand me as a person."

It's so segregated in this city that it's almost like a vicious cycle. There's no way we're going to break out of it. These kids see it and they know. And honestly, they know what's bad and what's not. They just don't feel like they can promote change alone.

I work with high-school kids. These girls aren't prepared for what's to come. Once they have these kids—that's it, they're stuck. They end up having a hard time going to school and working, so they drop out, and then here we go again with the cycle. These kids want love. They get pregnant and they think, "I finally have somebody that's going to love me." I see this so many times.

And the sad part is they don't have resources in the community to help them. It's like the system is designed for them to fail. Now that I work and serve as a youth organizer, there's times where I'm talking to these kids and I want to learn more about them. So I go to the parents—and the parents know less than what I know. And it's not that they don't care; it's that they don't know *how* to care. These kids are out there and they're just learning based on what's in the environment.

On the West Side, they run a drug deal right in front of our youth center, on the corner of the unit. And I have to talk them, like, "Hey, I know this is what you guys have to do, and I'm not telling you not to do it. But while we're meeting, maybe you could move it."

And they respect it. They do. I give it up to these drug dealers because—it's horrible—I feel like they're destroying the community and, at the same time, they sorta save it in some weird ways.

It's like they're destroying these people that are already addicted or heading down that path but then providing resources for these people that can't make it otherwise. That's what got my mom through. There were some times where we would have an uncle come through and be like, "Here's $100."

Honestly, I feel like the older guys don't want these kids out there drug dealing. They don't. They'll tell them, "Here's $20, man. Stay off these streets. Go do something." But when it comes to the gang thing, they need their numbers. They need their recruitment to be high. That's the only way they keep themselves safe.

These kids, they're not ready for it. They're recruited at a young age by gangs. They paint this cool image of like, "Man, you could be like us and we'll protect you." That's how they got this boy named Cornelio,[50] who was just killed this past year.[51] Cornelio, when I started working with him, he was 13. He was a tough kid, just this heart, and that's what they look for: that true, true heart. And Cornelio, they wanted him and they got him and he's dead. And that's how it works.

The police can't do much unless they have an actual incident that took place and they have the proof right there. As community members, we know what happened and who did what. But it's all hearsay. So these cops can't do anything with that information. Now, what I don't respect about the police officers is that you see these guys on the corner and you know they're up to no good, so you pull over. But instead of telling them to disperse, you sit there holding a conversation with them, get back in your cop car, and roll off. That's what I don't respect. I'm not going to say all officers do that. I see it a lot, though. They have to maintain a good relationship with the gang-bangers. They want peace on their clock.

My kids will argue that these cops are extremely crooked and in on all of this. So for these young people, it's like going against joint forces. You're fighting against people in the community and you're fighting against cops and you're fighting against family members—because for a lot of my kids, just like for myself, family's tied into this. So they don't want to cause controversy with family. They learn to dismiss certain things and just hope to try and be a little different than everybody else.

My biggest thing for these kids is exposure. Take them outside these communities. I take them to places that normal people would be like, "Oh, that's regular." But take these kids to a theater or a restaurant, they're like, "Oh my goodness, this place looks expensive." And it probably wasn't, but to them it's like, "Oh, we're downtown! We're eating downtown!" They make the biggest thing out of the smallest thing.

We take them on college trips, because they need to see other students such as themselves that came out of the neighborhood. They're in school, they're successful, and they're doing something major—as opposed to seeing their friends that are on the block pretty much the whole day.

I've thought about leaving Chicago myself. I thought about going to somewhere warm, like Miami. Oh my God, I visited Miami and it's just like, they hold on to that Hispanic culture. They all speak Spanish. It's something we lost here in Chicago.

I wanted to leave after undergrad. But my family acted like I killed somebody. I realized I could never leave. *La familia*—you know it's all about the family. We're all we got. Period. My mom says it and my brother says it. He even has it tattooed on him. We are all that we have, so to lose a piece is like breaking down a significant part of your backbone. There's no way you can function without it. If one person out of the family makes it and wants to achieve more, they're bound by the ties that they have to their family. So everything about me is just tainted. It's like choosing between where my heart is and what's right—and it's hard to make that choice.

—*Interviewed by Danielle Killgore*

ENDNOTES

49 The phrase describes someone from the older generation of Latin Kings.

50 According to the Chicago Police Department, Cornelio Farfan Jr. was killed on Dec. 5, 2010. See https://portal.chicagopolice.org/.../60502397208980E5E-040A5A7403B2187 .

51 Our interview took place early in 2011.

WHAT'S ONE BULLET?

ERNIE PURNELL

Ernie Purnell is a nurse in the Cook County Trauma Unit at the John H. Stroger Jr. Hospital, located at Ogden and Harrison on Chicago's West Side. Formerly known as Cook County Hospital, Stroger is a central hub for violence-related treatment in the city, and much of its patient population is economically challenged and without medical insurance.

Purnell is a tall, stocky 47-year-old who grew up in an impoverished African-American neighborhood on the West Side. His beard has a little gray and he wears glasses. Despite the difficult nature of his work, he is jovial and often laughs in amazement at what he has to deal with every day.

One of the favorite questions that my younger patients ask is, "What type of gun did I get shot with?"

And I answer, "I don't know. I just know you have a hole in you. We're going to assume a *big* gun because the hole in you sure is big!"

They're like, "Oh, did you get the bullet out?"

"Well, I don't know, we'll have to see." And one of the things I like is showing them the X-ray. It's like, "Okay, guess what that is! That's the bullet that's still inside of you!"

And they gasp and are like, "Are you going to get it out?"

"Mmmm, depends…"

When a young person comes in, we have to physically take care of them. So we need to figure out what's wrong and treat them. Because the goal is to save lives. So number one: Save their life, regardless of what happened before. You're here, you're a patient at Stroger Hospital, we just need to deal with this. We start an IV, draw blood for labs, get that X-ray, maybe a CAT scan, give them medications for pain, a contrast to light up their insides so that we can see what's going on. And then, we prep 'em depending on where they're going.

After we break through saving lives, the second step is getting past those trust barriers. A lot of our patients *don't* want to tell us what happened, who they are, what's going on, or their medical history—and those are really, really important things that we need to know about while treating them. They may not *want* any treatment. They may think like, "Okay, you're just holding me here until the police get here." And it's like, "No, not really." Or, "You're going to finish me off." Which is not true, but sometimes you have to deal with those types of attitudes. Or, "You're holding me until the *other* person can get here to finish me off."

Sometimes there's the one who walks out, or the one who gets really angry at the staff—but you can tell that anger is not really with *us*. It's the situation, and you're trying to get them to understand that. It can be kind of a rough transition until they realize that we just want to save their life. And we talk to them *always* within the confines of the trust—because once you lose trust, that's it.

For young adults, the reason they wind up in the emergency room is usually gang-slash-crime-related. I won't say everybody's in a gang, but a gang-related crime is usually the background of what's going on. You kinda want them to understand how serious it is, because a lot of our young people, they see these things on TV—people get shot and get up all the time, and then, in the next scene, they're okay. They have this idea that, "I can get shot four or five times and then *live,* so what's one bullet?" And then, when you tell them that one bullet didn't just go through you—it bounced, it ricocheted around inside of you, so it hit a lot of things—they're like, "What? Bullets can do that?" Uh, yeah. It's not like TV or a video game—at all. You don't get up again.

They don't realize that one bullet can cause massive damage to the human body. I like to bring them to the reality of it: "Okay, we took out part of your bowel. The bowel is responsible for digestion, which means that you may have to change your diet, particularly if we gave you a colostomy bag. You're going to have to learn what to do in social situations, because you can't eat everything that you want to eat." Or they had to take out a kidney, and then I explain what a kidney does. Or they had to take out a part of your liver, and I explain what a liver does. Or they had to take out a part of your lung, and I explain what the lung does. And it's like, "You're only 16. These are not parts that you should be missing at this time." And, unfortunately, sometimes you have to explain to them, "If your spinal cord's been transected, that's game over for your legs. I'm sorry." Or they'll ask, "Will I be able to have sex or have children?" That all depends because sometimes you lose your testicles, so that's *no.* They don't like that part. But those are the consequences of your decisions, you know. You went out there, you got shot. Unfortunately, this time it took out your scrotum, so it's a done deal.

And a lot of patients, when they find out that they've lost certain body parts, or when you have a patient who becomes quadriplegic or paraplegic, the support system that he thought he had—including his friends or his girl-friend—they tend to drift away before his hospital stay is actually over. And so he's forced to re-evaluate those relationships. And, usually, he'll draw closer to the ones who *truly* love him, which are the ones who are really actually vis-iting him—usually a grandparent or parent, aunt, uncle. It makes him think. Sitting in the hospital bed, the only thing you can do is think. Because you can't run the streets, you can't go with your friends, you can't do too much of anything, so you need to re-evaluate what brought you here to the hospital.

Our whole trauma team deals with the families. The doc may have to go out and explain what's going on with the patient. And I may have to play liaison between them and the patient, because the families want to see their loved one—and, depending on what's going on, they can't come in just yet. My job is to try and get them in, you know, and at least *see* the patient— maybe just see them on their way to surgery. At least you saw them—'cause there is the chance that this may be the last time you have to say whatever you're gonna say, do whatever you're gonna do with that person. And that's both ways. It's both ways.

We have met the parents who, you know, they're tired. They're like, "I have talked to him or her over and over and over and over again, and she just keeps doing X, Y and Z. I don't understand. Why am I not reaching my child?" They want us to talk to their children—sometimes the child just needs to hear it from someone else. And then, you know, it's like, "Well, you need to listen to your parents, because they kinda know what they're talking about." We try to encourage the parents: "Don't give up on them—'cause the teen years, they're just the crazy years. This is when you have to hold on a little bit tighter."

And then you have some people where it's like, "Yikes, your parents are nightmares!" You can see it in some of the things they say, some of the things they do, and some of the ways they appear when they come in to check on their child. It's like, really? Drunk? High? These are not good things. These are not good role models. One parent was like, "Don't worry about him.

He's just gonna die anyway." And I'm like, "You do realize he's only 15?"

So you want to tell the child, "Until you get away from your parents, I can't see you changing, because they're the major influence in your life and they're leading you way down the wrong path."

You will sometimes get the victim and the assailant at the same time, and the best thing to do is to try and keep them as separate and as far away from each other as possible. Because it's not them. They're injured, so they're not going to do anything to harm each other anymore. It's the families—and when the families get here, that's when things blow up.

Of course, everyone's innocent because, regardless of who the victim is, the family is always going to provide support. If they're the assailant, then the family will usually buy into the idea that the other victim must have done something to *trigger* the assailant to attack. If they're the victim, then the assailant must have attacked the victim for no reason. They never get down to the reasons of what really happened. So yeah, things have blown up here to full-fledged fights where we actually do have to call in the police and people do have to get arrested.

I'm hoping that more youth will be involved with education. I'm hoping that they'll understand that you gotta be educated to get out. I tell my gentlemen: Try nursing. I let them know there's something else you can do with your life. You don't have to sell drugs. You don't have to run with a gang. It's like, "Aren't you tired of your mother crying? Aren't you tired of that? You can do something that actually makes a difference, helping people instead of hurting people."

I just try to be a role model for them. When they say, "Well, you don't know my story, you don't know my life," I'm like, "Yeah, I kinda do. I didn't *live* your life, but I do *know* what's going on in your life."

I grew up over here on the West Side. I actually grew up in this neighborhood here at Congress and Central Park. Now I think it's called East Garfield Park, but back then it was all just called the West Side. I saw a lot of gang activity growing up, a lot of hopelessness, helplessness, a lot of drug activity.

There was this one girl I knew—I will always remember this one forever—she played Russian roulette and she lost. I was like 13 when that happened. And it's like, "A: Why are you playing Russian roulette? B: Why are you drinking? C: How did you get access to a gun?" There were just so many questions. And to see so many of my peers—because we were all friends—going in a different direction than I did, it was kind of depressing.

I went on to high school. Back when I went—I graduated in 1982—they opened up a program where you could basically go to any high school in the city.[52] Before, you were stuck to districts. So I went to Taft, which is up on the Northwest Side. Oh! Going to Taft as part of the first big group of African-American kids was like going back into the 1950s to civil rights times. We were met with protests. We were met with rioting. We were met with name-calling. People pulled their kids out of school. It was insane. I stuck it out—I made it through my four years and graduated—but I got to literally see what racism is all about.

I went to college, and then, once I graduated, I came back to the West Side to contribute back to the population that produced me. I knew I always wanted to help people. It was just a matter of *how* was I going to help people. My mother was a big influence 'cause her heart's, like, huge. One of the earliest things I can remember is, she allowed some of our family members to come up from Mississippi, and they lived with us for however long they wanted to before they moved on to other houses here in the city. And after that, I saw how she would always take care of homeless people or people in the neighborhood who just needed help.

So I started my journey in nursing when doors opened through the military. I became a nurse in the Army National Guard, and I transitioned from the military to my civilian life. That was back in 1988 or 1989. The military helps you to focus: You work as a team player and you learn not to complain *at all*. It's like, "Look, this is a job, this is what you signed up for, this is what you're gonna do. Go do it." And it gives you that mentality: "I'm here to work and I'm going to work to the best of my abilities. And, when it's over, it's over till tomorrow." I've been working at Cook County Hospital for almost 20 years and in trauma since 2002.

I always tell patients, "I'm not here to judge you; I'm just here to fix you. If you choose not to change, you know that's on you. If you know the things that can happen to you—jail, death, permanent disability—then you have the opportunities. If this is the life you're choosing, then I'm just here to try and put you back together again."

We take care of some of the worst injuries, some of the worst of the worst. But there are patients who you would think would never survive who actually survive—and it's just *amazing*. It's amazing. I just told a patient the other day, "I work in a land of miracles."

We do have patients die, of course. When it's happening, if the patient can talk, they'll let you know something's not right. Or they stop talking, which is a bad sign, but a lot of people are like, "Oh great, they're calm." And it's like, "Mmm—they're dying." The next thing you'll notice is the monitor: The patient's vital signs will start changing—and changing drastically for the worse. Then you contact the doctor, you make sure the patient's airway is okay, make sure he's breathing. And then sometimes you have to explain to him, "We have to put you to sleep. We have to put a tube in to help you breathe." But sometimes you don't have time to explain—you just have to do it. And it can be very scary for everyone involved, because we have to figure out what's wrong in a short period of time and then fix it. And sometimes we can't figure it out in time.

But I'm sorry, a lot of people think you can get used to watching a young person die. You don't get used to it. Young people have so much potential and, when you talk to them, you realize, "You've got so many other gifts that you could use, that you could contribute to the world." And then to kinda see that just ebb away, and you think about the people in their lives that it's going to affect because that person is gone. But for every 10 that we lose, maybe there's two that'll turn around and actually succeed and change their lives. And who knows? From that, maybe they could change the world.

—Interviewed by Michael Van Kerckhove

ENDNOTES

52 Before Purnell and other blacks integrated Taft under the city's "Access to Excellence" desegregation program in 1978, the Far Northwest Side school had only enrolled one African-American student in its history. On the first day of class, "some black students said whites threw rocks and crab apples at them," according to the *Chicago Tribune*. See Casey Banas, "Peaceful Return to City Schools," *Chicago Tribune*, Sep. 7, 1978.

YOU LIVE BY IT, YOU DIE BY IT

LATOYA WINTERS

Latoya Winters studies sociology and Family and Child Studies at Northern Illinois University. She hopes to eventually earn a master's degree and work with at-risk kids in a neighborhood much like the one she grew up in: East Garfield Park, an impoverished area that has seen its population decline from about 70,000 people in 1950 to about 20,000 today. As a child, Winters lost several family members and friends to violence and saw her own mother spend time in prison. But she was nurtured and inspired by her maternal grandmother and found refuge at the Marillac Social Center, a Catholic outreach house that has served poor families on the West Side of Chicago for almost a century.

In many respects, Winters shares similarities with other college students on the verge of graduating: She is neatly dressed, has big dreams and is a fast, passionate speaker. But her childhood experiences are far different from those of most classmates.

My grandmother, Carrie Winters, was born and raised in Mississippi. After her parents passed on, she moved to Chicago. She wanted to find work, and she wanted a better life for her children. She worked all these odd jobs just to make a way for her kids—two to three jobs at a time. She worked at Campbell's Soup forever, and that passed down to my aunt working there. My grandmother bought her house in maybe the '40s and lived there until she died in 2006.

I always smelled a sense of soulful in her. I could smell this perfume that she'd always wear, especially when she went out or went to church. When I say she was churchgoing, I *mean* churchgoing. She was always cooking, everything from the big dinners to macaroni to the chitlins. She had a kind of curl to her hair, because she always wore rollers when she went to the beauty salon. She was a hard-working, independent woman; I see that in her from as early as I can remember. It is still deeply rooted in her grandkids today. Oh my God, we are pieces of my grandmother.

A lot of my grandmother's kids strayed off—a majority of her kids, honestly. Some of them were alcoholics; some were drug addicts like my mother, Raquel. My grandmother raised me. My mother had nine kids, and my grandmother had custody of all of them, plus maybe 10 to 15 of my cousins. My uncles' kids, then my aunts' kids—my grandmother raised all of us. We had a two-flat building with a basement, a first floor and a second floor. There was always room.

My grandmother reached out and took care of kids that weren't hers. At Thanksgiving dinner, if we had a friend who didn't have anywhere to go, my grandma had enough to go around. She had her table set for everybody. If me and three cousins had to sleep in the same bed, we always had somewhere to sleep. My grandmother adopted all of us, because everyone had their different problems, and she refused to let us be separated. She never closed the door on anybody, including her own kids who didn't, you know, fulfill their parent responsibilities. I never even heard my grandmother talk down about anybody, no matter what.

Gangs always existed in my neighborhood. The majority of the guys in my family are affiliated with the Gangster Disciples; so are the majority of people in my neighborhood, actually. I never understood what it was about gangs, but then, as I grew older, I learned more. I've had these sociology classes about it, and I see the way gangs have destroyed people. I've talked to people like my uncles and cousins and brothers who say, "I got put into the gang when I was younger," and, "If I could have gotten out, I would have." But some of them wouldn't have. Like I always say, "You live by it, you die by it."

Growing up, it was terrible. It was all I saw, all I knew. I think that I was scared that I might end up in a gang or something. I look back now, and all I can say is, "I am thankful." I hate the lives that were taken, but I just thank God for the lives that were changed because they were given a chance to look at the positive and the negative and decided not to get involved.

I grew up not even a whole block away from Marillac House, where they have different social service agencies inside the building. Their main purpose is to make a safe environment for kids, so they don't have to be out on the streets. My big cousins and my big sister actually went there first, but I was too young to go. They always had their jump-rope teams going, they had their cheerleading, and they had their dance groups, and it was like the spark of a movement or something. They would come home bragging, "We did this and we did that," and I was just moping around, sad, because I wanted to do it.

That's how I became involved, with my cousin Shavontay and my two sisters. We were the four young ones who begged and cried and whined, and they opened up the age range for us. I came in through Hope Junior, an after-school program. It went from just the basics of getting help with my homework to being involved in everything you can name, just to have something positive to do. I played basketball, I played volleyball, I did poetry, I did choir—you name it, I did it. As soon as I walked into Marillac, it felt like home, and you don't get that everywhere you go. My Marillac family is like my second family, and the different things I've learned there, the many friendships I've gained there, are remarkable. I give them credit for me sitting here today. It's made some of the violence in the neighborhood invisible, like it doesn't exist.

My brother, my mother's firstborn child, his name was Lamont. Lamont started out in a gang when he was about 13. He was heavily involved. Heavily. He did a lot of negative things, lived a very dangerous life, and it caught up with him. I was 10 years younger than him, and young when all this happened, but I did have a relationship with my brother. I knew that he would only be going out one way: through the jail or, you know, dead.

It makes me curious, every time I think about him. I think about the day when me and my aunt and my cousins had just come from eating out, and he walked up to the car and said, "When I die, I want to be buried right here in front of this house." He lived to see about two or three more days, and then he was dead.

People said that he had killed somebody a week before that, and somebody was coming back for him. My family was telling him to leave town and just go lay low. He had been wearing a bulletproof vest for a week, but then to just take it off... Why was he wearing that bulletproof vest all the time and he all of a sudden took it off?

I was in sixth grade when it happened. It was a normal day, and I was in the house. Me and Shavontay were hanging out and watching TV, and I had fallen asleep. Then, she was shaking me: "Wake up, wake up. I just heard gunshots."

Gunshots in our neighborhood was like hearing the ice-cream truck, as sad as that is to say. I guess, when she told me, I kinda was asleep. Before I could fully get up, I heard people upstairs running out the door. I got outside and my mom's all broke down and fell out, and the mother of Lamont's kids is out there lying down on the street and she's crying, and my sister's crying, and my cousin—so I knew something happened to someone close.

Lamont had been standing with my mom and sister and all these chicks, so obviously, none of them were holding any guns. These two boys came up through the empty lot next to our house and shot Lamont at close range, about 15 times. My uncle had gotten his pickup truck and put my brother in the back of it. There was a hospital up the street from us, and my uncle was just speeding. The police got behind him but he didn't stop until he got to the hospital. The boys shot Lamont so many times, so I'm guessing my uncle already knew he was dead, but he still wanted to try and revive him.

I don't understand why people do the things they do, but then, I have to realize my brother did a lot of bad things. I was just happy that my mom and my family didn't do what some people do when they get on the TV news and act like their kids are innocent. My mom didn't do any of that. I'm sad to say I lost a brother, but it's just so much more than that. I'm sure that if he would have lived and been caught, he would have served time for more than just the murder. I'm sure they would have found all these guns somewhere, and probably drugs.

My cousin Andre was following in Lamont's footsteps, because he started gangbanging so early. And then, when he was 17, the same thing happened to him as Lamont. Some boys came up through the exact same lot, and they shot Andre at close range.

I can't forget that our other cousin Phillip was killed the year before Andre. So it was every year, we lost someone. It was emotional thing after emotional thing—a lot of death—and my grandmother was still standing at the top of us all. She raised them, she raised them all, and then to have to constantly bury them year after year? Everybody would look at her and say, "You are so strong."

My cousin Shavontay and I went to an all-girls Catholic high school through a residential scholarship program that Marillac had set us up with. We moved to Evanston. We didn't come home much, and my grandmother cried, but she thanked God for Marillac helping us get into the program. We had to get used to not seeing our family. It was hard, but I wanted to go to a good high school, get a real high-school education, because I wanted to go to college eventually. In my neighborhood, some people barely make it to high school, so you know how hard it is to go to college.

I ended up running for class president senior year and got it. So, by me having the top position in the school, I was the first to come out on graduation day. Graduation hadn't started before I was crying. As I was preparing for our song to play, I was looking at everybody in my family that was in the audience. I will never forget it. When I got my diploma, I just stood on stage like the graduation was all about me. I raised my diploma, and my mother was the main one that I looked at. She had been in jail for my eighth-grade graduation, and none of her daughters had even gotten a diploma.

When I was younger, I was mad and I cried a lot and wondered why my mother couldn't be involved in my life. She would stay at my grandmother's some of the time, but she wasn't stable. She was doing hard drugs, like crack, heroin, cocaine, stuff like that. I'd often see her, but she'd be hanging outside on the corner with the other drug addicts. It was like she'd rather spend time with them than me, and I always wondered if I did something wrong.

When I became old enough, I started writing her letters in jail—and as she started to better herself, she'd write me cute little cards back. As I got older, I got more of an understanding that this was just a problem she had. She had to take time to deal with it, to better herself when she was ready, not because everyone else wanted her to. I learned that it wasn't my fault, and everybody goes through problems. It just takes some people a longer time than others.

Since my junior year of high school, my mother's been doing good and has stayed clean. I wasn't always proud to say, "That's my mother," because I'd see my friends with clean mothers with the nice clothes and the nice shoes and the job and everything. Today, I am proud. I say, "That's my mother. Her name is Raquel. That's who brought me into this world. I love her unconditionally."

Her proudest moment was being at my high-school graduation and being able to say, "I'm here. I'm clean. I'm a mother. I've changed."

Looking back, before high school, I would have never thought I'd even make it to high school because of where I lived and all the people I have lost. I thought that I would have given up a long time ago, but I'm still pushing and fighting and I plan on making it somewhere. I feel like, as long as you have faith and you have some motivation, it will take you a long way, a way that you would have never thought it would have taken you.

I've still never met anybody like my grandmother. I was 17 when she passed away, and it was like Rosa Parks died or something. I would give it all up if she could be here now, but I know that she sees what I'm doing and I know she's proud. That's why, when I'm done getting my bachelor's degree,

I'm moving to get my master's degree, so she can say, "Everything she's doing, I taught her that. And she hasn't given up yet."

—*Interviewed by Danielle Turney*

TOMORROW IS NOT PROMISED
CHARLIE BROWN

Charlie Brown—an alias—is an 18-year-old who lives in the West Humboldt Park community on the West Side of Chicago. Residents of the area face high crime and poverty rates, struggling schools and "one of America's biggest open-air drug markets," in the words of a recent Chicago Reader *article.*[53] *Charlie describes his neighborhood as a place where you need to watch your back.*

Charlie is a tall, charismatic young man who loves to write poetry. He describes himself as artistic, cocky and intelligent. Charlie was adopted by a woman who is raising six children, five of whom are adopted. His biological father dropped contact with Charlie suddenly when he was 10 years old.

Charlie spent his first two years of high school at King College Prep on the South Side. For his junior year, he transferred to Urban Prep Academy, an all-male charter school on the West Side that regularly helps get 100 percent of its graduating seniors accepted to college. Despite the academic excellence of the school, Charlie doesn't like it. "The days are too long," he says. "I also don't like Urban Prep because of the uniform, which is a blazer, red tie and khaki pants. And I don't like it because it's all boys."

But an even bigger problem for Charlie Brown is trying to imagine a future anywhere outside of his own violent community.

I know basically everybody in the neighborhood, so if I see unfamiliar people, I get cautious. "Who is that? Watch out!" I turn around every few steps. I watch my surroundings. If I see cars drive slowly down the street, I get paranoid. If I am sitting on the porch, I go in the house. Everyone operates like this, even the drug dealers. No matter how many dudes you have with you or how many guns you have on your waist, you have to watch your back.

I'm also cautious of the dudes who hang on the corner. When you pass them, they often say, "Hey, you wanna work?" And I always think, "No, nigga, you need to work. You need to get a job." But I can't snap on them like that because I don't know what they got. Plus, I get kind of scared when I tell them no because I don't want them to start looking for me. Sometimes they follow you and wait for you to fall just so they can say, "Yeah, you should have come and worked for me."

I'm cool with a lot of the people around here, but my friends know that I'm not like them. You won't catch me sagging my jeans or saying to every chick, "Hey, shorty!" I am not like that. So if they wear their pants down, if they are about to go smoke, or if they be like, "We are about to go to this party and do this or that," they know I am not going to join them. So they just say, "All right, we will talk to you later." But I do like to have fun, get my laughs and jokes in. I make sure I live life for today and not tomorrow. Tomorrow is not promised.

I have been writing poetry ever since I learned to write. I realized that poetry was my thing when I started reciting it in front of the class in fourth grade. We were told to recite memory pieces. That's when you take somebody else's poem, memorize and recite it. But I would write my own and recite it. People started saying "You're real good," and I loved the attention.

Art makes me happy. I can express myself and let me be seen. When you express yourself, you don't want to be judged. You want somebody to listen and just hear what you have to say. You want them to see you for *you*, not how stereotypes see you or the media sees you.

At a poetry performance I had to write on the topic: What have my parents given me? The other kids said life, breath, lungs, beautiful eyelashes. I know my parents gave me those things, but I took it as, "What have they given me—given *me*?" My response was: nothing.

I never knew my real mother but my adopted mother has a picture of her in our house. I know how she looks, but I don't know her. I just know what I see on that picture. I did know my dad. I can't say I resemble him, but I'm tall like him; he wears glasses, I wear glasses; he always looks mean like I do. He stopped coming around when I was 10 so I only have a couple memories of him. What I do remember was he was my daddy until then.

My dad was a construction worker and had his own restaurant. One day, he took me and my granny there and we had spaghetti. When he picked me up he said, "You're my little guy" and my granny was right there. When I say my granny, I'm talking about my adopted mother's mom. I don't know what happened, but I never saw or heard from him after that day. Even though I don't talk to my dad anymore, that moment makes me smile because that was the last moment I remember having with him.

Sometimes I get mad and my granny will say, "Think about your dad." She tells me this because she knows that last time together was a happy moment in life. I don't know how to take it when she reminds me of my dad, because I'm like, "I don't see him anymore." But she says, "Don't judge him. You're still his little guy." I don't know what went on, so I don't judge him, but I do feel like he could at least call or something.

My mother adopted me at the age of 3. I don't even know where I lived before that. It's not a lot that I remember from my childhood, but it was all right. I wasn't getting beat up or nothing like that. She wasn't a drunk or had me with stepdads. She took care of me like I was her own. As I got older and started thinking about it and seeing everyone else with their mothers and daddies, all being so happy, we did get into a lot of arguments. I would sometimes tell my mother, "I wish you didn't adopt me. I don't want to stay with you." And I would walk out the house. I didn't mean those things because she did take care of me like I was her own. But sometimes little things get to you. My mother was single when she adopted me and still is, so I don't have a man around to say, "Don't get in trouble with the law, don't drink, strap up when you have sex" and things like that. But she raised me to the best of her ability and I'm not doing bad. I've never done drugs, been to jail or anything like that.

Sometimes I think about asking my mom and dad, "What happened?" But at the moment I just write a lot of poetry or I draw about it. If I'm in a real bad mood, where I can't stay still, I turn on some music and just dance. Now that I am aware of my talents and what I can do, I go draw, paint, dance or whatever. This is my way to get my feelings out. I don't go hit or yell at somebody, or smoke or sell drugs. Plus, if I do those things, that will just make me less of a person. I am going to be me. Peer pressure doesn't get to me. I won't let it.

There is not much I would change about me, with the exception of my social skills. I'm a good speaker. I perform poetry, but when certain people are talking to me, like if a white man or woman were talking to me right now, I wouldn't be looking them in the face. I would be looking down or something. When a person of authority talks to me, a police officer or white person, I don't look them in the face. Well, not just a white person. It depends on the type of authority and power. Like police officers, when I watch the news I see them get away with everything they do. They beat people for no reason, they can be crooked sometimes and then it is just like they get away with it. And then judges, they can send you to jail for X amount of years if you did the crime or if you didn't do the crime. And I don't want to spend my life behind bars.

I don't know what would happen if I looked them in the eyes. That's the part that scares me. I'm already placed in a box to be lower than them. If I go to school or if I don't go to school, they still see me as a statistic. It doesn't matter how many degrees I get, I would still be the minority to them, the black person, slave or whatever you want to call it. I can go to school and graduate and be at the top of my class, but it will always be that white man who has to hire me. Or, that college tuition that I would owe, how would I get it? There will always be that white man who has to put my life in order. Or, it doesn't necessarily have to be that white man who has to hire me. It can be a black man, but what's to say that he won't hire the white man over me?

I started feeling this way when so many of my friends were being judged and sentenced before they even did a crime. No one gave them the chance to speak up or speak out. No one listened to them and what they had to say. It starts in school. When something happens in a lot of the schools in my area, they don't suspend the kids or call their parents. They just throw them on the streets. Who's to say, when they are thrown on the street, that a drug dealer won't be standing there and say, "Do you want to make some quick money?" Before you know it, they are in gangs, they take this into the schools, it escalates, they get failing grades, are kicked out of school and are on the corner 24/7, and then jail time.

Trevon—like if someone was to ask, "Who is that?" I would say, "That is my brother." We were that type of close.

One day, in April of 2010, I was walking home from the candy store with my other friend, Mikey. We were just walking and laughing—then we hear two gunshots. We hit the ground and duck, wondering, "Where is this coming from?" We run the opposite way into the alley, give it some time and then go back around. It was like there was nobody outside because we heard the gunshots but don't hear any screams or anything. We turn the corner at Ridgeway and Iowa and see a body lying in the middle of the street. Then, we see dudes closing the doors of a car and driving off. There are people at their screen windows, staring, and others looking like they are calling the police. We walk toward the body and say, "Dang, who is that?" We go closer and we're like, "That's Trevon!"

Trevon is lying facedown with a blood-stained shirt. He looks as if he is sleeping with his eyes closed. I think, "What can I do? What am I supposed to do? Am I supposed to retaliate? Am I not?" I see the group of boys hop in the car—do I chase it? It's crazy, like out of a movie, *Boyz n the Hood* or something. I always hear about things like this happening but I never expect to see it in real life. Mikey and I scream, "Help me! Call 911!" We don't have a phone so Mikey runs off screaming for help and I just stand there in shock.

It's just crazy. I can't believe this. I just saw him that morning. It's a Saturday afternoon, and all three of us were just sitting on the porch talking. Mikey and I decided to go to the candy store; Trevon didn't want to go. So Mikey and I went and came back and now he's dead. I start thinking, "I was just with you. This could have been me if I was still with you." I stay there for a minute, and then go to my granny's house. I sit on the porch and then just walk around.

I don't know why they killed Trevon. Some say he was involved with the wrong people. Not involved like selling drugs or anything, but in the wrong neighborhood saying the wrong thing. He came back on our side of the neighborhood, they followed him, he tried to run, and they shot him. When things like that happen, I don't cry. I don't know why; all I do is think about it. I think about what will happen to me after I die. Will people remember me? Will people cry? Will people come to my funeral? What if there is not a heaven or hell? That's when I start to think about it real deeply, and I might cry then.

I dream of a community that has nice neighbors; kids that come outside and play; patios; old ladies on their porches in the summertime, smiling and being able to talk to the young kids; mowed lawns with real grass instead of potato chip bags and cans out front. Although, I know I wouldn't fit in this community; it wouldn't fit my life. Not having to worry about anything would just leave my mind to think about my personal problems like, "Where is my mom? Where is my dad?" Everybody would be all smiles and laughing in this perfect community, which would be phony to me. It would feel like I was living in Mayberry.[54] What comes along with me, my problems, my thoughts, wouldn't fit there. Like the saying goes, you can take the boy out of the 'hood but you can't take the 'hood out of the boy. I know I am not ghetto, but this is where I am from, this is where I live.

I dream of going to college, graduating, getting a nice job, getting my money right, paying back student loans, starting off small with an apartment, getting a nice job, getting a house. My home would be in the city, not in my current community, but not in a place like Mayberry. It would be some place in between. I would talk to youth, tell them what I did and what I came from. When I dream, I do dream of perfect communities and a perfect world. Even though I don't think it would fit my life, I do dream of it.

—Interviewed by LaDawn Norwood

ENDNOTES

53 Mick Dumke, "Besieged," *Chicago Reader*, April 25, 2012, http://www.chicago-reader.com/chicago/besieged/Content?oid=6141461&showFullText=true

54 Mayberry is a fictional community that was the setting for two popular sitcoms of the 1960s, *The Andy Griffith Show* and *Mayberry R.F.D.* The town was white, rural and violence-free.

THE DREAM CLUB'S CHIEF DREAMER
COLLEEN F. SHEEHAN

Judge Colleen F. Sheehan presides in the Cook County Juvenile Justice Division, one of the largest juvenile court systems in the nation. She is the daughter of Irish immigrants who taught her to work hard and pull herself "up by the bootstraps," encouraging her to begin delivering papers at age 8 and to get her first real job— in a restaurant kitchen—at age 13. After graduating from John Marshall Law School in Chicago in 1987, she began her career as an assistant public defender for the Cook County Public Defender's Office. In 1991, she went into private practice, representing clients in criminal and civil matters. She was elected as a Cook County Circuit Court judge in 2000.

Openly gay, Judge Sheehan believes that her sexual orientation often gives her empathy for young people from minority communities. "I am not saying that I know what it means to be an African-American 15-year-old or an African-American male," she says. "But I can understand what it feels like to be hurt from discrimination."

During the course of her career, Sheehan has become an advocate of "restorative justice," an approach that stresses conflict-resolution over punitive incarceration, often through "peace circles" that bring together affected members of the community, including the victim and the offender. The focus of this approach is to help young offenders understand the real harm that resulted from their actions, to take responsibility for those crimes, and to commit to repairing the damage they've inflicted upon others. Restorative justice also encourages the community to be a part of the solution and the restorative efforts.

In conversation, Sheehan is confident and animated, taking on many characters, each with distinct accents and hand gestures. Drinking sparkling water and twirling a paper clip, she leans back in her chair as she speaks.

One day I was coming out of Whole Foods, and a man asked me if I would sign his petition to be a judge, and I said, "How do you do that?" He told me how to get the petitions downtown, and I thought, "I could do that." I enjoyed being an attorney and did not want to abandon something that was so much a part of me. But I was searching for a different way to serve and needed to find the right path. I had secretly dreamed of being a judge one day, but didn't dare believe that it could really happen. In that moment, the barrier of self-doubt suddenly lifted. I knew that I needed to do something about making my dream a reality. I ran for judge in 2000 and was successful.

In 2006, I was asked to come to Juvenile Court. It was a very sobering experience. During my first year or so in Juvenile Court, five kids I sentenced to probation were murdered. When a child is sentenced to probation, I have an ongoing relationship with that child, and I am very much invested in their well-being. I receive periodic reports from their probation officer as to their progress. The kids often come back to court and let me know how things are going with them. So to have a probation officer step up on a case and tell you a child has been murdered is gut-wrenching and surreal. Here we all are, living in this beautiful city of Chicago. But for some kids, it seems like they are living in a war zone.

When I first came to Juvenile Court, attorneys argued that science shows juvenile offenders' brains are not as developed as adult brains and that's why they were making bad decisions. The science was sound, but I thought it was being used to excuse bad behavior. I mean, even a 4-year-old knows that it's wrong to break into somebody's house and steal something.

But after you work in Juvenile Court for a while, things aren't so cut and dry. You see everything here. You have kids that are cognitively delayed. They were born that way. Maybe their parents didn't have the correct nutrition. Maybe a child was born with drugs in his system. You get some kids that have been abandoned—and more than once. They've been abandoned by their parents, so their grandmother raises them for a while, and then their grandmother dies, and then a cousin starts to raise them. Now they're 14 years old, and they're getting in trouble, and the cousin says, "I can't take it anymore."

Then the state enters the picture. That may be necessary, but the state is not a decent substitute for a loving parent. These kids are in serious stress. There are real social, economic and race inequities stacked against these kids and their families. That is wrong. In America, the one thing everyone should have is a chance to succeed. I'm not saying that these children do not engage in bad or even criminal behavior, but it's complicated.

Sometimes all I can do is to acknowledge how painful it must be for them. I tell them, "I see you're in pain, and I'm so sorry. I'm sorry that all of us together—me, society, the system, your parents—have failed." You see a young kid who's so tough that they almost seem dead in the eyes. And then to see a single little tear just roll down their cheeks. Those are the kids that stick with me the most, when I make a profound connection to someone who is virtually a stranger to me, and connect with them on such a deep, human level.

In the past six years, thousands of people have come before me. And in only one case, the victim's family seemed out for blood. In the remaining cases, I have been so amazed at the generosity of the victims who come to court and don't want revenge or punishment for the minor. Time and time again I hear them say, "I want better for you." These victims have suffered serious pain, whether it's physical or emotional. I think it is the best in all of us that says, "If we can't save a child, how can we have hope for any of us?" There's just something about children that evokes empathy in people.

When I worked in the adult system, some defendants were as young as 17 years old. I'd ask them what they wanted out of life. What was their dream? The first time I asked a young man what his dream was, his face lit up. It was as if no one had ever asked them that question.

I was taken by the two responses I would get. Some young men and women turned into completely different people when they were asked about their dreams. They went from tough kids with an attitude to innocent and childlike. They opened up about what they wanted and how they were going to get it. Usually their dreams were unrealistic—playing in the NBA or the NFL—but they seemed happy dreaming big. The other response I would get was telling. Some kids didn't have a clue what their dreams were. They had a flat affect, and I saw the deadening of the hope inside of them.

I remembered those young men and women when I was asked to have a CPS[55] high-school student intern with me. That's when I hatched the idea of Dream Club. Basically, the idea was that, if you had an adult who worked one-on-one with a kid every single day—if you could help them identify their dreams, formulate a plan and then help them execute that plan—then those kids could achieve anything.

I ran the idea by my sister, who is a social worker, and she said, "You really should make it a group of kids, so they can support each other's dreams." So I called the teacher in charge of the intern program back and said, "I'll do it, but I want two or three kids." She called me back and she asked if I would take four.

So these four kids were with me for nine months, two hours a day. We talked about goals and dreams: What's a goal? What's a dream? Why do you want that goal? Why do you want that dream? Why do you want 22-inch rims on your car? What's the value of that? Maybe you want power. Maybe you want respect. Maybe you want notoriety. We discovered that what they wanted, even more than the rims, was what the rims represented.

Then we looked at how they could achieve those things in a way that was more meaningful and longer-lasting than owning 22-inch rims. I gave them movie cameras and sent them out to find out what other people's dreams were. They interviewed attorneys, probation officers, judges and their peers. They were surprised at what people revealed. One of the attorneys they interviewed said, "I don't want to be a lawyer. All I ever wanted to be was a writer. But I don't know if I could ever make that change." This shocked the kids. They looked at this young lawyer and thought he had it all. So they learned that what seemed to be an end-all and be-all wasn't, and that the dream keeps evolving.

I took them out to "business lunches" at fancy restaurants. We visited college campuses. I tried to expose them to things they didn't even know existed. On the day after the historic election of President Obama, we had a picnic in Millennium Park, in front of the Bean. Each of them declared their dream. At first, one girl said, "This is it. This is my dream. To be here, downtown, on this beautiful day, having a picnic in the park." She had lived in Chicago her whole life and had never seen downtown.

Finally, each of them said that their dream was to go to college and find a way to pay for it. None of these kids had parents that went to college. And one young man never had anyone in his family make it past junior year in high school. We went to work. I helped them with the applications and, in one case, literally raced to Loyola with my intern, making the deadline by three minutes.

When we were making real headway, one of the kids came to me and said he wasn't going to college because his father was giving him grief about being better than everyone else. In fact, he almost dropped out of high school. But in the end, they are all in college. Three of them are seniors now and they all still call and text me from time to time. My dream is to go to each of their graduations.

Once people found out about the Dream Club, they started asking me to share the experience. A probation officer asked me to speak to students. The topic was how to be successful on juvenile probation. So I went to this school, and I saw a bunch of kids who seemed fairly bored and not real thrilled to see a judge coming in to speak to them.

Then one young man asked me about a police shooting in New York City. "How did the police get away with that?"

A lot of people ask judges questions like that. But I couldn't answer that question because I didn't know all the specifics. I wasn't in the courtroom. I left thinking, "I did a horrible job and I am never going back to a Chicago public high school again."

Still, I was really taken by their passion. As soon as that young man brought up the issue of the police and community relations, the whole room came alive. I was ignorant that this issue was a concern for kids. I thought, "With all the things that they have to worry about—violence, teen pregnancy, drug use, incarcerated parents and high unemployment—why do they care about the police-community relations?" They didn't seem interested in talking to me about things that I thought had a more direct effect on their lives. Yet they were very interested in talking to me about the police and the community.

About a week later, the same probation officer asked me to speak at Fenger High School in front of about 100 kids. I thought, "Are you kidding me? Oh my God, this is nuts." When I told friends that I was going to Fenger to speak, they said, "It's a big a waste of time. Those kids aren't going to listen. They're going to act like wild animals. They're going to completely disrespect you." After all the stories I had heard, I was half expecting the principal to walk down the hallway with a gun in his hand and be like, "Okay, I gotcha covered, Judge!"

But Fenger was a beautiful school. It was clean, the floors were polished, and there was great woodwork all over the place. The teachers seemed energetic, and the students were in uniforms and seemed really well-behaved. I was really struck by that, because the principal told me earlier that day that a minor had been stabbed outside the school. So there was this contradiction that I was aware of as I walked the hallways.

The teacher introduced me: "All right, everybody, quiet down. Judge Sheehan is here, and she's going to teach you about civics." I was a bit shocked by that and said, "Thank you, but I am *not* going to teach you about civics. I came here today in spite of everyone telling me not to come."

I continued, "I am not here to speak to you. I am here to listen." You could have heard a pin drop.

I said, "I'm going to treat you with the respect that you deserve as young men and women. I expect the same—to be treated the same way—and if I'm not treated that way, I will leave. I will assume that you will behave like young men and women and that you and I can have a dialogue with each other."

Well, I could see them sitting up straighter in their chairs. I could feel sort of the honor that was somehow bestowed in the room, the respect from them to me and me to them, and it changed the vibe of the room. I spoke for a while and then, just like before, a young man started aggressively questioning me about the police and his community and how they get away with what they get away with.

I could feel that I was losing them as they aligned with their classmate. I tried to convince him, the young man, that there were good and bad police, same as with any group. But he just said, "You ain't out here. You don't know." And then he kept saying, "What are you gonna do about the problem? What are you going to do?"

And finally I looked him square in the eye and said, "What are *you* going to do about it?" And that stopped the room. I mean, the room was *quiet*.

And then he looked at me and said, "Well, what *can* I do about it?"

I said, "I don't know. I guess you can do what you just did. Speak up when you see injustice. But it's easier to be a victim and say what's wrong than it is to be a part of a solution. It's a whole lot harder, and it takes a lot more courage to be part of the solution."

And at that moment, I had a sudden image of police and youth sitting together at a round table to talk about their conflict, a safe place to deal with this pain. Because I saw that most of this was born out of pain and crisis. So I asked, "Would you be interested in sitting in a circle not invested in blaming someone, but invested in a solution to this problem?"

He said he would. And, after my talk, about ten kids came up to me and asked, "Are you really gonna do that?"

I said, "I guess I have to now." That is where the journey began.

I started talking about my idea to anyone that would listen. I was referred to a wonderful group called Community Justice for Youth Institute (CJYI). The group was very active in communities, using restorative-justice tools like peace circles. Since that day at Fenger High School, there have been many circles involving police and youth. Not long ago, I helped organize a daylong summit of 80 police and youth. They exchanged ideas, laughter and tears with each other. They lunched together and even participated in a "street yoga" session.

We created a video to share this success and to help cities from across the country find solutions to conflict. During a recent restorative-justice conference in Oakland, a Chicago team met with a member of the Oakland City Council, as well as the city attorney and chief of the school-district police, among others, to share the video. Later, officials in Oakland decided to show the video at a full city council meeting to demonstrate a way that all parties can address issues in a constructive way. I am not sure if the Chicago Police even know that they had that kind of positive effect on another city.

Organizing peace circles is rewarding, but the time has come for these kinds of restorative practices to be institutionalized and become an integral part of the system. In order for real change to occur, there must be joint effort from communities, restorative-justice practitioners and individuals at the highest level of government. If we value peace, healing and cooperation, we all must give our time and treasure to it. Like Juvenile Court, it's complicated and takes effort. But it's worth it.

—*Interviewed by Kaitlyn Willison*

ENDNOTES

55 Chicago Public Schools.

TRYING TO BREAK THE CYCLE

KIM

Kim—who asked that we give her a pseudonym—is an 18-year-old Vietnam-ese-American living in Uptown, a North Side neighborhood known for its ethnic diversity. Although it's not one of the city's high-crime areas, Uptown has been contending with pockets of gang violence for years.

Despite flirting with gang life and dating a Latin King who is now in pris-on, Kim became valedictorian of her high school class and is a straight-A college freshman at University of Illinois at Chicago (UIC). Her interview takes place at a local Starbucks—not Kim's favorite spot, due to her strong opposition to the gentrification of Uptown. "They actually want to knock down the building I live in," she says. "They're like, 'Oh, we need to put up some more condos.' And that's their approach to like, what? Helping their society? Just to push all the so-called bad people to another area? That's not effective."

Although the coffee shop is quite warm and comfortable, Kim leaves on her white puffy coat with its faux fur-lined hood and keeps it zipped all the way up for the entire hour. Except for an initial sip, she doesn't touch the hot chocolate in front of her.

I feel like somebody's watching over me.

Every single time somebody gets hurt or there's a gang shooting, I'm not there. Ever. It's like, "Wow, I could have been a victim if I would have left out the house a little bit sooner." Like last week, I was on my way to the train, and an hour before that, somebody had just gotten shot in the head—right at the corner of my house. It was a drive-by shooter, so that could have hit me.

I honestly feel like somebody's watching over me.

Anything could happen, and you never know when it's going to happen. I don't come outside. The only time you will find me outside is going to a train and then walking home. I mean, I have a younger brother and sometimes I find myself sitting in class and I'm like, "Oh, is he okay?" And then I'll text him because it's like, you know, I'm paranoid something's going to happen.

I live with my mom and brother. And that's it. I grew up right here in Up-town. We moved up and down the street, the same street—Winthrop. We just moved a couple blocks down, a couple blocks up and then back.

My mom, she doesn't have parents. She was raised in Vietnam and her father, an American soldier, died in the Vietnam War. My mom's mom, like, didn't even want her. I think the pregnancy was from a one-night stand. She tried to abort her with an abortion pill, but it wasn't effective. My great-grandmother raised my mother.

American soldiers' sons and daughters, they were being treated poorly over there in Vietnam. So in the late 1980s, the Bush administration, they had a program to send all the people who are mixed-race over to America.[56] So my mom was the sponsor for her family and they all came. She was in her 20s—probably 23. My step-grandfather, he lives by Kimball Avenue and my grandmother is in Kansas. They separated a couple months after they got to America. I don't talk to my grandmother. I don't mean to be disrespectful to my elders and stuff, but she didn't even raise my mom.

My mom told me that she met my dad when she was taking English and he was a math student in an adult education class here in Chicago. And he kept talking to her or something like that. He wasn't around that much. I don't know if he lives in Uptown, but Argyle's[57] right there and Asian people, they just, like, gather there. I see him walking outside.

My mom works pretty hard. She used to work two jobs. I mean, she raised two kids by herself. She's the only person that means anything to me.

About 12 years ago, my mom, she was a victim of attempted rape. This African-American guy, he impersonated a police officer. My mom doesn't speak that much English and she doesn't know her rights. She didn't know that an officer cannot come into her house without a warrant. So she let him in, and he attempted to rape her. She kicked him in his private parts, and he pushed her, and she hit her head on the wall. She had to get stitches, and now she forgets a lot. Sometimes she gets headaches, I guess. And she gets, like, crazy upset when she's not on her medication. Like, she would sometimes try to choke me for no reason. She can't work anymore. She's on disability pension. But she's okay with the medication.

I was at school when the rape happened. I didn't really know what was going on. They were using big words at the hospital, and I remember, even when I was translating for my mom, I was confused. But I was calm. I just remember that they said that this guy also had raped 11 other victims. My mom was the 12th but he was unsuccessful. They caught him.

That incident kind of changed my whole life because I didn't get to be a child anymore. I didn't get to be a kid, even though I wanted to. I had a rough relationship with my mom when I was probably 16 or 17. We was just constantly fighting and arguing. You know, I didn't listen, and I was kinda, like, drifting on the bad side of stuff. I was always smart; I always did well in school. But I was socializing with the wrong people. I guess it's kind of hard to avoid those kind of people, especially if they all grew up in the neighborhood, so you can't just walk past them and be like, "I don't know you." I think if my mom didn't get tough on me, I probably wouldn't be in college right now. I would not have graduated. Something could have happened to me where I could not have accomplished everything.

And it almost did happen. I met this guy named Corey, hanging out with some girls from school. We dated for, like, two months. And he was a gangbanger. And for some reason, at that age, I thought that was cool. He was a Latin King. Right now, he has 14 years to do in prison. He did armed robbery, grand theft auto and then assault.

One night, I almost went to jail because I was affiliated with the Kings. I was getting a ride from one of Corey's friends, Sal, to go to the county jail to see Corey. It was early evening, probably like 5 o'clock. Sal was dressed from head to toe, gold and black—the Latin Kings' colors. So if members of enemy gangs saw him, it was like, you know, a "shoot me, shoot me now" type of thing.

We were driving down—what street is that?—California. And there was, like, some other gang—I don't even know what it was—and we were involved in a car chase. I could have lost my life because they started shooting, but, at that moment, I was just, like, so careless about it because I was just so immature. And Sal was driving all crazy. I mean, like, he drove down the street on the wrong side, trying to get away, and he could have caused a car accident.

I was just like, "Drive! Hurry! Drive! Let's get away from them." Then he turned in an alley and we lost the guys. When we came out of the alley, the police stopped us. I was really scared because I was like, "I'm gonna get arrested. My mom's gonna knock me out." And thank God he didn't have drugs in the car.

Oh my God, I'm a horrible teenager. I put my mom through a lot when I was associating with those people. I think if I could go back, I wouldn't do any of it. But then again, I might go back and still be 16 and be stupid and do it again.

I was going through a phase, a need to fit into my environment, a need to socialize and be cool or whatever. That's why it was so hard to stop talking to people like Corey. I think the wake-up call was when my mom cried. I was, like, 17. She never cries, so when she cried, it was when Corey called me from jail. He called collect and I accepted the charges. My mom was there and I was trying to play it off like, "Oh no, it's somebody else." But the house phone's kinda loud, so she got pissed. I guess she felt disappointed because she raised me better than that. She yelled at me and she cried. I mean, I saw her cry about other stuff, but I wasn't the cause of that, so I didn't really feel guilty about it before.

See, despite all this stuff, I never really liked making my mother upset. I just wanted to be rebellious, but it caught on to me that I had to stand up and help my mother, take care of her. When I hit 18, I was like, "Really? I'm smart. I'm not going to be socializing with you people. Why would I put what I have on the line? I have scholarships lined up for me to go to college. Like, I'm a straight-A student." You gotta look at reality. Where can you get without an education? I mean, that stuff that people do on the streets, like, it's fast money, but I mean, you can't get retirement and pension to come out of that.

Now I'm a freshman at UIC. I thought about going to University of Michigan, but I couldn't afford it. But either way, I think I would have still chosen to stay home. I'm studying criminal justice. I want to be a detective. I mean, it's a lot of people that complains about a lot of stuff, like, "Oh, this is happening, that is happening," but they don't do anything about it. And what's better than getting paid for something you want to do? Which is, like, make a change in society.

I want to go into homicide because I feel like that's something that's most dangerous. And then I want to get my graduate degree because I don't want to be a cop my whole life. I want to go do other stuff, too, like be a prosecutor.[58]

I went to visit the county jail on my own. I wanted to see what was really going on in there, because, it's like, I hear people, you know, coming out of jail, like, "It was horrible" and I just wanted to see it. It's actually a wonderful place. They actually get help, but they can only give you so much so if you don't take anything from it while you're in there, you come back out and, you know, do the same stuff. And it's understandable that some people can come out and do the same stuff because it's not like they ship you out to Harvard University when you get out. They ship you back to your freakin' neighborhood. That's all you know, that's all you're exposed to. But there are people in my neighborhood that are in the same situation that I'm in and I'm doing better than them, so I guess they need motivation. But I don't know. I don't know how to help these people.

That's one reason why I want to move my family out of the neighborhood. If it changes, then I'll come back because, I mean, I grew up here, this is my home. All 18 years of my life, I've seen the same thing—the same cycle.

If my mom was able to have a good mother, like fortunately I have a good mother, she would have been able to come over here when she was younger and she could have went and got her education. She would not be in this neighborhood and the assault would not have happened to her and she would have gave birth to me somewhere else nicer where I don't have to deal with this stuff. In 20 years, I don't want someone to attempt to rape me like my mom. It's like a chain. That's why I say the change should happen now. Just break the cycle or it's going to happen again and again and again.

—*Interviewed by Stephanie Gladney Queen*

ENDNOTES

56 Congress passed the American Homecoming Act—also called the Amerasian Homecoming Act—in 1988. It allowed Vietnamese children born of American fathers to emigrate to the United States.

57 The West Argyle Street Historic District is known for its Vietnamese restaurants, bakeries and shops, as well as for Chinese, Cambodian, Laotian and Thai businesses.

58 When we last spoke with Kim, she reported that she no longer wants to be a detective. She has decided to enroll in law school after receiving her bachelor's degree.

THE GIRL WAS A FIGHTER

CRISTINA FIGUEROA

Cristina Figueroa has seen youth violence from many angles. The child of a Puerto Rican mother and a Mexican-American father, she grew up in a home where beatings and fights were regular occurrences. She also experienced bullying in elementary school. And, during her teen years on the Northwest Side, she explains, "a lot of my friends were gangbangers, because at the time, that's who I felt had my back."

As a runaway teen mother, she found herself in an abusive relationship, facing a dead-end future. Determined to turn her life around, Figueroa earned her GED at the age of 22. Since then, she has received a bachelor's degree in criminal justice from Northeastern Illinois University in Chicago and a master's degree in public administration from DePaul University, where she teaches part-time. From 2001 to 2006, she was a juvenile probation officer in Lake County, Illinois, counseling, supervising and helping to rehabilitate young people. Now she works with adult offenders as U.S. probation officer.

A short, dark-haired woman in her early 40s, Figueroa maintains a youthful appearance and has an abiding compassion and empathy for at-risk youth.

Kids are not born bad. There are very few sociopaths out there. Kids are not inherently bad. That's learned behavior. And I think that if people take the time to investigate kids' lives and what they go through, it will all make sense to them why they are behaving the way they are behaving.

As a child, I experienced a lot of domestic violence. There were a lot of fights between my parents. My mom was ultimately the victim. That started before I could remember, and it was pretty much all I knew up until I was a teenager.

I always knew when there would be a fight just based on how my dad rang the doorbell. I don't know why he didn't just use a key, but he always rang the doorbell when he came home from work, and I could always tell when it was going to be a bad night. It was almost like Pavlov's dog. You hear a certain ring and you know what your response should be. I knew where emotionally and psychologically I needed to put myself. That's not healthy for any child. People can't expect kids to be subjected to that type of environment and to grow up psychologically healthy.

Did I get hit? Yeah, we all got hit. I think my brothers got it much worse than I did. My dad definitely used corporal punishment. Sometimes he would go overboard. The thing about my dad is that he didn't take pleasure in it. I know that's how he grew up. He was subjected to very serious abuse, not only at home, but at school. And so that's how he dealt with my brothers. Back then, it was very difficult to handle and to understand, and I felt a very deep sense of hate. I was robbed of my childhood, because I always lived in fear.

Aside from the violence in the home, there were a lot of issues in school. I mean, fights and things of that nature. I was bullied all the way from first grade to seventh grade, just constant bullying. I remember having to run home from school. You hear people talking, and someone would come up to you and say, "Such and such is going to wait for you after school," because they wanted to fight. So I would then have to start plotting my exit strategy. I lived seven blocks from my school, Haugan Elementary, in Albany Park. So the moment the bell rang, I would take off running, and I would run nonstop, and I'd have crowds of people chasing me. And this would happen constantly.

The isolation that you feel sometimes, feeling defenseless, both at home and at school, when you can't stop it, being a victim of it, it's very impactful. At some point, you get so tired of it. You know, it's that saying, "When you can't beat them, join them." So it just came to the point where I said I was no longer going to become a victim and I became an aggressor.

My first fight was in the seventh grade. A girl and I just kind of got in a spat in the library. Her name was Alma. I will never forget that it was in the library. And I remember she said, "Your mother's a bitch."

And I just said, "No. Now you're going to wait for me after school."

She came out ready to fight, and we had a crowd, and I fought her. And unfortunately I wound up beating her ass. I say "unfortunately" because, all of a sudden, people started to be nice to me because they saw that I was able to fight. Then it gave me a sense of empowerment and I was no longer scared, so when things would occur, I wasn't running from it anymore. Now I was confronting it, but confronting it aggressively. I was ready to fight.

Although it empowered me, I hated it. I was very, very good at what I called "verbal judo," very good at talking my way out of things. Sometimes, when I could sense when something was escalating, I would quickly be able to de-escalate the situation verbally because I didn't want it to result in a fight. My biggest fear was that I would wind up in a fight and they would wind up killing me. So I didn't run around looking for fights, but I wasn't going to back down from one, because I felt that if I backed down, I'd become the victim again.

I was 17 or 18 when I left home. You know, I don't remember the exact situation. I know that it was a fight with my dad. I'm not necessarily going to blame him for the fight. I know that it was because of something that I did. At that point, I was just a rebellious, hard-to-deal-with teenager. And I'm going to take full responsibility, because I just didn't care. I went to a friend's house for a little bit, and then I kind of bounced around wherever I could stay. If I was able to sleep somewhere, I slept somewhere, and if I didn't have a place to sleep, I would just stay up all night. Hang out with whoever was willing to hang out. All night. I did that for about two months.

Then during that two-month time period, I met my daughter's father on a street corner. I was waiting for the bus and he was at a gas station. And he stopped. He said hello. We talked. We exchanged numbers—pager numbers. I didn't have a phone. We just started talking, and then we went out on a couple of dates with some friends. I didn't want to go out with him by myself. And I would say about two or three months afterwards, I found out I was pregnant. And in some sick kind of way, it was almost like, "Yes, now I'm pregnant. I got somewhere to live."

And so I moved in with him into an apartment where he had no gas and no light because he couldn't pay the gas or light. They shut it off. I'll never forget. It was February 1991 when I moved into that apartment, and it was horribly, horribly cold. I was still in school—Wells High School, which is in West Town. Even though I ran away from home, I was still going to school, but I was always afraid that my parents would show up there trying to find me. Now I was pregnant and didn't want my parents to find me, so I said that's it and I decided to drop out.

But I didn't even know this guy, clearly. After three months, he started to become physically abusive. And I didn't want to say anything to anybody. And at the same time, in some sick kind of way, I had developed a love for him. I was in love, or whatever that was, at the time. He wasn't only physically abusive, but he was psychologically abusive. He would do things like go out and not come home, and I wouldn't know where he was. There was this whole fear: Is he dead or is he alive? I would imagine that he would be with somebody else. That was very difficult. I couldn't sleep, and here I was pregnant. I had no job. I had no education. I had no insurance. I had nothing, so now I was fully dependent on him.

For months, my parents didn't know if I was dead or alive. But my best friend was in total disagreement with what I was doing. So one day, she figured out a way to get in contact with my mom, and my mom showed up at the apartment. My parents were basically, "We don't want you to struggle. We want this to be over and we want to help you." That pretty much mended the relationship with my parents. My dad just wanted to make sure that I was okay. And I let them back into my life and started over with them.

My parents helped us get a nice little apartment, and my dad gave us the security deposit. They gave us a whole bunch of furniture. We had a pretty nice place to live in Humboldt Park. But the day that I was giving birth, the moment I was giving birth to my daughter, I could hear him on the phone with another woman and that changed my life—I mean, big time. The rage and the violence just came back. I was tremendously hurt, because here I was having this baby. I was a mother, and now I had to deal with something I'd never dealt with. It affected me so much psychologically and emotionally that I found myself fighting a lot with him. And this time, when he would fight me, I would fight back. I'd come out really beat up.

And so in 1993, when my daughter Syra was 2 years old, we had a really big fight, and I called the police. And the police came and he was just wearing jogging pants, no shoes, no socks, no shirt, and it was winter. It was December 10th. And there was so much snow outside. And so they were going to take him into custody and he was begging me, "Don't let them take me. Don't let them take me. Don't press charges. Please, please just don't."

I was just done. I looked at the cops. I just said, "Take him." When I said that, all I felt was a fist right in my face. He punched me so hard and I hit the ground and there was blood everywhere. And the cops were struggling with him to handcuff him, so they started beating him to restrain him, to handcuff him. And they were walking him out the door, and, the moment they got out the door, they all slipped and fell because of the snow. So when the two police officers and my daughter's father slipped and fell, he jumped up and took off running. And he was handcuffed. They took off running and they couldn't find him.

They looked and looked and looked. They called other cops, and other cops came, and when they couldn't find him, one of the cops came in and said to me, "You're under arrest."

And I looked at him and I was like, "What do you mean I'm under arrest?"

"You're under arrest for obstructing the police."

And I'm like, "What are you talking about? What do you mean obstructing the police?"

And he's like, "Ma'am, just come with us."

Now, I had my 2-year-old daughter and my 4-year-old stepson with me, because at this point, his son was living with us because his mother had abandoned him. They put me in the police car with these two kids and took me to the police station. While I was sitting in the police station, confused, a cop came up to me and told me, "This is off the record. If you ever say it, I'm going to deny it. The only reason we are taking you into custody is that he escaped handcuffed, and we can't find him, and we need to blame somebody. If we don't, we could be suspended for two weeks with no pay. If you say it, I'll deny it."

When we went to court, I chose not to press charges. I was 20 years old with no money. I didn't know anything about the law. I didn't know anything about rights. I was threatened with two or three years of jail time if I didn't plead guilty, but if I plead guilty, they would plead for six months of supervision. So I pled guilty and walked out of there.[59]

I didn't leave him right away, but a few months later, when he went to work one day, my best friend and her brothers came with a moving truck, and in a matter of three hours we packed up the apartment and cleared it out. I left him with a mattress and a roll of toilet paper. We put all of my furniture in storage and I went to live with my parents. At that point, I decided I had to do something with my life. I said, "I can't live like this."

And that's when my best friend and I decided to go take our GED test. The moment I looked at those results, I went straight to Northeastern Illinois University in Chicago and I started college. From then until I graduated, I went to school full-time and I worked full-time in a pharmacy and I was taking care of my daughter.

My initial plan was to go on to law school, but I began to volunteer at the Juvenile Temporary Detention Center here in Cook County, and I would visit kids who didn't receive visits, and I became interested in kids that were involved in the juvenile-justice system.[60] So I applied in Lake County as a juvenile probation officer, but I couldn't be a probation officer right off the bat because I didn't have experience, so I had to work in the Detention Center. I came in with a law-enforcement kind of attitude. I was like, "I'm going to tell these kids what to do. And if not, there's a consequence." That was my thinking.

I walked in and got a wake-up call real quick, because now I was dealing with kids who had the same attitude I had when I was 13, 14, 15: "I don't feel. I don't care. Lock me up in my room." I mean, I had never been to jail or anything, but some of these kids had been in and out of juvenile detention, so me saying I'm going to put them in their room was not a threat. They would curse me all the way there and sometimes they would have to be restrained. What it did was change my attitude with the kids.

It involved me doing less talking, and I started doing more listening, just to kind of understand who these kids were, what they were doing, where did they come from. Because of legal reasons, I couldn't talk to them about the offense they committed. But where did they live? Where did they come from? Is there a mom? Is there a dad? I would notice the kids who didn't get visits or some of them that got visits that would be very contentious. The kids would come back very upset. And then there would be those who had visits every week, very positive visits, so I saw there were all different types of kids with different types of experiences.

And after I became a probation officer for juvenile offenders, I began going into their communities, into their homes. Here I saw kids who didn't have parents, or girls who had a dad but didn't have a mom, or Mom was a drug addict. What I realized is that people judge these kids on their behavior in the communities and schools, and they have no idea what they're going through at home. Just like how people judged me when I was their age, and I was acting like this, a little delinquent. But they had no idea what I was going through at home, no idea. I was not going to say, "Oh, poor kids, I know you're having a hard time at home. Go out and act a fool." But I felt a sense of connection with these kids.

I dealt with some of the most thuggish gangbangers. I dealt with some of the snottiest kids from the snootiest suburbs, and they were still kids that came from dysfunctional homes and were judged just by their behavior. That was a whole new awakening for me.

I wanted to have all of them understand that there is a better way, and that there is hope, and that there are things you can do to get out of your situation. You cannot make this the rest of your life. You have to change. And when I told them my own story, they felt like, "She understands. She's not okay with what I'm doing, but she understands."

So now I had them listening. I had their ear.

There was this young girl that I met. She was probably 15 years old when the case was first assigned to me and I'll never forget, when I drove up to her house there were all these gangbangers in front of her house. I mean, our policy was if you don't feel safe, drive off, but I was like, "No, no, no. This girl's not going to be hanging out with gangbangers."

So I got out of my car and I walked up to her and she just had this mean look on her face. I identified myself and said, "They got to go. We need to talk." I explained my role and told her what was acceptable and what was not, and then I set up appointments to meet with her at the office. When I started to get to know her, I realized she lived with her aunt, uncle and cousins. And then I found out that the mom was in and out of prison, and when she wasn't in prison she would just be gone. Mom was a crack addict.

This girl was a fighter. Oh my God! All this girl would do is fight. She was on probation for hitting a kid over the head with a padlock at school. She ran around with the Satan Disciples in Waukegan[61] and she got high. Smoked a lot of marijuana. That's what she did, smoked a lot of marijuana. She was this angry, angry girl, and it was almost like I was seeing me at her age. Me and her would butt heads all the time and I would give her a run for her money and she would get very angry with me. And then I started to realize that she didn't have her dad. Her mom had prostituted herself. She had witnessed this as a very young girl. I'm sure she went through some sort of abuse. She cut herself a lot.

In one of our moments, I said to her, "You know, it's not your fault. I'm sorry you went through what you went through, but it's not your fault." I think that was like a breakthrough for her. Somebody had given her permission to be angry. And I don't think anybody had ever said that to her. All of a sudden I discovered this little girl. This little girl. I just think she was just trapped in that traumatized body of hers. I mean, I have lots of stories, but for me that was probably the most impactful because that's where I knew that what worked for me was going to work for her. That was just accountability, structure and someone to listen, to say, "It's okay." And to celebrate the rewards, dish out the consequences when needed, and let it work for her own good. She was on probation for a long time. She would email me every so often to ask me how I was doing and tell me she was doing well.

The last time I Googled her name, just to see, oh my God, what am I going to find? Was she arrested as an adult or something like that? And what I found was an article of her with a bunch of other people in Mississippi after Hurricane Katrina. She was down there helping to rebuild homes. So it was a proud moment. It was almost as if she was my daughter, and I was like, "Wow! Here was this thug, wreaking havoc in the town of Waukegan and she's now in this town in Mississippi, helping people rebuild." That was awesome.

See, if you're not going to try to figure out what is going on or what has happened with a young person, then you're simply punishing the kid; you're not dealing with the behavior. So you can't restore. That's the real question: How do you restore?

—Interviewed by Emma Cushman Wood

ENDNOTES

59 Figueroa reports that, when she wanted to become a probation officer, her guilty plea "came back to haunt me. It was going to ruin my career." Luckily, she was able to get her record expunged.

60 According to the Cook County website, "The Juvenile Temporary Detention Center provides temporary secure housing for youth from the age of 10 through 16 years, who are awaiting adjudication of their cases by the Juvenile Division of the Cook County Courts. The Center also provides care for youth who have been transferred from Juvenile Court jurisdiction to Criminal Court. These youth would otherwise be incarcerated in the county jail." See http://www.cookcountygov. com/portal/server.pt/community/juvenile_temporary_detention_center/304/ juvenile_temporary_detention_center

61 Waukegan is a racially diverse suburb about 40 miles north of Chicago.

WHERE IN THIS COMMUNITY DOES IT SAY WE CARE?

DIANE LATIKER

Diane Latiker has been a resident of the Roseland community for more than two decades. This South Side neighborhood has one of Chicago's highest homicide rates and is plagued by poverty and unemployment. In 2003, Latiker, a mother of eight, opened her home to at-risk youth seeking a positive alternative to gang involvement. Her living room became a place for tutoring, mentoring and artistic expression for the young people of the neighborhood. Ten years later, Latiker's nonprofit organization, Kids Off the Block (KOB), has helped more than 2,000 kids.

In 2007, "Miss Diane," as young people call her, created a memorial near KOB that contains rows of carved red paving stones. Each stone bears the name of a child who was killed by street violence in Chicago. The memorial currently has 376 bricks and, even though she has already rebuilt it nine times, Latiker still needs to add the names of 118 murdered children. In October of 2012, the Chicago City Council passed an ordinance for a 12,500-square-foot site to be made into a public park and expanded memorial so that KOB can continue its work.

A charismatic woman with a quick smile and big laugh, Latiker is both passionate and resilient. In one moment, she welcomes a youth at KOB with a gentle greeting; in another, she pounds her fist on the table when advocating for change.

I grew up with unity. To me, unity consists of not just that word, but also love, caring, respect, relationship and trust. I grew up with Mrs. Stone down the block knowing who I was. And if I got out of line, she'd tell my mother when my mother got off work. If I came over there doing my thing, I'd hear, "Diane Latiker, if you don't get back over there, I'm gonna..." It was unity. I was surrounded by people and a support system. I'm not saying it was perfect because we always had knuckleheads. But growing up I always remember that it was this tight-knit community. I could walk through and not be afraid.

We had the gangs, but for some reason they were more like protectors. They would kill each other, but they wouldn't hurt the innocent people in their communities. If we had a barbecue or something, they would make sure nothing happened around that area. It was crazy, but it was beautiful to me as a child, because I knew that I was protected. I knew that I was supported.

I have memories of people wanting to come together. Barbecuing on the street, you know, eating together, laughing together. But the younger generation never saw that place. And the reason that they didn't see it was because we didn't teach it to them; we didn't show it to them. I say "we" because it was my generation that dropped the ball. And I don't only mean in Roseland. I mean, period. We dropped the ball on teaching our young people about how important it is that they help in the community and be a part of a community and not separate themselves. I know the young people thirst for that. I know they do because, when we do community events, they don't want to go home. They love it. They talk about it for days. That's what I would like to see. I think there are some good parts in Roseland, and there are some bad parts in Roseland. I want to stay here and make it all the good parts.

As a young girl, all I wanted was to be married and have a lot of kids. Well, be careful what you ask God for, because He'll give it you. I got pregnant on my 16th birthday, and my mom made me get married. I wanted to get married but was scared at the same time. I was married nine years to him and 25 years to my current husband. I have eight beautiful kids. I have four boys and four girls. My oldest one will be 38 this year. And my youngest one, she'll be 21. I love them. They are, wow.

I was a licensed hair stylist. Hated it. I hated doing hair. I did it because of my family. My daughter, she's the one that had the talent to do hair. She wanted to drop out of school. And I said, "Don't do that. What do you love to do?" And she said, "Hair." So I enrolled her in hair school, an after-school program. To keep her in there, I joined. I didn't want to. But in the meantime, my other two sisters went to hair school, so my mother said, "I'll open up a shop for you guys," and then I was stuck. I couldn't say no to my mother. My mother is my mentor, my best friend. She believes in everything we want to do. So for eight years, I did hair. But when I found KOB—well, when God helped me find it—I knew: This is me. This is it.

My youngest one, she was 13 when I started Kids Off the Block. I was hanging with her, trying to keep up with her because all my other kids were gone off to college and married and she was the only one at home. She had about nine friends, and they were running up and down the street all the time. They didn't have anything to do. They were just tearing up people's grass and fences and stuff. Not intentionally, just playing in it, you know?

I started to take them skating and fishing and swimming, all that kind of stuff. And my mother saw it, and she said, "Why don't you do something with those kids? They like you." And I was like, "No, no, no, no, no." I thought my youngest daughter would go off to college, and I'd be free.

But then I prayed about it for three days. I prayed hard, and I said, "Lord, is this it?" And yeah, it was. When I finally made up my mind to go out there on July 15, 2003, they were all in the front. Hottest day of the year. They were all standing out there, hollering at each other and playing, and I walked out and said, "Excuse me."

And my daughter said, "Oh, Ma. What's the matter, now?"

"Nothing. I just need to ask you guys a question."

"What, what?" they said.

"If I started something in the house, would you guys participate?" Because I didn't know what—I had no idea what a nonprofit was and all that.

And they were like, "Yeah!"

I asked them, "So, what do you guys wanna be? What do you want to do?"

And they all started jumping up and down: "I wanna be a doctor!" "I wanna be a singer!" "I wanna be a rapper!" "I wanna be a lawyer!"

And I was like, "Oh, so ya'll do want to *do* something?" And that's what inspired me. That's what excited me. The next day I invited them into my living room, and that's where it started.

I had a six-room apartment. My husband said we're not going past the living room, the dining room and one bedroom, which we made into a little studio for music. So we cut it off there. I gotta have my own bedroom. I looked up one day, and there were 75 young people coming to my house every day. We could barely move. I realized how big the need was, because these kids didn't even know me.

In the beginning of KOB, as I began to talk to the other kids, I realized all the problems they had. Oh my goodness, I was like, "Whoa, I couldn't be a teenager these days." They had so many issues. They had mothers who were on drugs. They had fathers who were on drugs. They had mothers who were locked up. They had fathers who were locked up. They had grandmothers who were taking care of them. They had sisters who were taking care of them. They had older brothers who were selling drugs to take care of the little kids. And then to do something with them and see them smile and play, because they missed all that, you know? The innocence. The playing. The laughing, the talking, the bonding. They missed all that.

The key to young people, by the way, is their interests. If they love something, they'll get involved in everything else. Last year, there was stuff all summer at KOB. It was so awesome. We had a three-day workshop on HIV/AIDS. We went to a workshop at O'Hare Airport learning about aviation. That was so cool because some of them had never been on a plane. We went to the Black Women's Expo. We did an event for the alderman, a barbecue. We've been to 20 cities, because the young people don't go anywhere, they stay on the block. Their whole life is on the block. They don't know what downtown Chicago looks like.

I had 53 young people working out of my house through the Put Illinois to Work program.[62] We walked Roseland and cleaned up vacant lots and alleys and seniors' yards. We had little groups go and see what the seniors wanted, because we have a senior citizens' building right on the corner. Like, if they needed stuff from the grocery store, cleaners, things like that. The young people had some great stories about the seniors, but I was just thankful that they even listened to what the seniors were saying to them. I keep telling the older people like myself that the young people don't know about the civil rights movement. They have no clue; they don't understand it because nobody has explained it to them. How many people died, how many people were injured, how many people were jailed, just so these young people can do what they're doing.

I found out my biggest thing with young people was that I listened. No judgment. I give advice if I'm asked, and sometimes when I'm not asked. If I know that they are getting ready to make the wrong decision, I will step up to them. But 90 percent of the time, I just listen. It has to be a relationship, you know?

When they believe in themselves, it's contagious. They pull along their peers and friends and everybody. But the hard part is getting them to realize their power. They've been told otherwise, and they believe it, because they've been told so long. Some of them since childhood, since birth. So that's what you fight against, too.

You see the young man—that poster over there? He was just killed. His real name is David Rodgers, but we call him Red. He was just killed on 115th, right here on this corner. And it hurt me to my heart. I still reel.

Red loved basketball. He ate, slept, drank basketball. And Red was really talented. I believe Red could have gone to the NBA. I really do. I used to tell him that. I used to tell him, "You're a superstar, Red." And he would be like, "I know, I know."

But he had a cousin. And when this cousin came, I knew that everything would change for Red. Red's grades in school had started coming up. We had got him a job. He was working with us. He was coming to play basketball. He was doing so good and then, all of a sudden, he got involved with drugs and gangs and robbing people. I would still see him. I would try to talk to him. But in the last couple months, I couldn't get to him. I just couldn't get to him. He was surrounded by negativity. So I did what I knew best, and that was to pray for him.

He had gone to a barbershop right up here on this corner. He got to arguing with another guy in the barbershop, and he told the guy, "Let's go outside." It seemed like a setup to me. When he got outside, three or four guys starting shooting at him, and he was trying to shoot back, and they caught him on that corner over there.

I was coming from downtown, at another event about youth violence. I had about 10 young people with me. And we see all these police cars on the corner, and we were like, "What's going on?" So we get out of our cars, and people are screaming and hollering. All of a sudden, I look right there at the sidewalk, and there's Red. He had been shot in the jaw, shot in the chest. I said, "That's Red." And I, oh, my daughter and I, we just grabbed each other.

I think, when Red first came to KOB, the way I was talking to him, he believed it for a minute because he got involved and started to do real well. But reality set in when he would go home. He'd be right back in his environment, and I could only go so far. Funding doesn't allow us to do a whole lot. We are good at what we do with what we have. Red loved basketball, so we could keep him going with the basketball, but you had to go beyond basketball. He needed other services, which we tried to get him, but it was a battle. It was a battle for his life.

And he chose. He chose to do what he was doing. His whole family was involved in gangs. I mean, that's all they knew. If you ride around this community, you will see what I'm talking about. There's nothing here for young people. There's nothing here. Where in this community does it say we care, we want to help you to thrive, we want to give you recreational activities? We want to give you the arts so you can express yourself? Nothing here.

Youth violence hurts me. I don't know how many times I've cried. I had to stop being so emotional about it. A lot of my friends were telling me, "You can't save everybody." And I used to say, "Why not?" I was being naive, I guess. You see, it's not that violence has escalated so much. It's the brutality of the violence now. And it's the ages. When you see an 8-year-old gunned down, and she'd been jumping rope? How cruel is that in the young person's mind who is getting ready to shoot? Does he think, "Maybe I'm not going to shoot now because that little girl is there?" No, he still shoots. What's missing here?

What's missing is that the young man who is doing the shooting has no guidance, and if he does, it's negative. He has nobody to say, "Look, man, you don't do that." That's the young man I like to get to. I like to get the ones who are the shooters, the ones who want to do the bad things to our community. Because I believe that's all they need, somebody to get to them.

We're losing a generation, right before our eyes. What's really ticking me off at this moment, the same thing that was ticking me off when I started: no outrage. If this were happening in a different culture, a different race, I guarantee you it would be different. And I'm faulting my own, because they're ours mostly. It's Hispanics, and it's black kids. And nobody is saying a word.

The black community is over here, and we're quiet. The white community is over here, and the Latino is over here, and it's quiet. I want to break it down. Tear it down! What purpose does it serve? Why is it so hard for people to come together?

I would love to walk into the Hispanic community, which is right around the corner from me, and say, "How you doing? Come on, let's sit down. Let's eat." I would love for them to come here. The Latin Kings and the black gangs are fighting all the time. Some of the Latin King boys can't come this way because they might get shot. But I would love for the Latin Kings to come here and be involved in the program, because they're suffering from the same things. They need somebody to talk to.

But you can't break down that barrier for the adults in the Hispanic community who say, "We don't like black people, 'cause all blacks are blah, blah, blah." And we over here in the black community are going, "Yeah, all Mexicans are blah, blah, blah." And we are teaching that to our kids, who then amplify it. "And all white people are blah, blah, blah, blah blah." So it continues, generation after generation.

If I got a 10-year-old, and he's out here running up and down the street, robbing old ladies and throwing bricks in cars, and I'm sitting on my porch going, "That's a bad little boy." Well, guess what? That bad little boy is going to grow up, and then he's going to be in your neighborhood. So when I see that, I say, "Hey! Come here." And then if they run, I call the police on them, because they've got to know they can't do that stuff. I probably saved that little boy's life, because after I call the police, then I go talk to his mama. Then, when I see him again, I'm like, "Yeah, I'm the one. I'm watching you."

Actually, that's a true story. Now when he sees me he goes, "Hey, Miss Diane," and he goes around the corner. He knows he can come in that door and say, "Miss Diane, I need help." And he got it. Whatever I got, he got.

Lord willing, in five years, I hope to be serving thousands of young people. Getting them jobs, getting them back in school, helping them fulfill their dreams. I also hope to have KOB over this whole city in different communities. I think we could be a help to others who are already established there. And in 5 to 10 years, I pray that we have touched a whole generation.

I don't want to offend anybody, but maybe I should. How in the world can people sit? We're all silent right now, but it's getting ready to get warm again, and when it gets warm, youth violence heats up. And then when it gets really hot, youth violence is really hot. We'll have bodies coming up.

But now, we're just sitting here twiddling our thumbs instead of getting ready to intervene into that violence that is about to happen. We're not intervening with those young people who are already standing on a corner because they dropped out of school, hoping to join a gang and have nothing to do. An organization like KOB has to fight to get funding to do things, to stop this from happening.

Help us help these young people! I'm talking to a city that needs to back up what they're talking about. They're always throwing youth violence out there: We're gonna do this, we're gonna do that. When you find somebody, an organization, that is really doing that, you should be, "Yeah, let's help, let's help!"

Where are you? That's my question. Where are you?

—Interviewed by Kristin Scheffers

ENDNOTES

62 Put Illinois to Work was a temporary jobs program that matched workers with private employers. It lasted only a few months in 2010 before being shut down by Gov. Pat Quinn. See Monique Garcia, "Quinn to End Temporary Jobs Program Next Month," *Chicago Tribune*, Dec. 13, 2010.

HELL BROKE LOOSE
HYINTH DAVIS

Hyinth Davis is a 20-year-old from Roseland. Growing up, Davis was surrounded by substance abuse, violence and poverty. Both of his parents were on drugs, and his father was physically abusive to both Davis and his mother. But unlike many young people in similar circumstances, he has resisted the temptation to join a gang. Instead, he spends a lot of his spare time at Kids Off the Block, a safe haven for young people, run by community organizer Diane Latiker.

Because of the 2009 beating death of Fenger High School student Derrion Albert, Davis' neighborhood has received a great deal of notoriety. To the countless people worldwide who watched the viral video of that murder, Derrion Albert became a symbol of street violence in Chicago. But to Davis, he was simply another lost friend.

I'm not trying to say it's a curse, but it feels weird knowing that five of your friends got killed within the same year. So it's kind of hard, even though most of them were gangbanging. I'm not saying they deserved it, but most of them don't want no help. I kind of like separated myself from them, because I didn't want to be a part of that crowd. I'm not trying to live like that, 'cause I'm not that type of person.

I grew up with my mother and my father, and both of them were on drugs. When I was growing up, my mother was beaten. Like beaten, you know? When it started, I think I was like 3 or 4. My father used to beat her in front of my face.

The biggest incident happened when I was about 5 or 6 years old. I was just not doing what I was supposed to be doing when I was in first grade. I mean, I wasn't a bad student. I just didn't do the work. So the teacher had called the house, and my mother had come up there, and the teacher was like, "Well, Hyinth is a good student, and I know he can try harder. I just know he can do better." My mother was like, "Okay." But my father, you know, I guess my mother told my father. He took it overboard.

He brought out the belt and he just started hitting me. So my mom, she tried to stop him. She was like, "No, no, don't hit him. You have to talk to him." But he got mad. My mother, she was blocking my way, so he hit her. And then it got to the point where he broke her leg and her arm. She was on crutches. She was on crutches. She had a cast on her leg and a cast on her arm, and she couldn't walk. She was on crutches.

It was kind of sad living in the house, but I really couldn't do nothing about it because I was young. I remember me running to the store at 57th and Sangamon, getting on the pay phone and calling 911. And I didn't know my home address. I didn't know the street or anything. I couldn't tell the police that my mother was getting beaten. I was panicking, crying. I was scared. I used to have nightmares every night.

My mother, dead. I thought in half my nightmares that he killed her. It was all bloody, and I used to see her just lying there in a casket. All I could do was cry. My mother, she's a loving person and everyone likes her. I don't think that she deserves what he's done to her. My family's been much better since she left him. My mom seems like she's happy, and she claims she's not taking drugs no more. She's really trying to get herself together, but it's kind of hard 'cause she's still living in that environment where people are slowly bringing her down. It's hard for her to just walk away, you know.

I could forgive my dad, but I won't forget. I don't have a relationship with him anymore, even though he's still around. He just recently got out of jail. That's always been an off-and-on thing for him—going back and forth to jail. When I was born, he was locked up. I don't know how long he was locked up, but he wasn't at the hospital to sign the birth certificate.

Me and my two sisters, 13 and 26 years old, we're close. My two little brothers, ages 8 and 10, they're in foster care. When my mother had them at the hospital, I guess, the foster people took them away. They got custody of them. It's kind of hard, because I don't speak to my two little brothers at all. I only saw them one time. They don't know who I am, and I don't know who they are. I would love to be in their lives, to guide them, do things that brothers should do. It gets to me. It really hurts.

The happiest moment that I had with my family, we took a vacation. We went to Florida. We went away for, like, a week. That was the happiest moment because there wasn't no type of negativity drama surrounding us. You know, we actually enjoyed ourselves and didn't have to worry about what's going to happen today, what's going to happen the next day. Happiest memory from my neighborhood? There's not much I can say, you know, about Roseland, because there was a lot of shooting. There's still a lot of killing. I think someone just got killed on 111th. I think it was yesterday. I'm not sure.

I got robbed three times. One time I was coming home from school— this was my sophomore year. I had these red-and-white shoes on. I was the only one in school that had them. So my friend and me was just walking and my friend had my phone, listening to my music. The next thing you know, the boys who robbed me, they was like, "That's my song. Play it again."

I'm like, "Don't play it again."

So they put a gun up to my head and was like, "You have ten seconds to take off your shoes." I had to hurry up and take them off. They was actually counting. Then they took my driver's license. They was like, "Just in case you trick, we know where you live."

It was snowing, and next thing you know, I was barefoot walking home. Then I had to go and get the locks changed on the house.

The most recent time I got robbed was my senior year. It was around prom time. I remember that I had $100 in my pocket, and I ended up getting jumped on by my friends—guys who I thought were my friends.

I'm mainly by myself now. I feel as though groups cause problems, so I'd rather be by myself because I don't want a target on me or anything. Always be by myself. Can't trust anyone. You know, people always tell me how you got to trust some people, but it's easy for them to say because they haven't been through what I've been through.

My biggest fear is getting shot or ending up dead. 'Cause I always think that the people that have something going for themselves, they end up being the one that's gone first. Like my friend Cordero, he was just walking, and then mistaken identity, and he ended up getting shot in the head. I think it was a drive-by. They stopped and they was shooting and then he ended up getting shot. On 111th, down the hill, by the park.

Red, which is what we called David Rodgers.[63] We graduated with honors from eighth grade, and he was real smart then. In our freshman year, we had honors classes and we was both getting A's and B's and, you know, he was doing something positive. And then hell broke loose. He started shooting people and robbing people. It just went from there. But I remember, like a week before he died, he knew he was going to get killed. He was like, "I know it's too late, because I messed up." And then, next thing you know, he died. He got killed. Right there on 115th and Michigan.

My one good friend, Gregory, he got killed just by walking. He was just walking. They was shooting, and then I remember we was in front of my grandma's house. We all run in the house and my friend, he was walking, he was trying to run in the house and, next thing you know, he got shot in the face and just laid straight down. In front of my grandma's house, on 65th and Washtenaw.

My other friend, Derrion Albert—you probably know about Derrion. We was all at a party the night before, and so, the next thing you know, Derrion got into a stupid argument. Um, I didn't know it was going to wind up being that serious—you know, where they could just beat you to death.

Me and Derrion, we was close in his freshman year. I was a junior and he was a freshman. And we just clicked from then on. We was so cool. So cool and close. His killing affected me real bad. I mean, I couldn't even sleep, 'cause I'm like, "I just spoke to Derrion that day before."

For a person to have that much hatred in their heart, where they have to hit you and beat you with a stick—it's just sad. But I'm trying to not let what happened to him bother me. I could never forget it, but I could just erase it out, you know—just keep living life, just doing something positive. I mean, I'm trying to live a productive life. I'm still young. Life is too short, and life is passing by. So I'm not trying to waste time.

I live with my auntie now. She's supportive; she's real supportive, but she lives off the first-of-the-month check. She's never had a job. I don't want to live life like that. I don't want to live life half-the-way and get $674 a month just to pay the bills and then you don't have no money left over. It's like, your life is not going anywhere, 'cause you settling for less than you could be.

I want to buy my own home someday. I don't want to just live in someone else's apartment. I'm going to move to a better place, like hopefully the suburbs somewhere. I'm just looking out for the better and the self in my life. When I look in the mirror, I see a positive person. I see me striving for the best in the future. Hopefully, I mean I was in college at Olive-Harvey, but I took a semester off because I needed to get a job. So I'm planning on going back in the fall. But right now, I'm just looking for a job. It's kind of hard because I'm like, I don't have no one to take care of me. I want to take care of myself but it's like, a lot of jobs say they're not hiring or, you know, call back next month. It's, like, very hard.

I see a lot of teens my age, you know, they out here robbing, smoking, gangbanging, drinking. I'm just trying to live life and just stay away from all of that, but it's kind of hard because it's like we trapped in the environment. You can't just play basketball, hang out with friends, go shopping. You can't do that without getting robbed. Without getting shot at. So it's basically like we living in a prison. We have to watch ourselves. Sit in the house and look out the window before we step out the door.

—Interviewed by Olivia Karim

ENDNOTES

63 This is the same "Red" whose killing Diane Latiker describes in her narrative.

I ONLY WORK HERE

THOMAS McMAHON

Retired Chicago Police Capt. Thomas McMahon was with the force for 37 years. From 1980 to 1996, he worked on gang homicides, a job he describes as tough but rewarding. During his career as a detective, McMahon worked on some of Chicago's most high-profile cases, including the 1984 killing of Simeon Vocational High School basketball star Ben Wilson, the federal conspiracy case that led to the 1987 conviction of El Rukn gang leader Jeff Fort,[64] and the 1998 rape and murder of Ryan Harris, an 11-year-old Englewood girl. He operated under fierce pressure. Just a few days before his retirement in 2010, in fact, he was running errands in his family minivan, when he heard gunshots and spotted two assailants who, he would later learn, had just killed a 20-year-old man. Unarmed, he chased the suspects in his car, drawing their gunfire as he called 911.

Now in his 60s, the white-haired and bespectacled McMahon drives through that same neighborhood in his brown Toyota, offering a tour of the streets he used to patrol on Chicago's Far South Side.

I'm taking you to 111th and Vernon. A kid was killed here back in the middle of November. At 10 minutes to 12, not too far from our time frame right now, in broad daylight, two kids came out of the alley with .40-caliber guns and fired 25 rounds at this kid who was just standing there by the pole and killed him instantly.

The street corner here has a police camera on top. The assailants completed the job right under it. There's a tape of them fleeing. They were 15 or 18, probably. They weren't that old. They weren't men. They didn't wear hats or cover their faces, either. They could not have cared less if their faces were seen. They just came out and blasted. That case is still not cleared. We don't know who did it.

You can see the flowers and flags and the signs over there on the pole. That is a memorial for the victim. It used to contain bottles, teddy bears, other flowers, with R.I.P. written on everything. We'll see R.I.P. LeBron, R.I.P. Chico, or R.I.P. whoever it was that got killed, spray-painted on the side of a wall.

Let me tell you how police work works. For me to have a successful day, someone has to die. When you think about it, it's a paradox: Someone has to suffer something major to them for me to have a successful day. Point blank, it's a paradox.

So now I will present the problem to you. I can't present the solution. (Should I have ever come up with a solution that would work, I would have written a book, made a million dollars and been long gone out of this city.) In order to understand gang violence, you need to understand the school situation. It will all happen in the school and carry over into the streets; something that happened in the streets the night before will be brought back into the schools. It gets to a point that no matter what the discipline level is in the school, the gangbangers do not care. They will walk into a classroom and attack a kid right in front of the teacher. Will they take a 10-day suspension for fighting? Absolutely. They do not care. It's just that way. The gang becomes more important than the school. Besides, many of these kids who come to school don't come for an education. School is where their friends, their girlfriends are; it's about the socialization. When it all mixes into the school, and you have three or four different gangs all operating in the same school, the potential for gang violence is very high.

Michigan Avenue and 103rd—this unassuming, very idle street corner at 3 o'clock is the epicenter for gang violence. When school lets out, we have police officers literally at every corner. We have a new security program with guards patrolling Michigan Avenue for any gang activity. We have a police helicopter that flies overhead focusing right on this corner. CTA brings a number of buses, so we can get these kids on buses and out of these neighborhoods right away. At dismissal time, there's an enormous amount of police resources that are used to create safe passage for the students to go back and forth. It's unfortunate: You would think that even with all of these resources that it would create a safer environment.

There's no one on the street right now because of the time. Normally, they would be out all over the place, but the kids are in school, and those who are gang members who aren't in school are laying up in their crib. Their break time is from school to 3 o'clock. But there will easily be 100 kids around at 3 o'clock. The most critical time is between 3 o'clock and 8 o'clock. If you can find something for a kid during that time, I can tell you it would keep kids away from gangs. If you even had an after-school center that kids could go to, and what you do is have them work on homework,

work on a computer, socialize, play some games, whatever it is they do, they won't have that fear of being threatened by a gang.

The question is, do gangs recruit members or are the members recruiting gangs? Some members will actually join the gang without being recruited. In the nature of how kids are, their streets, their alleys, their little area becomes their area of influence. They can't control that block and that whole street; they can't control the whole neighborhood, but they can become part of an organization that does. This is their world: "This is my block. I run it. I own it." If those guys standing on the corner are all Black Gangster Disciples, then why would he go out and join another gang? These gangs are prepared because over the years, more than likely, they have offered the kid some kind of protection. He sees this as his peer group or the group that he looks up to.

Think about this: You're 12 or 15 years old, and an older guy says to you, "Hey listen, shorty, if anyone ever messes with you, you come see me. I'm gonna take care of it for you. We're out here and we're running the street." To a 12- or 15-year-old, it certainly puts an impression in his mind. He's not getting that kind of support at home or at school. A gang gives a kid a sense of belonging, a sense of self-esteem that he's not getting from anywhere else. Plus, you get to hang with a 21- or 22-year-old who's been to jail, so it's like, "Hey man, if he's a bad guy and you're hanging with him, then you must be a bad-ass too, you know." The kid thinks, "Yeah, that's right. I am somebody you don't be messing with." And that's the only thing this kid has got in his life. If you think about it, he derives no other benefits from life except in the street gang culture.

In other social strata, you don't see a 21-year-old hanging around with a 15-year-old. However, in the street gang culture, it's not uncommon to see a wide range of ages of people who gather together in certain locations for camaraderie, for safety, for income. And everybody has a role. You're a shorty; you're a new guy; you're going to be the lookout, and eventually then go to jail or get shot, and that's how you come up in the order. And then you can take over my role as the drug dealer and become the beneficiary of the income that the gang has. Of course, everyone in it makes a little bit of money. The kids who are lookouts can make $50 to $100 a day.

It's ironic that sometimes we find that a particular guy serves a four- to five-year sentence and then he comes back to their corner and wants to take over the corner. "Man, I'm back. This is all mine now. I'm running this corner." And a guy who has been out there for four or five years ain't ready to give up his role, so you have internal gang conflict. Somebody is going to get killed, either the boy who came out of jail or somebody on the corner to re-establish himself. The young buck goes, "You know what? Screw you, pal. While you've been inside, we've been out here dodging bullets." And he'll take the other guy on. I call this thinning the herd.

You see this guy over here with the hat on standing there with all those clothes on? He'll be yelling something as people walk by. He's the salesperson telling them where to buy. He doesn't have anything on him. You can stop him and go all the way down to his underwear; he ain't got it on him. If I ask him what he's doing there, "I'm waiting on my cousin." We're not dumb. We know what he's doing there. Or you'll pull up to a kid standing there with two pairs of gloves, three hats on, four pairs of pants, boots. He is so insulated and freaking immobile that he's been out on the corner for over an hour, and a cop pulls up asking, "What you doing?" and he says, "I'm waiting on my cousin. He's coming down the street. He should be here any minute." You drive off and come back an hour later, and he's still standing there.

Why should they continue to go to school or get a job at McDonald's for six or eight bucks an hour? It's easy money. They just have to work two shifts. It's a 24-7 operation. So $100 cash money, $500 a week, $2,000 a month, he buys his own gym shoes. In this case, he becomes the breadwinner in the family. He's important. He's bringing them the bacon. He's 15, and mama won't fight it. She won't ask him what he's doing. They need the money. It's more than a welfare check.

It really starts with more economics. It starts with parenting. You're looking at remarkable facets that are influencing this problem. Even then, you're looking at street gangs in more affluent suburbs. People think street gangs are just in the city, but let me be the first to tell you, they are in the suburbs. They still have kids who establish street gangs out there. Sometimes there are actual branches of the original gang, and sometimes they are copycat gangs. It's just a phenomenon, a cultural thing, that bad-boy image taken to another level. The question I always ask is, "If a wannabe gang member shoots another wannabe gang member, do you have a wannabe murder?"

Now this street, called Kensington, is Latin King territory. From this point forward—Michigan Avenue all the way east to the riverfront—is their territory.[65] This is a Mexican food mart, a taco stand next to it; you have a lot of Hispanic people here. They have been here for years, I mean 30 to 40 years. We're talking about third-generation Latin Kings. No one's out here now, but if this was the summer or a Sunday afternoon, people would be all over. This is Prairie Street. This is definitely one of their locations.

You see the 7-4-11? Here's one for you. What's the seventh letter of the alphabet, the fourth and the 11th? G.D.K., Gangster Disciple Killer. It's a warning to the Gangster Disciples that if they enter this territory, the Latin Kings will try and kill them. So with three numbers you probably wouldn't pay attention to, the Latin Kings are identifying their territory and warning their rivals to stay out. Like I say, you can read it like a newspaper.

The local gangs all know that this is their neighborhood. They know the yards they can run through and they also know what houses they can run into. The streets are where they live. They are going to control that. No doubt about it. This is their territory. I don't live here. I only work here.

—*Interviewed by David Cueman*

ENDNOTES

64 Jeff Fort was one of the founding members of the Blackstone Rangers, later known as the Black P Stone Rangers, the Black P Stone Nation and the El Rukns. In 1986, while in federal prison, he was indicted, along with other high-ranking El Rukns, for attempting to purchase high-powered weapons from Libya to commit terrorist acts against the U.S. government.

65 This corner is only a block and a half from Kids Off the Block, Diane Latiker's community organization at 11621 S. Michigan Ave.

THE WALK HOME
JUAN AND ESTHER PITTS

For nearly three decades, Juan Pitts and the Rev. Dr. W. Esther Pitts have shared a life. They can tell endless stories about their relationship—including the one about being divorced once and married three times, and about their busy life mentoring children in Jeffery Manor, a South Side neighborhood with winding, mazelike streets and a history of gangs, guns and drugs.

The Pittses have raised two biological daughters and six children adopted from foster care. They have also taken in 14 other children in need of a stable home. Esther Pitts wears a flattering blazer and still has the flawless skin of her days as a model. Juan Pitts wears a sweater and slacks, and sports a subtle goatee. They are friendly and dignified, but their smiles appear weary. In February 2009, two of their teenage sons were killed within two weeks of each other. The Pittses stay busy with family life and church work, but they are in the process of leaving Chicago for the warmth—and the new memories—of Florida.

Juan: When we first moved to Jeffery Manor,[66] we was actually the first blacks in the area. I remember the neighbors used to come up in front of my house, singing Christmas carols and everything. We actually used to sleep in front on the yard. I remember going to some of my school friends' houses for lunch, or they'd come to our house for lunch. It was pretty much okay until more people started moving in, and then it got kind of divided.

Esther: When my mom and dad purchased their home on the West Side, it had a cottage in the back, so we felt wealthy. It was a mixed community, predominately Caucasian and a few black families. I remember my mom would put on talent shows in the backyard. Her house was the type where all the kids, throughout the whole community, would come and sit. She taught the Bible, there in the basement.

We would ride our bikes to the Brach's Candy Company. At some point, Brach's decided they wanted to buy up all the homes so they could expand. It hurt so many people in the community. That's when we moved to the South Side.

Esther: We met working at the Tropical Hut restaurant at 91st and Stony Island Avenue. It was a Hawaiian-type atmosphere. Very homey. People were so attached to this restaurant that they would come from as far as Carol Stream to eat there.

Juan: We all worked there: all my brothers, my mother, my whole family.

Esther: I think I was 23 when I met Juan, and then I ended up pregnant by him. I was only kicking it with him; we weren't really a couple. I was modeling back then, and it took a lot of people for a shock, because I was so career-oriented. But I stopped working, because it was a high-risk pregnancy. After the baby was born, I was about to marry somebody else.

Juan: She wasn't about to marry someone else.

Esther: I was. Because I knew enough about God to know that what I had done was out of God's wishes. I was raised in a two-parent household, and I was really serious about marrying someone. Juan was like, "No, no, no, wait. Don't do anything until I come over!" So he came over and changed my mind.

We had a big wedding. Then I lost the marriage license, so we had to marry again. My uncle was a pastor. He married us twice, and he was like, "When are you all going to get this thing right?"

We filed for divorce in 1997, and it was final in April of '98. He did his thing, his life with someone else, and I had someone. We ended up back together because the man I was with died in 2000, out of the blue. Actually, the day that he died Juan said, "What do you want to do? Do you want to get back together?" Isn't that funny?

Juan: Actually, the third wedding was the best wedding.

Esther: It was the best one. It was outside. I wanted that island look, so we had tropical trees. We had a waterfall we had put in. We had so many people, even the people we didn't send invitations to were there. It was really nice.

Esther: My godmother was a foster parent and Juan worked with her. She kept pressing on us to be foster parents. She said, "Get a place and do it."

Juan: When she closed her group home down, all the kids just went out of the house crying, because some of them had to go back into the shelter. They didn't have any place to go. And that's when I told Esther that, if we get a house, let's consider doing this.

Esther: We took in a family of four girls, and they would say, "We don't want to leave here." When it was time for them to go, it was so heartbreaking. We had to take us a vacation because it hurt us so bad.

Then Hull House[67] called us like three days later saying, "Can you take another family in?" I told them no, I'm not. And then, about two weeks later, they said, "Can you please take them in, because you all have available housing and you're good." So we took them in, another family of four. After we divorced, I ended up adopting three of them.

Juan: I kept being a foster parent, too. First, I adopted two brothers from foster care, one of them being Carnell, and then I adopted Kendrick a year later. He was 8 when I got him. He was born into the system.

Esther: So when we remarried, we brought the kids together. I first got the townhouse, and he bought the adjoining one. We ended up knocking the wall out and raising four boys and four girls together.

During the time we were divorced, God had called me. I woke up on my couch and there was a note: Matthew 10:22. It reads, "And you shall be hated of all men for my name's sake: but he that endures to the end shall be saved." I understood that to mean even though you won't be accepted by a lot of people, you still push.

God told me to start a Bible class, so I started it in our house. I was in the process of being licensed and ordained. And we had all these kids come over, it would be like 54 kids, spending the night on the weekends to go to church. There were so many kids came out to that house, they would be sitting up the stairway, all over the living room and the dining room.

We work with kids and whatever bad that's within them—I don't mean to say bad, but whatever disturbs them, we get to the root of that. I never, ever believed in whupping them—but what I did say is, if you do wrong, you're going to be washing these walls or you'll be doing dishes. We call it the KP—kitchen patrol. I can find chores for you all day long. And, I promise you, things would be different by the time they finished those chores. I think we did a pretty good job with God in the house, because all our kids graduated from high school.

Juan: We had a deck on the outside. While she was out there ministering to the kids, I'd be in the house cooking for them. I'd just make all types of appetizers and little fancy things for them; stuff that they probably have never seen. I loved it. Actually, it kind of, like, took over our life, because we was in church just about every day.

Esther: We was a very tight-knit family. We didn't allow them to run the streets. If we'd go to Walmart, they were there. If we went away, we did a whole family thing for the weekend. If we go to Florida, they all went. And I'm talking about 18 to 20 kids. For real. I'm telling you, we turned some heads. People would say, "Did you actually have all these kids?" I'd say, "It's a long story."

The kids always played so much. Some tears over little things, but for the most part, it was a lot of laughter. A lot of laughter.

Juan: Of course, it took years for the other kids to be close to Kendrick.

Esther: 'Cause Kendrick was ripping everybody off. He'd get their stuff—shoes, clothes, iPods, cell phones, whatever he could find. And he'd stand there and say, "No, I ain't got it. I ain't got it." And later on he'd say, "Yeah, I took it. And I sold it."

Juan: He was a good-hearted person. He was the only one who would volunteer to help, like cutting the grass. Only problem was, he just couldn't keep his hands to himself. If he'd see something he wanted, he believed that it was his.

Esther: We'd talk to him constantly about this. He'd go to school; he'd do a petty theft. He'd go in and out of court, in and out of the juvenile system.

Juan: When he went to court, they just kept giving him a smack on the hand and letting him go. So I went to court, and I asked the judge to give him a couple of weeks up there in juvenile detention and let him see where he was headed. The judge gave him two weeks. Kendrick didn't like it, but I did what I thought was best.

He got back out, and took somebody's gym shoes at school, so he went right back in that same day. So he was there for, like, three months. And then, when he got out, he was like, "That's it, I'm not doing nothing else. I'm turning it around, I just want a job." And for those 10 days he was out, he actually started going to school.

Esther: Every morning, from the time he got out, he was sending me texts—"I love you, I love you"—throughout the day. He was saying, "Mom, I love you," every morning before he left out the door. That specific morning, he was late. He's never late for school. So I said, "Why don't you just stay home? It's after eight, you're supposed to be at school at seven." He said, "I can't, Mom. I got to go to school."

I got a text that day from him at school, saying, "I love you." And I texted him back. I said, "Why are you telling me you love me so much? Are you okay?" He said, "Yeah, I'm okay."

Three texts that day, the day he was murdered.

Esther: That afternoon, we was all at home. And I had just walked away from the computer and went upstairs. My daughter came screaming up the stairs and hollering that Kendrick was dead. And I ran down the stairs, and she said Carnell had just called her and he was crying so bad, saying that Kendrick is on the ground dead.

Apparently, Kendrick was walking these younger boys home, because one of the boys had an altercation with another boy, and he was afraid. So Kendrick said, "Okay, I'll walk you home." They never made it.

I guess when this 21-year-old shot them, he shot the boys first, then he shot Kendrick. He chased them down in a car. Kendrick was running for his life when he was killed. He was protecting the other boy. Protecting him. Some of the kids saw that Kendrick hid behind a dumpster, and then, when the shooter came back, he tried to run. He didn't make it far.

Juan: I left and went to the area where they said he was shot at. But police had it blocked like two or three blocks each way, so you really couldn't see him. They wouldn't let me in to identify the body or nothing. It wasn't until 8 o'clock that night, and the reporter from the *Chicago Defender*[68] was at the house. He called the morgue for me. Then, the next day I went down and identified him. The police never did come to the house and say, "Okay, that is him."

Esther: It was all over the news.

Juan: Oh, yeah, they swarmed our house. For days.

Esther: Two weeks later, I opened his death certificate in the mail. It looked just like a birth certificate. But it said "death certificate," and Kendrick's name was on it. It stopped me for a while. I sat on the couch and looked at it.

Esther: The same day Kendrick's death certificate got to the house, Carnell was killed. He was killed around 11:30 at night, after going to a party.

Juan: He was shot. He actually made a phone call to our oldest daughter...

Esther: 'Cause they was really, really close.

Juan: ...to tell her he got shot. And, I guess, he was calling out for help...

Esther: He was trying to talk...

Juan: But he couldn't talk, 'cause he got shot in the back...

Esther: She couldn't hear him...

Juan: Well, he got shot multiple times, but...

Esther: Both of them were shot multiple times.

Juan: It was just unbelievable. You know: not one, but two children? I just think I was in a daze for a while, not even believing that it's really happening. I haven't grieved yet, I don't think. I haven't even really cried yet.

Now, when I do my prayer at night, I pray for everybody, even them. Then, I have to think, "Oh, wait a minute, they're not here no more."

Esther: God was really holding me, keeping me, sustaining me during it. I did break down, when I was at the computer a few weeks later, looking at their pictures on the Internet. I'm still finding pictures that people are posting of Carnell and Kendrick. Carnell was so smart. He was an honor roll student; he stayed in "Who's Who" every year. He won scholarships; there's pictures of him with Mayor Daley when he earned a scholarship. Carnell was prom king, president of his class at Bowen High School. He had dreams, expectations, he desired so much out of life. He wanted to be a judge and make it to the Supreme Court. It doesn't make sense. Him being so young, he didn't get to accomplish the dreams that he wanted.

Esther: I still don't understand whatever happened. I know there was something, because Kendrick, three days before he was killed, three boys saw Kendrick on the street. And they came up on him and they hit Kendrick in the back of the head with a brick. And I know Kendrick told Carnell about what happened. They left the house together, and they came back later. I asked him, "Do you need to call the police?" "No, Mama, don't call the police." So I don't know if they went and made matters worse.

From what I gathered from Carnell after Kendrick was killed, he said, "Mama, the police knows, but they wouldn't do anything to stop it. I don't trust nobody."

I'm not going to say that I'm blind, that they were perfect. I think they might have got involved in some stuff, and God saw it, and they knew better, 'cause they knew the Word. I'm praying. I'm hoping that they made it to heaven. I just love them so much, and I don't want to think anything else outside of that, but I've got to be real.

Juan: At first, when it happened, I tried to blame myself, you know. But then I have to think back: "Well, they was raised, they knew better." I had to let them go 'cause they was grown. I can't keep them with me every minute and watch over them.

Esther: I guess I never thought it would happen with them. They were very active in church. Carnell preached in church. Kendrick was doing the audio control of the PA system. They were also on the young men's drill team, and on the hip-hop praise team. I had heard how it happened to other parents. But you never, ever think that it will happen at your door.

It's still hard. We was used to seeing our kids out playing football and basketball in the streets, and there'd be so many of the kids come together. And every time I look out there now, there's two vacant places.

The house is real dreary looking. It feels like sometimes you can't breathe in the house. You just want to pack up and leave, and never come back. We've been talking about moving to Florida for a while. I love Florida. It takes your mind away from here. I always want to have the memories in my heart, but I don't want to keep looking.

Juan: One of the kids from the first set we fostered found us after Kendrick and Carnell were killed. We were saying, "We don't think we're going to do this no more." And she said, "Oh, no. You all gotta do this. If it weren't for you all, we wouldn't be the way we are."

Esther: She said, "You made me the woman that I am today. And my sisters. I got to give honor where honor is due. Please don't, don't let kids like us go." It was a blessing to hear that.

Juan: Our youngest is 17. When you're used to be in a house with 21 kids, and now it's getting down to zero almost, it's kind of hard. We're definitely going to be foster parents for some more kids.

Esther: I'm going to Florida. That's what God wants me to do now. I'm going to open up a church in Florida. But I think that God would eventually like me to come back and open a church in Chicago, too, because the need for the youth is heavy here. They need help.

—Interviewed by Lisa Applegate

ENDNOTES

66 Jeffery Manor—which is sometimes spelled "Jeffrey Manor"—went from an overwhelmingly white area to an overwhelmingly black one in the late 1960s and early 1970s. According to author Jason DeParle, "The first black family in Jeffrey Manor encountered a burning cross." See Jason DeParle, *American Dream: Three Women, Ten Kids, and a Nation's Drive to End Welfare* (New York: Viking Books, 2004), 44-46.

67 Established by the legendary social reformer Jane Addams in 1898, Hull House was the nation's most influential settlement house—an institution that provided community services to underprivileged areas. In recent years, its largest mission was to provide services for foster children. Declining revenues forced Hull House to close for good in 2012. See Liam Ford and Kate Thayer, "Hull House Association to Shut Door," *Chicago Tribune*, Jan. 22, 2012.

68 Founded in 1905, the *Chicago Defender* quickly became one of the most important African-American newspapers in the United States. In recent years, it has faced declining revenues and staff cuts.

WHEN A BULLET ENTERS A BODY

NANCY L. JONES

The Cook County Medical Examiner's Office is located in the Illinois Medical District, west of downtown Chicago. A large white building, the Medical Examiner's Office is the third-busiest in the country, processing 4,500 to 5,500 cases per year. Anybody who dies in an unnatural, unusual or suspicious way—suicide, homicide or accidental death, for instance—is brought in.

Victims' families or friends, who come in to identify the body, enter through tinted doors. A woman sits behind a protective, glass window where people check in before identifying a body. After they fill out the required paperwork, they are taken into a small room with a wide-screen television. In the morgue, the victim is placed underneath a camera attached to the ceiling. The face is displayed for families or friends on the television screen, which is how they make the identification.

Until July of 2012, when she retired as Cook County's chief medical examiner, the office was run by Dr. Nancy L. Jones. During an extensive interview, conducted several months before she stepped down, she offered a tour of the morgue. A petite woman with fading red hair, she spoke with assurance and carried herself with confidence.

Here is our cooler. You okay with this?

We can store up to 300 bodies in here. Anybody who is dying from anything other than a natural disease process has to be brought into our office to be examined and have a death certificate issued by us.

These two bodies here—gang violence. Well, actually—do you see the arms? See the wrists? This could well be a suicide.

My first autopsy was a man in his 50s who died of alcoholism. I was in residency at the University of Chicago, and the mental preparation starts in anatomy lab when you're working on your cadaver. Although, with a cadaver, it's a lot easier to separate because they smell so much like chemicals and the tissue is hard—it's like working on a plastic doll.

That first autopsy was very hard, both emotionally and physically. It took a few minutes for me to just make the first incision with the scalpel blade. You don't realize how difficult it is to actually make that incision through human skin. Human skin is pretty tough. It requires a lot more pressure than you think, but it also requires a lot more mental stamina—at least the first time you do it.

The problem was that I was focusing too much on the fact that this was a human being. But once I made that first incision, the scientist part of me took over. I did it, I dictated it, and that was the end of it. You cannot dwell on these cases. You can't think about it.

The way we deal with what we do is very similar to the way the police deal with what they do. In the autopsy room when you're doing the examination, you talk about other things. Part of the separation process and part of maintaining your sanity is actually carrying on conversations about other things. It's a survival instinct.

Nobody likes doing children. *Nobody* likes doing children. One of the things that makes us nervous is when the economy starts to go bad, because we tend to see a lot more infant deaths. We're not sure why. We're hoping they're not smothering or neglecting their babies. When the economy started turning a couple of years ago, we had a little uptick in the number of babies we were seeing, which was hard.

The teenagers that we tend to examine are usually non-natural deaths. You know, traffic accidents, gunshot wounds and suicides. Most teenagers are relatively healthy, so in a typical week, there aren't many teenagers. If there are, they are usually suicides and homicides.

When I started working in the 1980s, most of our homicide victims were in their late 20s, early 30s. Over the years, the ages have been creeping down. We even have cases where 12- and 13-year-olds were homicide victims, but 12- and 13-year-olds were also the offenders. The gangs were using the 12- and 13-year-olds to carry the guns and to deliver the drugs. They were using the younger members, recruiting them younger, because they figured the police wouldn't hassle them as much.

On Saturday, I did two homicide cases. Both single, simple gunshot wounds. One was a 16-year-old Hispanic male and the other was a 16-year-old black male. One of the kids was just sitting with his friends and they heard what sounded like firecrackers. They turned to look and he got hit in the right side of the head. Totally innocent bystander. Never been in trouble a day in his life. The other one was a gang member. He had been arrested at least twice: one for a stolen vehicle and one for drugs. But, of course, I'm sure his family is saying that he was an angel and that he has never been in trouble a day in his life.

You find out that, if you look into some of these reports, they give gang affiliations. They usually find out by tattoos or witnesses, things like that. You get to recognize some of the gang tattoos. I mean, the 16-year-old has tattoos, but one of them was his name and, like, praying hands. A lot of the people that we work on have tattoos, and a lot of them have gang tattoos that can easily be recognized.

If it's the number 4, it's the Four Corner Hustlers. If you see crossed pitchforks, it's GD, which is the Gangster Disciples. There are so many different factions now that even some of the bigger gangs have broken up into smaller factions and fight each other. The crossed pitchforks I see a lot. But a lot of those are on people that are in their 40s and even their 50s. They're older gang members that have survived and they're dying from drugs or natural diseases. They're not into the gangbanging; I guess it's not exciting for them anymore.

This is the working hallway where they're doing autopsies. Want to see?

It's a gunshot victim and there's the victim himself right there. We have digital X-rays now, so we're able to locate the bullets and recover them. All of the bullets in the body have to be removed.

When a bullet is fired from a gun, it has kinetic energy, and kinetic energy is determined by its velocity—how fast it's traveling—and mass. The more kinetic energy that a bullet has, the more damage it's going to do. So if you have a low muzzle velocity handgun—a .22 or something like that—it's not going to do as much damage as a higher velocity gun, like a .22 rifle.

As the bullet goes into the body, the small piece of lead isn't really going to do all that much damage. If I threw a bullet at you, it wouldn't do anything. But as the bullet is entering the body, it's sending kinetic energy out in a circumferential manner around it. So a bullet that's the size of a pencil eraser may create damage in the body that's the size of a softball. What happens is it creates what's called a temporary cavity, and that cavity pulsates and becomes smaller, smaller and smaller, until you finally just have the hole the bullet has left in the organs. That hole is surrounded by a larger area of damaged tissue.

So depending on where the bullet goes into the body and what organs it affects, it's going to create far more damage. If it goes through the heart, it can kill you very quickly because you need your heart to pump your blood.

Where you're hit determines how quickly you may die or succumb. Now, I've done autopsies on victims that have been shot in the head and have run 75 yards or have driven their car for several blocks before they succumb. It all depends on what part of the brain and what the kinetic energy is. You could shoot somebody and, if it goes through the frontal lobes of the brain, they're not going to lose consciousness until the brain swells enough from the damage to cause them to become unconscious and die. If you shoot them in the back of the head where the vital centers are, they're going to die much faster. It's not like on television when you get shot and you go down. In some cases it's true, and in some cases it's not true.

The length of an autopsy depends on how many times they've been shot. I've been doing this for 25 years, so it usually takes me about an hour, an hour and a half. We always X-ray our gunshot victims, examine the outside of the body. We do height, weight, hair color, eye color. Are your teeth natural? Are your ears pierced? Do you have any tattoos, you know, scars, identifying marks? Then we locate and measure the wounds. We look for evidence of close range fire, like soot, gunpowder or stippling.

After you do the external examination, then you do the internal examination. If you're shot in the head, it doesn't matter; we're going to do a complete autopsy. We usually start with the chest and abdomen. We collect toxicology samples: blood, bile from the gall bladder, urine from the urinary bladder if there's some there; we usually take fluid from the eye. If they're shot and the bullet is still in the body, then we remove it and photograph it for the investigating officer.

What happens when they do IDs is they set it here under the camera. So if you stand right here and come a little forward—there you are.

The intake attendants and autopsy technicians get the body on the cart and they usually have a blue sheet over them and just the head is shown. We do identifications by close-circuit television. We don't pull a drawer out, like you see on TV. The family's not standing right there.

We have the family fill out an affidavit when they come in. We take them in the order that they come. We ask them who are they here to see, what their relationship is to the victim, you know, as much demographics as we can get. We make a copy of a photo ID. Then, they sign it. After they're done with that, we ask them to sit down and we'll call them back and take them into the viewing room.

This is the room where we bring the families to make the IDs. We ask them to sit down, ask them if they're ready. When they tell us they're ready, we turn the TV on and they see the face of the body. They can sit here as long as they want. They can look at it as long as they want.

We used to let anyone come in and as many times as they wanted to see the body, but we found that people were using us as their funeral home, and I don't have enough staff. This is a very difficult part of the job that we do—helping the families. I don't have a grief counselor or a minister or like a chaplain or anything like that for either the families or my staff.

Now this painting, this picture is very non-denominational and is usually hanging on the wall over there. But if you look at the wall you can see a ripply area. Somebody punched three holes in the wall while they were doing an identification. I don't even think it was a homicide victim. So we've restricted the number of IDs that we do. We've cut back, especially after the damage was done to the wall. Some of my staff have been threatened. We now restrict IDs to homicide victims, as well as unidentified and those tentatively IDed. It's made a big difference. Everyone's stress levels have gone down quite a bit.

In this job, we see the best and the worst of human beings. We really do. I've had mothers truly devastated by the loss of a child, of course. But others—well, we just recently had a young homicide victim, and the mother came in and she was making loud, wailing noises and dramatically falling to the floor and things like that. But when you looked at her closely, there wasn't a single tear in her eye. You know, they give an over-dramatic performance out of guilt. Some of our victims are 10-year-olds or in their early teens who were out on a school night at 11 or 12 o'clock at night. What were they doing out on a school night at midnight? Why aren't the parents enforcing curfew? Why aren't they in bed sleeping? I think that's part of the guilt. The parents realize that they weren't there for them when their child was young and needed them.

My parents lived through the Depression and World War II, so it was the nuclear family, the whole thing. When I was a kid, you were held accountable and learned to become self-sufficient. I grew up around the time where the drug culture and free love and personal freedom started coming in. Those parents raised their children differently, with maybe a little too much free rein, as opposed to what we had when we were kids. It has progressed to where society believes you should really allow your child to express themselves and you really shouldn't discipline your child.

I think the problem today is that parents are trying to be their children's friend and not the parent. And you have to be a parent; you have to set limits. Bribery doesn't work with kids, because they're just going to want more and more. You have to be a parent.

Everybody is like, "The police need to do more. The schools need to do more. Society needs to do more to prevent youth violence." But very rarely do you hear that the parents should be doing more. Ultimately, the parents are responsible for what their children are doing.

I know that there's a lot out there about joining gangs. Why does somebody join a gang? Well, because it's their family. The gang means much more to them and provides them with more than their parents did, than their family did. If you have a tight, cohesive family who are cared for and everything, then there's no reason to join a gang.

But I've had mothers where their sons have been nothing but trouble from the day they were old enough to leave home on their own. I've actually had a mother say, "I'm glad he's gone. He's been nothing but trouble his whole life." I understand that you can do everything in your power to try to raise a child correctly and make them socially responsible and everything, and it doesn't make any difference. There are evil people and, unfortunately, for this lady, her son just was evil.

Don't misunderstand me. I am a human being with feelings and emotions, just like everyone else. There are times where, for whatever reason, particularly if the victim is an innocent bystander and the family did everything to protect the child and raise them properly and they still end up dead, it just breaks my heart. Even if we don't talk to the parents or meet them at all, it still touches you.

Every day is a struggle for us to focus on our job and not focus on the social and human aspects of the job, because, if you focus too much on that, you lose sight of what it is that you're doing and you're not going to do your job properly.

Don't think I'm a coldhearted person, but I know how to separate the person I am from the work I do. When you're doing an autopsy, it's not a person. You're working on a case number. You're working on a case.

Even with gang members, I try not to think about them because that's personalizing them, making them more than a case number. In order to survive, in order to be able to sleep at night, in order to come to work day after day after day and do what I do, I choose to not humanize victims by not knowing their stories. Yes, even the gang member has family out there that cared about him, but I can't perform to the degree that is required to do a good job if I allow myself to get involved emotionally with what I do. As the examining pathologist, I don't want to know about his life, because my job is to focus on his death. I'm very comfortable with death; I'm very uncomfortable with dying.

I really love what I do. It's fascinating seeing how the human body was put together and to see how little it takes to cause it to cease to function. I can't cure what happened to this person; I can't bring them back to life. But what I can do is help the family.

When I was an assistant medical examiner, I thought of the morgue as a place where the work I was doing was bringing peace to family members and bringing justice for the victims of crime—to be the voice of victims and to tell their families and their friends what happened to them and what brought about their death.

I still think of it as that.

—*Interviewed by Jacob Sabolo*

BOTH FEET OUT

BENNY ESTRADA

Benjamin "Benny" Estrada believes he is doing God's work. A former gang mem-
ber in the Mexican-American neighborhood of Little Village on the Southwest
Side, Estrada uses his own experience to help at-risk youth. He spoke with us in
2011 at the YMCA's Street Intervention Program in Pilsen, where he worked[69]
as a program coordinator with Jorge Roque, whose narrative also appears in
this book. The program, which operates in neighborhoods throughout Chicago,
attempts to keep young people away from street violence through services such as
recreational activities and in-school visits.

Estrada—who, prior to joining the YMCA, worked for the anti-violence
group CeaseFire—is a small man with swift gestures. He has a casual air, but
when he becomes passionate about a topic he is prone to smacking tables and
using his hands to emphasize his points.

Little Village is divided by two major gangs, right: the Latin Kings and the
Two-Sixes. And where I grew up, which is like the east side of Little Village,
there was a real lack of resources, a real lack of after-school programming,
a lack of green spaces, parks in general. If we wanted to go to the park and
stay in the Latino community, you can either go to Pilsen, which is out of
your way, or you can go to Piotrowski Park, which is based in Little Village.
But there being two major gangs, if you're not from the community where
Piotrowski Park is at, there's guys that know that.

So what happened was I tried going to Piotrowski Park. I played Little
League baseball over there. At this time, I wasn't involved in gangs. I was just
a kid that loved sports. I was a pitcher. I think it was at the age of 11 that I
got put on the Pittsburgh Pirates team. And the Pittsburgh Pirates team uniforms are the colors of the gang in my part of Little Village. It wasn't even the
gang colors, but it was something that was very similar to the gang colors.[70]

So I went to the other part of Little Village to play a game. I pitched a
real good game and I'm walking home. I get to the boundaries of both gangs,
where this is this side and this is this side. And the gang from the other
neighborhood approached me. And I'm like, "Aw, man." I had a friend, and
he was a chubby kid and he just took off running. So that already invoked
suspicion on them. They're like, "Well, why's this guy running? He must be a
gangbanger." And I didn't run, you know, 'cause I didn't feel like I had to run.

And the ringleader asked me, "What you be about? What gang are you in?"

I'm like, "Man, I don't gangbang."

They're like, "Yeah, yeah, but what's up with them colors, man?" I was 11 years old and this 16-year-old goes and slaps me and he takes my hat. He's like, "Yeah, yeah, you're in a gang, punk, with those colors on." He took my baseball jersey too from me. I'm like, "Aw, man."

And that was like my first taste of what it was to be affected by gangs. And it invoked hatred in me for the other side of the neighborhood. I came home and threw my glove away, like threw it in the garbage, and my mom's like, "What's wrong with you? Why you throwing your glove away?" I just stopped playing baseball altogether. I'm like "Man, 'ef' baseball." I mean that's how much that day affected me. It just—it planted a negative seed in me, is what it did, and that seed upon time, you know, it grew and it grew and it grew.

From that point on, I didn't go to the west side of Little Village. I didn't go back over there. At all. For nothing. And that's where the park was at.

I really wasn't gang involved up until I hit my freshman year at Farragut High School, but my stepfather was one of the major players in the community. He was already involved at a young age in gangs; I think about 14 or 15 years old he was already involved. Everything that he did, I pretty much did; I wanted to emulate him.

And when I hit high school, it was like a culture shock. You got the Gangster Disciples, you got the Vice Lords, you got the Travelers, all African-American gangs. And the guys that were already involved in the Latino gang from my neighborhood in Little Village, they pretty much just cuffed me and took me under their wing. There was this one guy in particular, he seen me in the lunchroom like my second day. He's like, "You're gonna be cool; you're with us. Don't worry about it." He was like this big muscular dude; it was probably like his fifth year in high school, and he probably had like sophomore credits, and he just took me under his wing. From that point on, it was like, "All right, well, I guess I'm gonna be involved." I didn't really have a choice.

He was one of those guys that, you know, if there was a fight, he's right in the middle of it. If there's an argument, he's coming, he's showing up. That's just who he was—the guy that always managed to have his hands on anything that happened in the school in terms of guys getting into gang fights. Nobody would mess with him. And 'cause nobody would mess with him, nobody would mess with me.

I was with him once when a well-known rapper came to the school to perform a concert. So I sit down and the concert starts and some back-and-forth banter starts going on in the stands. The blacks and Latinos be gang-banging to each other. Signs here, signs there. All it took was one swing and it was over. Everybody started fighting.

And that was my first experience, man. I hit a couple people. Our assistant principal got hit with a chair; it busted his head right open. I got a black eye; I got a fat lip. It really started to invoke that hate, and that seed was already planted from the Latino gangs, but now it was planted from the African-American gangs. That really took me off course. It put a bad taste in my mouth.

It was tough, man, because I played basketball and all the African-American students, they would see me in the gym. And I had a real good friend that was a black student—a real good friend. I mean, we used to hang out after school by the gym and we would play ball. Saturday mornings, me and him would be the first ones there. And in my junior year, there was a big fight and everybody's running around the school. They were taking students and locking them up. I'm walking in the hallway and he's coming up the stairs. He's got a big old bandage on his head, and he's just bleeding profusely. He's like, "Why the 'ef' your boys got to do that, bro?"

I just looked at him, and that's when I knew: I just lost a friend. And it wasn't even something I did. It was something the guys did, but I didn't try to repair that relationship. I left it alone. That's just the way it was.

I didn't have a father growing up. I was about five months old when he passed away. And my uncle through marriage was a positive person in my life. He's like one of the biggest influences in terms of why I do this work, because he was a social worker, too.

He loved working with the kids and he took a real liking to me, even though I was heavily involved in the gang in the neighborhood. Basketball was always something that attracted my attention—and my uncle, he fueled that passion, man. He would come to the block in his little Honda. He'd double-park in the middle of the street and jump out in front of my house, which at the time was like the epicenter for all the guys. But he had no fear.

He would be like, "Hey, I'm looking for my nephew." People would pull out guns on him.

They'd be like, "Man, what you looking for him for?"

He wouldn't be afraid of the guns. He'd push them out of the way and go knock on my door: "Man, we got a game! Get your shorts. Let's go, man."

I'd be like, "Man, I don't wanna go play right now."

"Bro, we got a damn game, man. You got a commitment to me. You're gonna stick to it. Now get your ass up."

And I always had this tremendous talent to put the ball in the basket. It was a God-given gift, you know. I mean, people that know me can tell you I'm just one of those guys that just picked up the ball and it seemed like it was second nature to me. So my uncle seen all that, he seen all the potential. He never really pushed me to get out of the gang, but he just told me, "You're gonna see that eventually all this stuff is not gonna get you anywhere, but basketball is gonna get you somewhere."

And, I mean, it did. There was a Latino tournament that was strictly for the Midwest and it was like a 20-city tournament, so every month there was another tournament to go to. So I started getting exposed to all this other stuff that I just didn't know was out there. Here I am living in Little Village and closing my mind off to all these options, 'cause I thought just the gang life was all there was for me. And getting out there and seeing Latinos doing all kinds of other stuff just blew me away.

My son, to this day, has about 50 to 60 trophies that he just has put in his room, 'cause now he's starting to like basketball and he thinks his dad is like this big-time star. And I tell him, "I never made it to the NBA, and I didn't go to college to play basketball, but I did make a name for myself."

I even got offered to go play in Mexico on a professional team. There was a scout that had came to watch somebody play, and I ended up dropping like 50 points on the guy, and the scout just forgot about the dude and came to ask me. But I thought, "I don't wanna go live anywhere else, especially not for no three months. I'm making money doing my side stuff in the neighborhood." It just didn't seem like it was an option to me. I closed myself off to it.

I was in high school for four years. I had credits, enough credits to be maybe a sophomore at most. It wasn't a big deal to me. The gang culture and the gang life just took a real hold of me for a lot of years of my life. A lot of years, man, I lost a tremendous amount of friends, and, as I lost my friends, my hate for other gangs just grew and grew and grew.

I was on probation for possessing the cannabis. I spent about two months in the county jail. I was sentenced to two years' probation, but I was off of probation after a year and five months. Being on probation, you know, it started to change my attitude a little bit about not wanting to get into so much trouble. But what helped me decide that this road I was on was a destructive one and it was gonna end my life, is when I had my daughter.

At the time, me and the woman who is my wife now had broken up, and she had left the city, and I was just on this destructive path. I was just like, "I lost my girl and I loved her." So it made me drink even more, party even more, go out there and even be more of a … Then her mother called me.

She's like, "Come to the house. I need to show you something."

I'm like, "Show me something?" 'Cause I always had a good relationship with her mother, and her mother always kept in contact with me.

And she says, "Just be ready to see something that's gonna change your life." And I figured, like, she had money or something. And she opens the bedroom door, and there's the—there's the little baby, my daughter Leslie.

And I'm like, "Who's that?"

She's like, "That's your daughter."

"That's my daughter?"

It blew me away. By looking at that baby, I could already tell that she was my daughter. She had the same birthmark as me, everything. But I had so much anger in me that I was like, "No, man. I want a DNA test."

She's like, "If you don't stop, I'm gonna slap you, 'cause that's your daughter." And it hit me like a ton of bricks, man: "I'm willing to die for what I believe in, but am I really going to do that now that I have this little girl in my life?"

I went and I signed up for GED. And it took a while to get my GED, I can't lie. Because I had so much stuff going on in terms of just being in the neighborhood and dealing with stuff. I got my GED, and I got hired by a display company and, like, within a year that job just took off for me. I went from just being the driver for the company to getting the manager's job. That was my really first job-job, you know, and it took off from right there.

I started working on the railroad. I got the call from CeaseFire,[71] and I still don't know how they got that number. They wanted somebody that could get in there, get in touch with individuals in Little Village, and let them know that they're trying to promote a culture of nonviolence. And I started doing a lot of detachments for them, which was kids that wanted to get out of gangs. I knew everybody in the neighborhood, and I would say, "Look man, the kid's not going to pose a threat to you. Let him get out, man." Kind of negotiate some things. And I started pulling kids out. Not a lot of kids out, but four or five kids out of a gang a year to us is a huge number. Ultimately, God has his hand over who stays and who goes, but the threat of being killed by gang violence shoots down once you're not in it.

And it just sparked something in me. It just did. It always felt like there was a burden in my heart, 'cause I would be in the community and I would try to volunteer and do things, but I also knew that in this line of work you cannot, you *cannot*, have one foot in and one foot out. Kids see through that. The kids that you work with are gonna see that.

I've been on board with the YMCA's Street Intervention Program for I'm gonna say about four to five years. My days here, they can just be overwhelming. During my mornings, I could be at court or I could be at the high school or I could be checking up on one of my kids and making sure he went to school or talking to one of the school counselors. At night, I do recreational activities and run peace circles with the kids. I put in at least 65 hours this week. For people like me, it's important that we make time for our own kids, 'cause we don't want to lose our kids while we're trying to save somebody else's. I try my best to call my kids at least three times a day and talk to all of them, see what's going on, tell them, "Daddy will be home late so just make sure you take a shower, get ready for bed, and I'll kiss you when I get home."

My weekends I try my best to just dedicate it to my kids. Even during the week, if I can sneak away, I'll tell my boss, "I gotta go home for a little while and help my son with his homework or I gotta see my daughter, who is in the choir." She sings like a bird. I don't know where she got it from 'cause I don't have that voice and neither does my wife. But I like being there to support her. So those are our days, man. We just do all this and that. All of it.

—*Interviewed by Mollie Diedrich*

ENDNOTES

69 Estrada left the YMCA shortly before this book went to press. He and Jorge Roque both now work for CeaseFire and for New Life Community Church in Little Village, where they mentor young people who are on probation.

70 The Pittsburgh Pirates' uniforms are black and gold—the same basic colors as the Latin Kings.

71 CeaseFire was founded by Dr. Gary Slutkin, an epidemiologist who maintains that violence should be treated like an epidemic and can be prevented by stopping the behavior at its source. The group—recently renamed Cure Violence—was the subject of *The Interrupters*, an award-winning 2011 film by Steve James and Alex Kotlowitz.

HOW DARE I STILL BE HAPPY?
TU-TU

Tu-Tu, who asked that we only use her nickname, was born in Kingsville, Texas. At a very young age, she and her older brother were taken to Chicago to be raised by relatives. Her brother went to live with their paternal grandparents, while Tu-Tu moved in with their maternal grandparents, who lived in Englewood, a South Side neighborhood characterized by violence and a rapidly declining population.

When Tu-Tu was 12, her mother came back into her life to raise her and her brother. She and her mother did not get along, however, so after two years, Tu-Tu returned to Englewood. The Conservative Vice Lords, one of Chicago's most powerful gangs, became her de facto guardians, providing her with a studio apartment and financial support, as well as with protection in the area.

Tu-Tu has two daughters. She credits them with motivating her to return to school as she encouraged them to pursue their educations. She is currently working toward a bachelor's degree at DePaul University. Tu-Tu speaks in a soft tone with a touch of a Southern twang that hints at her Texan roots. She is witty and quick to let you know if she thinks you're pretending to be something you're not. She keeps her hair in a short, natural style, and often wears large hoop earrings. Although she has endured many hardships, she looks much younger than her 40 years.

My mother went into labor early with me because of a flying cockroach. I like to tell that story. A hissing cockroach came in the house and scared her so bad they could not stop it. I think it was almost like two months early. This was in Kingsville, a military town, where my dad was in the Navy. I don't really remember how long I lived in Texas. As a child, we went back and forth, so I'm not sure. I'm always in between.

I don't even know the date my parents sent me back here to live with my grandparents. My folks were married and everything, so how could they not be ready to be parents? There's a lot of stories that I'm not told. So as far as my childhood, like, "Why did we go here?" I still don't know that. I don't know why my grandparents took us and separated my brother and me, either. It's the biggest secret in the family and, now that everybody's pretty much passed that could tell me, I don't think I'll ever know.

I called my grandparents "Mom" and "Dad." I helped my grandmother cook. We cooked everything. Everything you can think of. Soul food. Everything under the sun. And we always had to watch Lawrence Welk blow the bubbles on TV. Why? I don't know.

I didn't see my father, but I used to call my mother "that white lady." She's very pale and fair-skinned, but she's black! She'd drop off stuff for me every once in a while, but nobody would ever tell me who she was. She'd just drop by. I kinda think I was just like, "Who are you? Thanks," and would move on. She's not very affectionate, so I wouldn't have really talked to her anyway. She's not my mother, you know? My grandmother is my mother. So I'm like "Who are you? Thanks for the Big Wheel."

I stayed with my grandparents until around 12 years old. My grandfather passed, so my grandmother moved to senior housing. After that, I went with my mother. By then, I knew she was my mother, but I didn't have a good relationship with her. We stayed in Chicago, and my brother came, too.

My mom sucks. Yeah, we just didn't get along. Never really had a fight. I never argued or yelled at my mother. It was constant nagging, browbeating, demeaning, little stuff like that. Just stuff that, as a child, you have no stand. You just have to take it. She would come home from work and maybe she would cook or I would have to cook, and the dishes better have been clean and rooms better have been clean. Don't let her come into the house and your work isn't done kinda thing. Complete opposite of my grandmother.

I dislike my dad even more than my mom, because he probably could've been the other parent that was responsible. Somebody should've been responsible. So for both of you to not be responsible? Y'all have issues. I don't wanna say my mom didn't try. At least, I think she tried, because she did come get us. He did nothing. I know him, but he has another family now—another little precious daughter and everything.

I wasn't with my mom very long—about two years. My reason for leaving depends who you ask. If you're asking me, she put me out. I just know we didn't like each other. If you asked her, she'd say that I was a unruly, spoiled brat that she couldn't control and blah, blah, blah…

I'm the only gang affiliation in my family. My mother and my brother are saditty[72] black people, so they would never affiliate. I'm called "the ghetto child"; I'm the black sheep of the family. I've actually been affiliated, like, 90 percent of my life with the Vice Lords. Not even on purpose, either. I just happened to be around those types of people.

So when I left my mother's house, I took all my stuff, as much as I could get, and I went to the streets. I never went home. I went back to my grandparents' neighborhood. A few guys in the neighborhood—Vice Lords, pretty much—got me a studio apartment in Hyde Park. So I was pretty much living on my own at 15. But the guys took care of me. I was like a little sister, I guess. They gave me financial stability and security. If I got hurt, they took care of it. I think I'm super spoiled. For me to have had such a rough life and the things I've been through, I've always been financially stable. You have to have some sort of association to survive.

The guys weren't old. They was just older than me. But to me, back then, they would've been old, because I was so young. Somehow, I've always dated the big-time guys in the neighborhood, and I didn't look for them. I mean, like, the biggest guys, like, newspaper-bound guys, but I never would've dated the original guys who took care of me. That would've been perverted; I do not like older men at all. Skin hanging and stuff. I have a phobia. Nope, no older guys. That was strictly big brother, little sister.

But I was still a little bad. I had my moments. I had to show I was worthy of the support. You have to do stuff. Nothing like initiation; just show that you are down. I've never had to, like, shoot anybody or anything. I remember, there was a new girl that moved into the neighborhood and they said that she was coming over there and telling our business to her old neighbors, something like that. So I had to go in her house, like, I walked past her mom and everything, snatched her out of the house, and, like, we all jumped her and beat her up. But I had to be the one to go get her. I know, I even feel stupid saying it, but that's childhood.

The Vice Lords, they watched you growing. They know their neighborhood, they know their kids, the families. Back then, it was about protecting your area. It wasn't about fighting each other. So anybody that was in the area was protected, pretty much. It was more structured in those days. You don't bring heat to your area because it brings police. So you keep it quiet. I hate saying this out loud but there was *order* in their gangbanging. I know it sounds crazy, but that's how mobsters made it or still make it: structure. You can't move without getting approval. You can't go just shoot up somebody without having a reason behind it. I'm not saying there's ever a reason to shoot somebody—it's hard to say what I'm saying without sounding like I'm condoning it. It was more of a protection-and-retaliation kind of thing.

Even though I was living on my own, I never went to the guys' places. I think they stayed on their own, but I saw them a lot on the block. You know, you hang out, talk junk, play basketball, hang out on the monkey bars, neighborhood stuff. I was just lucky. My life could've been worse. Because I don't do drugs and I don't drink. Never done it. No! Ain't I lucky?

The guys was like, "That's not ladylike. You don't do that." There was the hos and there was the ladies. Don't go over there. Stay here. They knew what my background was, they respected that. The "not ladies," I'm gonna call them that, they, you know, drank and smoked, and had sex, and partied, and didn't care. They thought they were being cool, but the guys don't respect that. It's still like that today. I try to tell these little girls, "Don't think, because they drink and smoke with you, they like you. That's just the category that you in now." The guys determine the categories, but the girls put their selves in it.

I ended up leaving high school my senior year. It was too much at the time. I didn't even really care anymore. I just wanted to go to work, make money. I got a work permit at Andy Frain.[73] I will never forget that job. It was ushering. So I worked all the Bulls games, all the concerts, the auto show. That's the best teenage job you could ever have.

Once I made money, I started paying for the apartment. I'm definitely independent; I'm definitely go-getting. I have to because that's the only way I made it. You can't slow down; you can't get weak, because you don't know what'll happen. You share something with someone and they throw it back at you, in your face, in a very inappropriate time. Yeah, I can't handle that so I just stopped talking. I kinda lost contact with a lot of people. They thought I was too good, a couple of my friends or whatever you wanna call them. So-called friends wanna bring up my childhood and, you know, who picks that? Nobody picks to be outside at that age. I was just trying to eat.

When I was 19, I became a mother and an adult. And then I moved in with the dad, and I was stuck with him forever. No, I'm just joking. We didn't get married, but we had two kids, two girls. We had a family and I was stable for the first time since my grandparents. We were all living together 10 years—maybe 15 if you count the back and forth. Yeah, we were together for a long time. We moved twice: Englewood and Calumet City.

My daughters were born in '91 and '95. Their nicknames are Skinny Thick Girl and Thick Skinny Girl. One is curvier than the other. Skinny Thick Girl is my oldest. She's skinny and just thinks she has a body out this world. And then my youngest one, she's thicker and thinks she's a size zero.

It's an extreme blessing to be a mother. You gotta do everything that your mom didn't do. Actually, it's the hardest thing I've ever done in my life to not mimic her ways. I'm still working on it, but their dad was good, so I had a good support system.

Their dad and I, we grew apart. We grew up differently, but we're still best friends. I moved back to Texas once, and they didn't wanna go so he kept them for three years. My youngest lives with him now so I can finish school, finally. She's a straight-A high-school student, high honors. She gets all kinds of awards and internships. She's going to be a neuro-neuro-some-thing-something-something. She's just everything. And the oldest, she's in Texas. She's studying education. She is living on her own; she pays her own rent. Every blue moon, she asks me for, like, a piece of money or something, but they are doing excellent. That's why I'm able to finish school. They're making me. I had to beat them because I pushed them to go to school, so I have to have my degree before they do.

I went back to high school maybe at 25 or 26. I went through a program. It's an actual diploma.[74] It was hard, too, because I was like, "I'm not going in there with these kids!" I started at community college in 2008, Harold Washington. I needed to be babied back into this. I was originally studying business. Now, I'm double major: African and Black Diaspora Studies and English, so I don't know when I graduate. I'm finally doing something I want.

Once you start growing and wanting different stuff, people don't see you anymore. It's, "Oh, there goes Miss Going to School, School Books, White Girl." I'm like, "How am I a white girl?" Even my daughters' dad calls me a white girl; he doesn't understand a lot of stuff. Just because I don't do what they do, they think I think I'm better than them.

I quit my job so I could finish school because it was too much. I was work-ing for Nike. So I took a big risk. But I'm doing good. Now I'm working at a beauty shop. I do natural hair two days a week: Fridays and Saturdays. It's on the South Side. Stressful, but it's taking care of everything.

I'm actually back where I started: in a studio in Hyde Park. It's almost on the same block, too. It's about me again. I actually don't know what to do. It's a lot more peaceful. Not looking over my shoulder. It's almost like I'm getting a second chance to be peaceful, but I don't even go to certain areas anymore.

The original guys, there were three or four of them, aren't around anymore. They passed away or gone to jail. A lot of the leaders are locked up, but I've never been to any jails. Not county, nothing. To visit anyone. I refuse to see people like that, but it's still people I'm connected to. You branch out, you know other people. I still need the security. I have rank, so if I need something I can get it done. I don't know everybody, but I have close ties with a few people, ranging from maybe 14-year-olds and up.

The younger kids are completely out of control. But if you can corner them, you can have a conversation with them. I think they trust me because I don't talk at them. I know what's going on in their heads. I know what they're going through. It's really big for me to not judge someone. These guys out here, with their pants sagging, they look rough, they look scary. But they might've had a mom like mine that put you out early. You never know what the backdrop is. I'm not saying trust them, because they are different now. They're on pills and stuff. Back then, if you did any kind of drugs, you was an outcast because you was a crackhead or something like that. For some reason, it's more acceptable now. You see these kids doing stuff on the news and are like, "What the hell is wrong with them?" But what's happening is they're on Ecstasy and drink, so they have an upper and a downer clashing with each other. They're literally frying their brains out. It's stuff back in the day the guys would not let be in their 'hood. So I'm more alert when I go to the 'hood than I used to be.

I've survived a lot, and it amazes me that I'm still able to be happy and laugh. I've dodged a lot; I'm not bitter. I know every single day that I'm extremely lucky. I don't understand who I am. I'm not normal. I have to be, like, an alien. I've been through so much, how dare I still be happy? I'm scared if I ever figure it out, my favor is gonna go away, so I don't really worry about it, don't wanna jinx it.

I'm gonna break down eventually. I'm just waiting for it to crash. I'm getting softer. My ex-best friend said I was getting too soft for her to hang with because I actually care about stuff now. I probably started caring like six years ago. I don't know what happened. I'm living in Atlanta and she calls me and tells me that some guy she's dating, some other girl that he's dating threatened, like, my god kids or whatever, so she's like, "You need to come up here so we can…" and I'm like, "I'm not gonna come from Atlanta to Chicago to whoop some girl's ass because ya'll both having sex with the same man." Is that soft or is that common sense? So then she calls me back maybe two days later like, "She just threatened to come shoot the house up!" So of course I'm a little more worried, but I'm still not on my way there. I can get people to do stuff for me, so I call and had somebody watching the house for a couple days and she's full of shit. So she's been mad at me ever since that, but the code, I mean that's common sense: You don't call for help like that unless you really need it. You don't wanna cry wolf because, when you really need it, they won't be there.

I'm not as numb now. While I was in hair school, I worked part-time at a funeral home, doing hair on the dead people. You only do the front of the hair, but I think I was able to do it for the short amount of time because I used to be super numb. Now I refuse to see anyone like that. I just want to remember them the last time I saw them. I don't go to anyone's funeral.

I've made it through a lot. You name it, I've probably been through it. Shot at, all kinds of stuff. But none of it is really tragic because I'm still here.

—*Interviewed by Ashley Bowcott*

ENDNOTES

72 "Saddity" is a slang word that refers to uppity-acting African-Americans who put on airs.

73 Andy Frain Services provides security at sports stadiums and other large venues.

74 Tu-Tu received her diploma from Benjamin Mays, a now-defunct alternative high school that operated out of Kennedy-King College in Englewood.

HOME WAS THE THREE OF US

JEFF MALDONADO SR.

Jeff Maldonado Sr., 41, is a teaching artist who grew up in Chicago. He and his wife, Elizabeth, live in Pilsen on the West Side. Formerly a neighborhood of European immigrants, Pilsen now has a strong Hispanic identity and is decorated with mosaics and murals by Mexican artists. The neighborhood is also home to the National Museum of Mexican Art, one of the many places where Maldonado has exhibited his work.

Sitting on his couch at home, Jeff Sr. has a commanding yet gentle presence, with a warm smile and tattooed arms. His left shoulder proudly displays the face of his 19-year-old son, Jeff Maldonado Jr.—J-Def to his friends. On July 25, 2009, Jeff Jr. was gunned down in Pilsen. As an aspiring hip-hop artist, he had hoped to be a part of the revival of underground, socially conscious hip-hop. Born Christian Devon, he decided to change his name to emulate his father when he was 9 years old. For Jeff Sr., the loss of his son, together with his Mexican and Native American heritage, are major influences on his art and community activism.

I was in seventh grade when I joined a gang. I was approached by a good friend of mine, and we actually formulated our own branch called the Satan Disciples of 24th Street. I was probably in it for a good six years or so. I was smart enough to know that it was not a true lifestyle for me. It was more about taking advantage of my teenage years and just doing my thing. It was kind of in response to my home life; my parents were divorced. But I have to say this—if it wasn't for me actually making the decision to be in a gang, I would have never met my wife. That's how we actually met—through another guy in the gang.

Back then, there was a level of ethics to gangbanging, as weird as that sounds. I would only engage with the enemy. That was it. I wouldn't jump on somebody when he's with his mother or girlfriend, or something like that. There was an honor system, and now it's completely gone. Now it's like the dirtier, the better.

During that time, I was getting in trouble for various things: fighting, stealing cars. Finally, I got caught with a gun, and when I went to court, the judge looked at my record and said, "I'm surprised that you haven't been dealt with." And so what he decided to do was to put me on a year's probation, with the stipulation that either I had to be out of the state entirely, or that I would have to spend the time in juvenile detention.

I ended up staying with my aunt and uncle on an Indian reservation in Texas. I'm half American Indian; my mother is full-blood Alabama-Coushatta. My grandfather and great-grandfather were both chiefs of the tribe.

When I was in Texas, I actually returned to drawing. Growing up, my interest was always in visual art and creating comic book characters. When I was a teenager, I found my older brother or sister's art history book, and I started just reading through it. I was fascinated by it. But it wasn't until Texas that I made the decision—I'm going to pursue my dream of being an artist. I'm going to drop this street identity, and I'm going to move toward what I want to do.

When I did come back, I went to high school and graduated. When I was 20, Jeff Jr. was born, right before I started going to Columbia College. Right out of college, I moved to Pilsen when I got my studio here, about 17 years ago. My head was really into the art scene. I felt like there was a level of freedom that we hadn't had before. Elizabeth and I had a sense that it was our time to run the show and make our own decisions. We were raising Jeff in a really good way. We all grew up together, you know? And that was part of us being a successful family.

I had daily things I used to do with Jeff, like a daily hug, even when he was big. I was like, "Come here, it's time for that hug." Just for a minute. As he got older, he was like, "Ah, man." And then it's like, "All right, all right." And when he wouldn't give me a hug, when he was sitting at the computer, I used to come up behind him and smell the back of his head. You know, smell is a powerful memory energizer. Obviously, he was 18, he didn't like that either. But I didn't care. I didn't care. Because it was for me.

At times it was difficult for him growing up because people would always say, "Oh, is your son an artist? He has to be an artist because you are an artist." And Jeff was trying to find his own way. When he tried music, he really found his voice. Jeff started out freshman year of high school with his friend, Rich. Over the years, they recorded, they practiced, they worked together. They were actually doing their own original work. And over the years, they got better. They got really good, as a matter of fact.

The two of them kind of split off, because their styles started to become different. Rich gravitated toward the more gangster, kind of like he had something to prove. I think the difference came from their home lives. Rich didn't have his dad around, and I know he had a lot of problems in school and in the neighborhood with gangs. So it was natural for him to kind of thump his chest, and say, "I'm here. What are you going to do?" Jeff Jr. was more introspective and had greater range.

And the great part about that was Jeff would see me as a resource. So he would call me up at the studio with questions about the Patriot Act,[75] or this, that and the other. He ended up incorporating it in his music, and so it gave his work just so much more depth.

Jeff's music was really honest. When I play his music to the different schools, these kids can all relate to what he's talking about. These kids are like, "Yo man, he hit it right on. He's got balance. He's a little gangster, but he's a little this, and he's a little that." That was really reassuring to me—that Jeff was really on the right track to achieving the highest form of art that he could.

Jeff wanted to be a performer; that was clear. However, he realized that he needed to have a handle on the business aspect of it. So his intentions were to get his associate's degree and then transfer over to Columbia College and study music management.

We all knew he was going to make it. Elizabeth and I used to joke with him and say, "Yeah, when you're a millionaire, you can buy your mother a house." And we sacrificed part of ourselves. I took time from my career to focus on raising him. It was definitely worth it. He found himself and that's a great thing. He was very confident. Things were really moving in the direction that we had hoped.

The day before Jeff's murder was his 19th birthday. Since he was older, we weren't going to get him a birthday cake, but we decided that we were going to get him a pizza. So we hopped in the truck and drove to Freddies in Bridgeport. We ordered pizza, and it came out, and we climbed back in the truck. Jeff was in the backseat. We gave him $40, you know, spending money because he was going out that night. Jeff had warm pizza in his lap, money in his pocket, and he just said, "The universe unfolds as it should." That was a good day for us. We were really happy.

But Jeff's murder happened on the next day, on July 25, 2009, when he was going to have his first public performance at a block party. My God, I'll tell you about the day. He wanted to get his birthday gift, like really bad. He wanted a White Sox Carlton Fisk commemorative baseball cap, right? He wanted to look good for his performance.

I drove him to Foot Locker and bought his cap. And he was just so happy. Then he asked me if I could drop him off at the barbershop, because he wanted to get cleaned up. I remember that was unexpected. I thought we were all gonna go out and grab a bite. But I dropped him off and he climbed out, and he asked me if I was going to be home. And I said, "Yeah, I'll wait for you at home." It was a Saturday. It was sunny out, a beautiful day.

The next thing I know, I hear banging on my front doors. I open the door, and it was one of the guys from the block who is a gangbanger himself, and he was beside himself. He says, "Hey man, hey man, hey man. I think your son got shot."

And I was like, "What? That's impossible. That's impossible." And I remember just fumbling around.

He said, "Hurry, man, hurry!" I was looking for my shoes, and I couldn't find them, so I just threw on some flip-flops. We both ran down the street. He led me to 18th Street. I'm thinking, "This is a mistake. This is impossible." I turned the corner, and I came onto a crime scene. There was yellow tape. There was a van with doors swung open. There were crowds of people on both sides of the block. And there was a lot of blood.

I broke through the tape. I said, "I'm looking for my son. I'm looking for my son." The cops were immediately like, "Whoa, whoa, whoa." The sergeant actually grabbed me and pulled me aside and started asking me some questions. I was still thinking, "This is a mistake." The sergeant ends up finding out the hospital that they had taken this person to. So he gets my information, and he says, "You need to get over there, right now." I ran back home. I was running at top speed, and I was still thinking this has to be some mistake.

I climbed in my truck and called Elizabeth, and I asked her where she was. She told me she was walking on 18th Street, so I picked her up because I didn't want her to see what I saw. When we finally made it to the emergency room, and I was led back there, it was this moment of complete shock. He was still alive, but the doctors had induced a comatose state because of the level of damage that was done to him. He was struck by one bullet in the head. It entered his left side, and it went through and came out.

We were together with Jeff, and he was still alive, and we started talking to him, and we were telling him, "You're home. We love you." We were just trying to reassure him that he was with us, that we were together. Because that's what home was. Home was the three of us.

And he heard us. He tried to get himself up. I mean, the strength of this young man to wake himself up from a coma, to attempt to get up... The doctors went to work on him some more, and we sat two beds down, just devastated. And wondering why this happened. And what we were going to do. Just the thought of living without him—it was unimaginable. And he hung in there. He hung in there for a little while, for a few hours more. And thank God that we had that time with him. I mean, if it wasn't for this guy that came and got me, we wouldn't have had those final moments with our son. I actually did see this young man about a year later and I stopped and thanked him for doing what he did.

Right before his murder, Jeff Jr. walked into the barbershop, got his haircut, and then his friend, Angel, asked him if he wanted a ride home. They stopped at a red light. There was a gang member on the corner who saw the van, saw two guys in it, and just pulled out a gun and opened fire. Angel said he hunched back and could hear the bullets break the glass and puncture through the door. The gunman ran the opposite direction and cut through an alley. He was caught by an off-duty police officer. There was also an off-duty Cook County sheriff, so they caught this guy red-handed—the weapon and everything.

A friend of ours, who has a shop right there, later described to us how she saw Jeff when he was let out of the van. Jeff walked off on his own and got up on the gurney on his own, you know. She thought he was going to be okay.

This was the middle of the day. Broad daylight.

And the backstory to this is the gunman grew up in a completely opposite way that our family had. His family had a history of gang activity, and his father was a gang member who was murdered the year before by people who were in a white van. So the white van was really who he was shooting at. He could not even see that these two in the van were not gang members. It's just nonsense, nonsense, nonsense.

That weekend after Jeff's murder, we weren't able to come home. We stayed in a hotel downtown, but when we did roll back in, one of the first things we saw was "J-Def R.I.P." bombed everywhere in the community. That was something that his friends had put up as markers or reminders.

But what blew us away was when all his friends got together and started a car wash. They washed cars for four days and four nights, in an effort to help us out financially with funeral costs. They actually managed to raise more than half.

My God, we got letters. We got letters from strangers. We got a card from the Chicago Police Department. Cops see this kind of stuff every day, so for them to take the time out to write a letter of condolence was really saying something to us.

There was a peace march that was organized by a group of friends a couple weeks after his death. The community was outraged, and it was like, enough is enough. This has to stop. I don't know if there's been a response like that in Pilsen. There are marches. A lot of them have to do with political issues like immigration, but I don't know if there's ever been one that's been sparked by gang violence or by murder. The route of the march actually was Jeff's last ride home. It ended up here at Dvorak Park. It was a really healing thing.

We are artists, and we had to do something in our own way. So that meant focusing it on making a documentary about Jeff and sharing his music. The film is part of a greater enterprise that we call the J-Def Peace Project. The J-Def Peace Project has a couple components to it: One is a visual art component, so that means painting murals and raising awareness of Jeff.

For me, these past two years have been about trying to keep myself busy enough, but in a creative way. I feel a very clear sense of intention in what I'm doing right now. I'm the most creative I've been. I've produced a series of drawings called "Secret Language," and all the drawings were inspired by Jeff. The goal was to create work that commemorated Jeff but also was really about how the three of us communicated at home. There's all kinds of imagery, from a june bug to a juniper tree, to a scooter, to two vinyl albums. That was just a way for me to work through loss, and do so in a way where I wasn't throwing Jeff's story down people's throats.

After Jeff's death, I got called by the Mexican Art Museum and asked if I wanted to paint an *ofrenda*, an altar, in one of the gallery spaces. It was for Dia de los Muertos, Day of the Dead, a three-month exhibit. I didn't want to do it, but I needed to do it. It was just part of the process.

The final piece of this installation included a six-minute music video and handwritten notes written by Jeff's friends and people who wanted to say good-bye in their own way. Some of the messages were really personal. Some of them I couldn't read. It was almost like reading someone's diary. I just took pictures of them, and someday I'll read them.

In the *ofrenda*, I used vinyl albums to spell his name out. I used about 80 albums and painted them gold. The idea "the universe unfolds as it should" is represented in the clouds and in this passageway. Everybody in the museum had to go through this portal to exit, so the idea is that this symbolizes the transition from earth to heaven that everybody has to go through.

When visitors would come to see the *ofrenda* and spend time listening to the music, and then read the handwritten notes, I felt like they had achieved a sense of fulfillment. They knew who Jeff was now. They connected with him. Now they were ready to move on. And it was good for me, too, so that I can move on.

It's easy to lose faith in humanity when something like this happens, you know? And Elizabeth and I, we have definite questions about why this happened to us, why this happened to Jeff. The least likely person. But we do believe that he has fulfilled his role and is still fulfilling his role. Things are happening because they're supposed to happen this way. It's tough. But there's a greater purpose to it. Now, we have to figure out what that is.

—*Interviewed by Kristin Scheffers*

ENDNOTES

75 Signed into law in the month following the September 11 attacks in 2001, the Patriot Act expanded the government's authority to secretly search private records and monitor communications. It has been controversial ever since.

THE FUNERAL HOME LADY
CATHLENE JOHNSON

Funerals have increasingly become the settings of gang-related violence in Chicago. In November of 2012, for example, one man was killed and another critically wounded outside a service for a slain gang leader at St. Columbanus Catholic Church on the South Side. In the aftermath of that tragedy, Mayor Rahm Emanuel declared that police would begin to have a stronger presence at the funerals of reputed gang members.

As general manager of the Johnson Funeral Home in the Austin neighborhood on the West Side, Cathlene Johnson has a unique view of gang-related murders—and of their tragic impact on the people left behind. When we spoke to her a few weeks after the shootings at St. Columbanus, she had just completed two high-profile funerals at which police stepped up security in order to make sure there were no revenge killings. "We've had an eventful few days around here," she said.

Johnson has been in the family business at Smith & Thomas Funeral Homes for 10 years. Her people are from Arkansas originally, and although she is a native Chicagoan, there is a slight twang in her voice. Despite frequent interruptions and visitors poking their heads into her office, Johnson is never too busy to address a concern. The 40-ish Johnson, who has old-fashioned views about the etiquette of discussing her exact age, dresses in suits with minimal jewelry, and describes herself as a no-nonsense problem-solver. She talks animatedly with large hand gestures.

It's always kind of funny when people walk up to you on the street or in the grocery store. Of course, I know where I know them from, but they don't always remember. So they say, "Hey, I know you…" I give them a little time, and we talk. And then it comes to them. "Oh, you buried my father," and I'll say, "Yes," and I always try to remember little details about them. It's a chance for the community to connect with you. Just as a person.

Smith & Thomas has been a big part of the Austin community since 1984. I worked downtown for so long and, just being here in the Austin-Oak Park-Forest Park area, it has that downtown flavor without that hustle-bustle. It's kind of artsy and diverse. It has a simplicity about it that I like. And there's a lot of openness, too. Openness of people. It has a small-town feel to it.

I think it's important to get to know your neighbors. These are my neighbors, and they call me the Funeral Home Lady. We are part of this community whether the people want us here or not. Death is a part of life. And so the funeral home is a part of the community. We will handle the death part, but we participate in the life part of the community, too. That's what I want you to know about us: that we are an essential part of the community.

I left the *Chicago Tribune*, where I was in human resources, in 2000 to start my own business. And I did that, consulting, for a little while. Then my aunt here at the funeral home, Miss Williams, got sick. She asked me to come over and manage the financial and accounting operation while she was doing her recovery. And so I came over here to help out, and I've been here ever since. So that's how I got integrated into the family business.

When people come in here, they have no idea what to do. It's just an emotional shock, a spiritual shock, a physical shock. And I have the opportunity to help somebody who's very distraught, walk them through a process, be gentle, have them come out with an end product that's celebratory of somebody's life, something that they're proud of. So, just to help somebody through a very, very difficult time—there's a lot of satisfaction in that.

To be a general manager—I like to think of myself as insurance. I am Miss Smith's insurance that everything is gonna go well. I do a lot of trouble-shooting on issues. One of the things about funeral service—you only get one chance to do it right. There's no do-over.

Now, at services, people have all kind of things going on. They have musicians, they have choirs, they have video presentations. So you're doing a lot of little things. People not being here on time—you rework the service sometimes. Keeping things orderly, which I would say is the most important thing that we do during a service. Because people sometimes respond to grief in a violent way, you can have a service that gets emotionally out of hand. You have to call the police. You have to escort people out. You also have to be sensitive to what's going on with your staff. You got to be looking to see if you have a problem, if somebody is a problem.

Man, we've had a couple services. We have learned our way through young people's services, especially when it's related to violence. Because we've had lots and lots of incidents at the funeral home related to violence. One of our policies is we don't do night services for young people who have died of violence. The family has to have a day service. We have undercover police who come to do security. We have emergency buttons throughout the funeral home so, if you have a situation, all you have to do is push the button. During those services, we're all on high alert.

Crowd control is so important. You may need to bring in additional staff, because they come out in droves. I mean, you get these really large crowds and a lot of young people congregating. We had one service where people were lined up from the funeral home about five blocks to see this guy in a single-file line.

I always call Mr. Thomas over to work the front door because, all these young guys, they come in with their hats on. We have a no-hat policy. Mr. Thomas, he says, "Young man, remove your hat!" A lot of their hats, they have gang affiliations. And then some of them say, "I ain't taking off my hat!" And then Mr. Thomas says, "Young man, you got two options. You can remove your hat and go into the viewing or you have to leave the premises." We are never disrespectful no matter how disrespectful they are to you. And some of these people—they get really mean. It's not because they're bad people. It's because they're overwhelmed by grief and they don't know what to do with it. And sometimes, my staff gets the brunt of their anger.

We've had fights at the funeral home. One time, we had a shooting. This was at the other location, on Madison. It was a huge night, so many people there. I heard shooting, and then the next thing I heard was just total confusion. I mean, people ran and scattered everywhere. The good thing about Madison is they're right across the street from the 15th District police station.

I had a family, we had some problems with them going to the cemetery in terms of the procession. They blocked off the traffic. They escorted themselves, which they can't legally do. It's their boy, and they're out there drinking, and it's just crazy. I told my staff, "Don't pass words with these young men. If it got to be aggressive, just walk away." You never know what people might do in response to their grief.

The number-one question I get is, "What happens to dead people? What happens to you after you die?"

Young people will ask that question. That's one of the saddest things for me—seeing children so torn by death. And the easiest thing is to go to a religious answer, but I always ask them, "What do you think?" Because what they want to do is talk. You don't necessarily have to push your beliefs off on anybody else. All you have to do is sit there and listen.

The kids think that they're invincible. And so then they're faced with someone they know who they also thought was invincible, so it challenges everything they thought they knew. All of a sudden, you realize you don't know nothing.

The young people have different ways in which they express that grief. There is some of the traditional crying and mourning, but I see a lot of artistic type of things. Lots of poetry and, you know, they have raps. You have to give them a voice, incorporating young people into the service so they could have a form of expression, so they could have closure, too. I definitely see some changes in the industry in terms of how younger people funeralize people. They don't want to do traditional things; they want to do their services their way.

When younger people die, memorial T-shirts are a big item. The kids wear them the day of the service, but then they frame them and they put them up in their rooms. The shirts actually become a memorial. But the other thing that I saw, too, was older people will buy them because it's an easier way to dress young people for the funeral. They can honor the memory of that person and they don't have to spend so much attention on what are the kids going to wear. It's kind of an appropriate thing to do now at the service.

I have nieces and nephews, and I definitely don't want them to show up in this funeral home with these issues. So I spend a lot of time with them.

My nephew CJ is ten. My sister Tesa let him get braids and he has the cornrows going to the back of his hair. When she let him get the braids, I really objected to it. I said, "Tesa, he looks like a little thug." And she said, "Well, he's not a little thug." And I said, "Well, I know that, and you know that, but the way that he looks…"

I tell CJ all the time, "I don't like your braids. I don't like 'em at all." So he'll say, "Auntie Cat, I want some new gym shoes." And I'll tell him, "If you cut your hair, I'll buy you some new gym shoes." My sister gets mad at me because I do that. I just don't want him to get in the wrong crowd. If it looks like a duck…

I'll tell you this. I saw somebody breaking into one of my neighbors' houses, some young men. I knew that my neighbor was out of town. And so when I saw those guys back there, I knew that they didn't belong there. I immediately picked up the phone and called the police.

The police called me 10 minutes later and they told me they had picked up three guys who fit the description I gave them. The men that were breaking into the house, they had on standard teenage stuff: red or white T-shirt, pair of jeans. So when the police officer drove me over to where they had stopped them, these guys were younger, but they were dressed exactly the same. Now, if I wasn't so certain about what I saw, I could have said, "Oh yeah, that's them," when it really wasn't.

So I told my sister that's why I don't want CJ to have braids. And he's gotten beat up a couple times. He's been bullied the last couple months on his way home from school, and I told him it has a lot to do with the way he looks. That visual is very, very powerful, so I think we have to send our kids some other messages. There's no way I want my nephews rolled in here one day.

What I hear from the kids these days is that they're bored. And I'm sure they are bored—TV and video games, that's not a lot of satisfaction. There's nothing for the kids to do. And all you really see is them walking around, sitting on the porch. My little nieces and nephews, they'll say, "I'm bored." And I tell them, "That's because you are bor*ing*. You're a boring person. What kind of interests do you have? What kinds of things interest you?" They say, "I don't know." Well, you have to figure that out.

One of the funeral staff here was telling me about a house party in Austin. Three people got killed at the party the other night. She said somebody turned off the lights, and two boys and a girl were shot. And to me, they got to have more creative things to do, you know? We got to give them outlets that produce something else. I don't have the answers, I don't know what they are, but a house party? That's not it.

Do I believe in ghosts? No, not really. I believe that there is a spiritual world along with the physical world, but I don't ever expect any of these dead people to get up and walk around, you know? These people who have died are so peaceful, they're not gonna bother you. You just have to know what you believe about dead people, and what I believe is that the dead have no power over the living. I think of it as an egg. Your egg is your body and you got a yolk and you got the whites. Those are the inner parts of you. And what we're left with at the funeral home, what we deal with, is the shell of the egg. That's it. And the rest has gone on.

When I get burned out from the emotional piece of the funeral home, I go home to Pine Bluff, Arkansas, and my mommy. It's a really emotionally burdensome job. When you're drained, you're drained. Because you have to show up, you have to be present, you have to be there for the family. And you can't turn away from that.

I wonder all the time: "How in the hell did I get here?" I never really planned to stay. It's really the people that keep you here. It's an experience like no experience you could ever have. And, a lot of people, they think it's weird. They think it's strange until they've had the experience themselves.

Funeral directors, we're really happy people on the inside. I think that's the biggest misperception, that we're this gloom and doom. I've had people say, "Why are you smiling?" Some people find it offensive, actually. That's one of the things that I tell new interns and people coming on: "People are mad and angry, but they're not mad and angry at *you*. They're mad and angry that their loved one just died. And every once in a while, one of them might take it out on you." People who work at a funeral home, they see just how short and fragile life is, and so they're happy not to be on the back table.

Don't delay anything. Because you never know. You never, never know. I'm happy because I got another day to live my life. Because death is a non-discriminator. Young, old, black, white, purple, green—it doesn't matter.

Oh my God, I don't even watch the news. Violence just walks through the door every day; the news happens here. I see what it does to people.

One of my clients comes back and we talk all the time. Her son was killed, and she is just so hurt. She just comes and she talks and she cries. You can't really do anything; you just listen. You carry the burden. Here's a person that feels comfortable enough with you to say some things to you that she could probably never say to anybody else.

I try to let people have their moment. A lot of times, they're trying to reason it out in their own heads. I've been with mothers where their children have been the victims, and mothers whose sons are the perpetrators, and neither one of them can understand it. Sometimes it's like you're talking to the same person.

—*Interviewed by Molly Tranberg*

THE SCAR TELLS A STORY
DAISY CAMACHO

In Chicago, violence and poverty go together like bullets and guns. According to The Chicago Reporter,[76] *nearly 80 percent of recent youth homicides (kids killed under the age of 21) took place in 22 low-income black or Latino communities on the city's South, Southwest and West Sides—even though just one-third of the city's population lives in those areas.[77] The report concluded: "It is nearly impossible to curb youth violence without addressing the underlying social conditions" including "limited access to higher education [and] violence-plagued and under-funded public schools."*

As a doctoral student in developmental psychology at UCLA, Daisy Camacho studies the "achievement gap"—the disparity in academic performance between kids from richer and poorer communities. The 24-year-old Camacho focuses on the role mentoring and after-school activities play in overcoming this divide. As the daughter of Mexican immigrants and first member of her family to graduate from college, she brings to her studies a passionate firsthand understanding of the subject.

Unfortunately, Camacho also has direct knowledge of youth violence. On Halloween night of 2009, she and fellow DePaul student Frankie Valencia attended a party at an upscale home in the traditionally working-class Puerto Rican neighborhood of Humboldt Park.[78] When members of a local gang tried to crash the gathering, they were asked to leave. They returned with a TEC-9 semiautomatic pistol.[79] Valencia was killed; Camacho was shot through the neck but survived. A petite woman with penetrating eyes and quiet charisma, she still has a small scar under her jaw.

In the ambulance after I was shot, I kept trying to explain to people, "Me and Frankie are not involved in gangs; that is not why this happened to us. We go to DePaul. Yes, we're Latinos, but, you know, give us a chance."

And that's when the paramedic was like, "You were probably just in the wrong place at the wrong time. It's just a bad neighborhood with bad kids."

And I was like, "No! No! Humboldt Park is not a bad neighborhood. Why do these kid have access to guns? And why don't we have activities for them so that these things are prevented?"

And, to this day, I have a really hard time thinking about the guys who shot us. I kind of just feel like they're a part of some system that turned them into this, you know? So it took me a long time to not view them as that. To view them as, you made this choice, and because of your choice, my friend is no longer here.

People try to say that you can do anything you want in this country, and that there's this American dream, and that whatever you aspire to, you can accomplish it. And it's true that, for some people, that does happen. But for a lot of people, it doesn't. There are certain things that are not even awakened in you because of the context that you're in. If you're in a low-income community, for example, you might not have access to role models.

Elgin, the town where I grew up, is one of the bigger suburbs of Chicago. It's not the most affluent of suburbs, but you're not living in the inner city. It's diverse. It's very diverse: racial-ethnic diversity, but also socioeconomic diversity. My parents were Mexican immigrants. They didn't speak English when they first moved here. My mom worked in a factory and my dad worked in construction. And then they got their real estate jobs, and they had their own office. And by then, we were doing really well. I remember they bought me a car when I was 16. Brand new. Over the years, however, more economic troubles hit my family, due to my parents' divorce and the market crash. Lots of times, it felt like we were worse off socioeconomically than when my parents raised us together with blue-collar jobs.

Sometimes discrimination could be bad in Elgin. You would hear stories about people saying mean things to Mexican-Americans, just very overt. Even when the animosity wasn't blatant, there were definitely micro-aggressions. But my parents were like, "Sometimes people will have negative perceptions of you because of your heritage, but you just have to keep working hard."

They weren't going to settle for what society dictates. I knew since I was very young that I was going to go to college. They made that very clear. Both of them are very ambitious, so if you ever said something like, "Oh, I want to be a nurse when I grow up," they would be like, "Well, why don't you want to be a doctor?" Or, if I said, "I want to be a teacher," they would say, "Well, why don't you want to be a principal?" It was always *do more.*

But I also benefited from other people believing in me and challenging me to do better. Although my high school was a little less than 50 percent Latino, minorities were underrepresented in the honors classes and the after-school programs. A lot of times, I was the only one. And I wound up in those classes almost by accident. When I first got to high school, I kind of got lost in the shuffle. I was taking all regular classes, and one of my teachers said, "You should consider taking honors classes."

So I said, "Okay," and I went to my counselor, and my counselor was like, "Oh yeah, your scores are way above everyone else's. You should definitely be taking honors courses."

I was like, "Man, if that teacher hadn't told me, I would never have come in here."

I also took part in a high-school program called Upward Bound, which gave me the tangible skills you need so that you can get into college—an understanding of how to apply and what kind of financial aid is available and what types of colleges are out there. I mean, there's just so much that you don't know when your parents don't go to college; it's difficult to even articulate it. But fortunately, there were people around me who had high expectations for me.

It was similar once I got to college. I had a lot of good mentors at DePaul. They recommended that I join the McNair Scholars Program, which helps low-income and minority students get into doctoral programs. Taking part in McNair helped me get to different labs, get research experience, present at conferences, things like that. At first, I didn't know that I wanted to get a Ph.D. I mean, it just *sounded* cool, but I didn't know what it was for or why you would do it or whether I would like it. It was sort of the same thing as in high school—people along the way making me aware of opportunities.

But how many other kids like me get lost? Many of them are very capable, but because they don't have these expectations, they're not going to rise to meet them.

I met Frankie at the end of our sophomore year at DePaul. We were applying for the study abroad program. And I just started talking to him, and he was like, "Oh, what are you doing at school?" And I just told him, you know, the standard "I'm a psychology major and I'm, you know, whatever."

And he was like, "Oh, I want to be *mayor*. I want to change Chicago politics!"

Which was kind of cool, you know?

After the shooting, some people thought I was Frankie's girlfriend and blah, blah, blah. But it wasn't like that. He really was just a friend. We connected over family, the value of family. We connected over wanting so-cial change. Sometimes we would try to do homework together. It never really worked, because we would start talking about things that we wanted to change or wanted to see happen. We went to a lot of cultural events at DePaul—like oh, there's this speaker coming, or this poet, or this author—anything like that, we'd try and go together. And ask tough questions and probably discuss it afterwards—nerdy fun.

Frankie was a dreamer, but he also did things. It wasn't just, "Oh, this is what I *think*." He engaged with people. He was active. He was doing things like volunteering for an organization that helps low-income preschool kids with literacy and other skills.[80] After a while, he and I began to share a dream about improving our education system and breaking the cycle of inequality from one generation to another.

See, I was passionate about research, and Frankie was passionate about politics. So our dream was that I would come up with some kind of re-search that would be useful in making the education system better, and then Frankie would implement it. It was probably a little over-simplistic, but I think we would have made it work. Yeah, we would have made it work...

For Halloween, Frankie and I were like, "Let's do something." And a few days before Halloween, my friends from Elgin had posted a message on Facebook. They had rented a ginormous house in the city for a weekend, and they were having this party. And then, I think one of them texted me and was like, "Hey, you should come by." And I was like, "I don't know. We'll see."

And that night, Frankie and I were supposed to meet one of his friends. But then his friend ended up canceling, and we were like, "Okay, now what do we do?" And I was like, "Oh, well, here's an option." We were planning just to say hi to people at the party, and then we were going to go hang out with his family. I think his parents were at a bar or something. I don't really remember.

We walked in, and it felt like Elgin High School because everyone looked familiar. It was mostly Latino kids. People were kind of shocked that I was there because I didn't really go out often. So it was like, "Whoa, it's crazy that you're here! How cool!" and stuff. And this whole time, Frankie was with me, so I just kept introducing him to people.

There was a dance floor and people were dancing. There were a lot of people, but it wasn't packed, like where you're sweaty and trying to get through a crowd. It seemed like a nice house, but it wasn't really until my friend started giving us a tour that it was like, "Oh, okay, this is a really expensive house. This is a luxurious house. Look at this indoor waterfall." I mean, I was aware of gentrification in Humboldt Park, but I didn't put everything together until afterwards.

What I found out was that, when we were on the tour, three guys from the neighborhood tried to get into the party. And I guess when they came in, they got kicked out. But we didn't know anything about it at the time. On the tour, it was just me and Frankie and my friend Manny. Then Manny, he got a phone call from another friend who was waiting outside and needed somebody to let him in the front gate. So the three of us went outside.

There was a gangway on the side of the house, and this whole time, Frankie was behind me. So Manny opened the gate, and we were walking back in—and that's when it happened. I heard four or five pops, and Manny yelled, "Oh, shit!"

I threw myself on the ground, and when I got up my neck just felt numb, so I grabbed it, and I was like, "Oh, man, I probably fell to the ground too fast and I sprained my neck or something." And then I saw my hand, and I was like, "Oh man, somebody got shot, somebody's splashed blood on my hand." And then I was like, "Oh, it's me."

The bullet came in through the back of my neck and then came out through the front on the left-hand side. My neck is really small, and the bullet missed everything—my spine, my jugular vein, my esophagus, my trachea, my voice box. And, I don't know, maybe because I had already survived a couple crazy car accidents, I wasn't like, "Oh my God, I'm going to die." I was like, "Oh, this is going to be so tedious to deal with. Trying to explain to my family that I was at a party. Ugh, this is going to be inconvenient, basically." That was my first thought.

There were suddenly a lot of people around, and everybody was calling the police. And people were staring at me and stuff, and I remember yelling at them, "Hey, stop staring. This is not a show. Keep moving." And there was a guy from the party who was like, "Just breathe. It's going to be okay." And he kept calling me "baby." And I was like, "Can you stop calling me that?"

And Frankie was sitting near me on the side of the house. I guess I kind of assumed that he had been shot, but I thought, "I'm okay; he'll be okay." And then the police came. And I just walked over to the ambulance. And I kept asking them, "Is he going to be okay?" Just to make sure. "Is he going to be okay? Is he going to be okay?"

They were like, "We're going to do the best we can."

Then they put him in an ambulance. And I didn't see him again.

A friend visited me in the ER. It was three, four, five in the morning. I'm not sure, just really late. She came in and was like, "Oh, I just wanted to check up on you." And I was like, "I'm fine. I don't care, as long as Frankie's okay. I just want him to be okay." Because I hadn't heard anything. And that's when she told me that he didn't make it.

After she left, I was by myself. So I was just alone with that…

The funeral and the memorial service were hard. I just felt guilty. I was the last person that he was with. And he didn't know anyone at this party except for me, so I felt like it was my fault.

I've been to a lot of therapy since then, and I've just kind of learned that guilt is not helpful because it's inhibiting you from dealing with other emotions. So like if you feel angry, if you feel like this was unjust, if you feel sadness, if you feel grief—it's almost like guilt is preventing you from feeling those things. So you have to kind of like peel off the guilt, and then deal with what you're really feeling. Those bad feelings don't really go away; you just learn how to live with them. But sometimes I do still feel guilty. Depends on the day.

The scar in the front of my neck was swollen, kind of 3-D, but now it's pretty much flattened out. I have a big laugh and if I find something really funny, I tilt my head back. And that's when people see it. I like scars, because I think they tell a story. And this one, it's bittersweet. I don't think you can avoid thinking about the pain. But it also tells the story of my friend—my friend who I was able to dream with, my friend who I hoped for a better future with.

And I think that makes it beautiful.

—*Interviewed by Lisa Applegate*

ENDNOTES

76 *The Chicago Reporter* is an investigative news organization with a distinctive focus on race and poverty. This important resource rarely gets the public recognition it deserves.

77 Kari Lydersen and Carlos Javier Ortiz, "More Young People are Killed in Chicago Than Any Other American City," *The Chicago Reporter*, Jan. 25, 2012, http://www.chicagoreporter.com/news/2012/01/more-young-people-are-killed-chicago-any-other-american-city

78 Chicago developer Anthony Mazzone designed and built the $1.2 million luxury home on a blue-collar street in Humboldt Park. Unable to sell it, he decided to rent it out as a weekend "vacation rental." A website advertising the property boasted that it was "located in a serene family neighborhood." It failed to mention that the block was controlled by the Maniac Latin Disciples. See Mark Konkol and Frank Main, "Killing Puts Spotlight on 'Vacation Rentals'—Aldermen Push Crackdown on Short-Term Deals for Vacant Homes," *Chicago Sun-Times*, Nov. 15, 2009.

79 The TEC-9 assault pistol has no military use. It was designed and marketed to kill civilians. Capable of unloading a 50-shot magazine in seconds, it was used in the Columbine massacre. One writer called it "the perfect implement of mayhem, because it does nothing well except spray bullets into terrified crowds." See Robert L. Steinback, "Gun Advocates Often Rely on Self-Delusion," *The Miami Herald*, Nov. 18, 1997.

80 The Jumpstart program at DePaul is aimed at helping overcome "the state of inequality in early educational experiences in America." It was one of several social-justice and service programs that Frankie Valencia took part in at the university.

HOW DO YOU LEARN TO LIVE AGAIN?

JOY McCORMACK

The stories in this book don't end with these final few pages. For many people we interviewed, there is no such thing as "closure," much less a happy ending. But that doesn't mean they have lost hope. So perhaps it's fitting to end with Joy McCormack, the mother of slain DePaul University honor student Francisco "Frankie" Valencia.

On Oct. 21, 2011—the day a Cook County judge sentenced 21-year-old Narciso Gatica to 90 years in prison for her son's murder[81]—McCormack told the court she still suffered from "unimaginable despair, pain, rage and deep grief."

"On many days," she added, "it seems like this darkness is stronger than I am."

Two years after the conviction, she continues to fight a day-to-day battle with that "darkness." But that has not stopped McCormack from throwing her considerable talents, energies and organizational skills into a new effort aimed at helping other survivors. Frustrated by the lack of resources available to her in the aftermath of her son's death, McCormack founded Chicago's Citizens for Change (CCC), an organization designed to address the needs of families devastated by youth violence. In addition to serving as a citywide clearinghouse for information and resources, her group provides referrals for grief counseling and funeral services, guides families through court proceedings and helps them keep in contact with police about criminal cases. Through a CCC program called Chicago Survivors, families find a real community with other people who have lost loved ones.

An intense and restless 40-year-old, McCormack embodies the struggles of so many people we spoke to for this book. "We all come through this life with some battle wounds," she says, "and sometimes those don't allow us to be as whole as we'd like to be as we walk through the world." Nonetheless, she keeps moving forward.

I had a very non-traditional background. My mom was a hippie; she and my father divorced when I was about 1. The last memory I have of him was when I was 4. I haven't seen him since.

My mother wasn't always around, either. She went to South America for a few years when I was a child, and that's how I came to Chicago to be raised by my grandmother. Then my mom came back to Chicago and we stayed here. Drugs, alcoholism—I grew up around that. It was all part of my childhood. I never remember having that kind of pure innocence that I remember seeing in other kids. I never really went through that phase of believing in the world.

I met Frankie's father when I was 12. I was still in elementary school at Nettelhorst, on Broadway and Melrose. Chico[82] was older than me; I was best friends with his cousin. He gave me a ride home from her house one night, and that was it. We became friends, started dating and stayed together.

Chico came from Acapulco, Mexico. A bunch of the family had migrated here, and so he had this beautiful network of people who spent time together and raised kids together and ate meals together and did all of these things that were just not part of reality in my own dysfunctional childhood. And I fell in love with that. I wanted it. I think that was one of the driving forces behind us getting together.

I was 15 when I found out that I was pregnant with Frankie. I was a freshman at Lincoln Park High School, in their International Baccalaureate program. I was having some irregular periods and my best friend was saying to me, "Joy, I think you're pregnant." And I was like, "No, I don't think I'm pregnant." There was really a part of me that kind of knew that I was, but I didn't want to deal with it because I knew that my mom would really be upset.

Although she was a great friend, my mother was never a great mom. Being a parent was always secondary to the other parts of her life. So when I told her the news, her reaction was like, "I'm 32; I can't be a grandmother." She really wanted me to have an abortion. She tried convincing me; she tried bribing me. But I decided I was going to have that baby.

I used to read *Goodnight Moon* to Frankie at night when I was pregnant: "Good night moon, good night stars ..." And at the time, there was this theory about how classical music would develop the child's brain. So I would put on the classical music station. Sometimes I would even put the headphones on my belly and hope that he was getting it, you know?

I had complications in the pregnancy, and there were a couple of times when it wasn't clear that everything would be okay. He was 3 ½ weeks late, and I was very sick with toxemia[83] by the time he was born. I was in labor for 2 ½ days. It was such an emotional experience, because I had been going through it for so long and the whole pregnancy had had all this turmoil. And then it all just kind of went away because there's this beautiful thing that I was holding.

He was 8 pounds 12 ounces when he was born at Illinois Masonic. He was a big boy. And he had very dark hair, and he had very red skin. And some of his hair was standing up. And he was very angry. He came into this world very angry.

I was 19 at the time my second son, Victor, was born. As an only child myself, I wanted Frankie to have a sibling. I didn't want him to be alone in the world.

But by then, my relationship with Chico was not healthy. He is a great person with a good heart; we are still great friends. But he never learned how to be a husband. So I chose to leave when Victor was a baby. My husband had closed the door on our commitment by the choices he was making. And once he did that, I felt like, "Okay, I owe nothing to this relationship anymore. I gave it my best; it didn't work out." And so very quickly after I left, I allowed myself to be true to me and began dating women.

I think I had known that I was gay for a very long time, but I rebelled against it. I didn't want it to be true, because of the stigma that went with it. And there were not examples around me of gay parents, so it was challenging to see myself both as a parent and as a gay woman. But when Victor was about 3 years old, I met my life partner, Siu.[84] And six months after we started dating, I had a conversation with the boys about whether or not they thought it would be okay if Siu joined our family, and they both said yes. By then I had graduated college and was building a career.[85]

We don't fit in to what most people's families look like. We don't even look like each other. I am Irish, Scottish, English and Russian-Jew. The boys are of Mexican and African heritage, because their father's grandfather is part African. And Siu, her parents were originally from China, and they migrated here.

Early on, we recognized that and we wanted to have something that would allow us to feel like we were connected, so we came up with this family acronym of the MMV family, which is the McCormack-Moy-Valencia family. It was a way to feel like we were a team. On a family trip, we once found T-shirts, which for some weird reason said, "MMV, a team that can't be beat!" That's how we felt—together, we were invincible.

It was a very open, very honest, very down-to-earth, very caring home environment. We ate dinners together most nights of the week. We always had a family day, which was our day not to do work and our day to play together and go do things and hang out. We made a big deal about all the special stuff in life, the holidays and special occasions and milestones. We just had an incredible energy. People were like, "Wow, this is amazing." And it *was* amazing.

I mean, it's destroyed now. But it was really amazing while it lasted.

Frankie was a fireball when he was little. And I had to be very intentional about parenting him, with behavior modification and all kinds of things to give him channels for that energy.

He really loved learning and he loved information and he loved facts. He was just so analytical and inquisitive and ready to challenge things at such a young age. And people were really attracted to his energy. People wanted to be around him. He was a leader at school. He just had that confidence.

My goal was to stop the cycles of dysfunction and chaos I grew up with and to be the first person in the family to raise a child who could actually have a childhood. And I felt like I did that. He had a great childhood, other than going through the divorce. But that was hard for Frankie. He really wished that his father and I had stayed together. It was really hard for him to give that up.

Frankie loved playing basketball and football, so he was hanging out with a lot of testosterone, a lot of guys who were all about being guys. I think it was in high school when he finally started to see examples of people being gay, other than Siu and me. And after he stopped feeling like he had this big secret, he started to not only be okay with it, but he started celebrating it, going to the gay-pride parades and wearing T-shirts about his gay family.

When he was around 17 or 18, he really started to question life. And he started coming up with these crazy things, like, "Mom, what if I decide to be homeless for a year?"

And I'm trying not to react to that, right? "Well, why would you want to have *that* experience, Frankie?"

And he's like, "I want to know what it's like to live a life where you're not connected to material things. What would that be like?"

You know, he just started questioning himself. What did he want to be? What did he want to do? What was important? That was the big question for him: What kind of man do I want to be?

Barack Obama—that was the first place he started to find the answer. Back when Obama was still just a state senator, Frankie fell in love with him. Literally. He had, it was a little bit of an obsession over this guy. He felt like he could relate to him because Obama had this really unique background, and he used that background to his advantage. Frankie was very inspired by the idea that a man of color could challenge the status quo in the way that Obama was willing to do.

By the time he was a senior at DePaul, Frankie's plan was, "I'm going to take a year off and do service abroad, volunteering in a Latin American country. Then, I'm going to go to law school, so that I can eventually have a political career. I'd like to start out as an alderman. Then I could be mayor. And then…"

This kid was such a planner, such a planner. He believed he was going to change the world. And I know that you hear people say that, but I'm telling you: Frankie believed that he was going to change the world.

Halloween in our family—you know, we just did it up. Every year, my partner and I would have all the little cousins come over and we'd have a party. And they would color pumpkins and bob apples, and our house was one of the most decorated on the block. So that night, Frankie came over and he went trick-or-treating with his little cousins, and put on a mask and was being very silly.

But I remember him being tired, and he seemed kind of down. We stood in our kitchen, and I looked in his face, and he said, "You know, Mom, I don't know if I'm going to go out tonight."

And I held his face in my hands, and I said, "Frankie, you're 21. This is the time to go out and have fun."

And he said, "Yeah, I'm going to go to school and see what everybody's doing. I don't know if I'm going to go out or not."

I thought that he had just overextended himself, because he always overextended himself. A couple of weeks earlier, we'd gotten word that Frankie had won the Lincoln Laureate Award.[86] He had also been nominated to do an internship at the White House. And he had been the featured speaker at the annual Diversity Brunch at DePaul,[87] hosted by the university's president. He was very excited about that because he liked seeing himself as a public speaker. It's what he saw himself doing in the future.

So when people would ask me, "How's Frankie?" I would say, "He's on fire. Nothing is going to stop him now."

And I really believed it.

That night, for the first time in 10 years, my partner Siu and I decided to go out for Halloween. A bunch of us—my ex-husband and my brother-in-law, my best friend and her niece—went to a Halloween party at a bar in Wicker Park, right there on North Avenue by Damen. My costume was like a witch-type, black cape thing that was very long and a little sexy. I felt pretty good. Dancing was always something I loved to do. So I danced. I was on top of the world.

While we were there, Frankie and his dad started texting each other, and he tells us that he's going to this party and that he would let us know when he was leaving so we could all meet up. We thought he was going to a party in Wrigleyville with a friend from high school. We had no idea that hadn't happened. I just assumed we'd see him later that night at another party, at a bar in Lincoln Square.[88]

But once we got to that other party, Siu started not feeling well, so she and I decided to leave. When we came home, Victor was sleeping on the couch in the living room. I was still wearing my Halloween costume. Then Siu gets a phone call.

She says, "Joy! Go change out of those clothes right now! We've got to go. Right now! We've got to go."

And I was like, "What's going on?"

And then she said, "Just do it, just do it now. Just do it!"

And so I ran upstairs and I changed my clothes. And Siu doesn't tell me what's happened. So we're in the car, and she's driving, and she's driving crazy. And I'm like, "Siu, what is going on? I'm freaking out."

And then she said, "Frankie's been shot."

The next thing I know I'm in this room, this big room upstairs at Illinois Masonic Hospital and there's a bunch of people already there. So then this,

I don't know who came, a lady, a nurse, something, and I was like, "Where is he?" And I started trying to slam through the door to get to him and a bunch of people started holding me back.

They said, "No, they're working on him. You can't see him."

I'm like, "No! I have to see him. I have to be there with him."

They would never let me go back and see him.

Until he was already gone.

The scene at the hospital was a nightmare. I was out of control. I was begging people to kill me. I tried killing myself several times. I kept on trying to find objects to cut my wrists. I tried to take shoelaces off of people. Finally, I got a key chain and I got into the bathroom and I locked myself in and I twisted it around my neck as hard as I could until there wasn't any more give. And the key chain broke and a security guard and the police busted the door open.

Eventually, Victor got there, and we went back to see Frankie. I was numb by then. I was beyond any feeling. I tried to give Frankie a hug and it was just ... They had tried to clean him up, but there was blood coming through the sheets and ... And then I walked right out of the hospital, and walked down Wellington, towards the lake, and I was planning on jumping in and letting myself drown.

They found me before I got to the lake, and they got me to come back. And we came home and went to Frankie's room and lay in his bed. But things just got very bad after that—worse than you could imagine your worst nightmare being. I didn't eat for 11 days. I couldn't connect to Victor. I couldn't connect to Siu. You know, as far as I was concerned, I pretty much died. All I could think about was the fact that I felt Frankie suffering. I physically felt Frankie suffering. I felt like I could hear him in my head, in my heart. And I felt like he needed me. I felt like, I really felt like Frankie was struggling with dying, like he was kind of lost in between two worlds, two universes.

I kept saying, "I know people think I'm being selfish, but Frankie's alone, and Victor's not. And this is the toughest decision I've had to make. But Victor has two parents here, and Frankie doesn't have any. And I'm gonna go with Frankie."

How do you learn, how do you learn to live again? I don't know how to express it, but after this happened, I couldn't do the simplest of things. I struggled going up and down stairs. I couldn't walk down the street by myself. I couldn't take a bus or a train. I couldn't go into a store without having a panic attack, breaking down crying. I mean, it took a lot of really hard work to get to the place that I'm at right now. And I continue to find ways to challenge myself to do things that are difficult. Like I recently went to the zoo with my family, and I saw all these children playing there. Being in places that have so many fond memories for me is still really hard.

But working with other survivors on a daily basis reminds me that, even though I'm in pain, there are other people who are in just as much pain. What Chicago's Citizens for Change allows me to do is keep this tragedy, and my experience of it, in perspective. I don't know that I would say it's been healing to get the organization up and running, but I would definitely say that it gives me a source of motivation and strength.

And I think Frankie would be proud that I've become more emotionally vulnerable, so that I can love a bit more openly those that I'm closest with, especially Victor and Siu. I mean, definitely there's still a lot of numbness. I don't dance anymore. And I don't celebrate any holidays. If something feels too celebratory, I just can't do it. But I have had moments when I surprise myself.

Not long ago, Victor, Siu and I went to the ocean, and she and I were standing in the water and a wave came up from behind us and splashed us. And apparently, I smiled and I laughed. And Victor took a picture of it. And he said, "Mom and Siu, I want to show you something."

So he shows us this picture of both of us holding on to each other, laughing and smiling and standing in the ocean. And I was surprised because I didn't know I had the capacity to do that anymore.

I just thought I would never, ever smile again.

—Interviewed by Miles Harvey

ENDNOTES

81 In June of 2011, Berly Valladares, a self-admitted member of the Maniac Latin Disciples, had been sentenced to 70 years in prison for supplying the gun to Gatica.

82 His full name is Francisco Valencia Sr.

83 "Toxemia" is an older term for preeclampsia, a medical condition characterized by high blood pressure and excess protein in the urine of a pregnant woman.

84 Siu is pronounced like Sue.

85 For the past 15 years, McCormack has worked as a financial investigator for the federal government.

86 The Lincoln Academy's Student Laureate Awards are presented for excellence in curricular and extracurricular activities to seniors from each of the four-year, degree-granting colleges and universities in Illinois.

87 The event took place on Oct. 17, 2009.

88 Wrigleyville and Lincoln Square are affluent neighborhoods on the North Side.

FINAL WORDS: TAKE A RISK

My last message. For the … young folks out there, I challenge you to take a risk. Take a risk in dreaming about a better world. Take a risk in dreaming about everything that's possible for your life. Dream about how to improve it. Dream about bettering the lives of people around you. Dream about the need to build a better world. Dream about all the opportunities to do just that. Sometimes we may not see them, but they're there. Maybe we need to ask questions, maybe we need to get pushed—but they're there. Take a risk and dream about leading—leading your families, your friends, your networks, your communities. Lead them to do good, to be loving and caring people. Lead by example. Don't let doubts, fears, pressures, concerns—don't let that hold you back. Dream, lead and take action. We need you.

—*Frankie Valencia, speaking at DePaul University two weeks before he was murdered*

ACKNOWLEDGMENTS

How Long Will I Cry?: Voices of Youth Violence is grounded in "collaborative storytelling," an ancient form that is taking on new importance in an age when online and mobile platforms allow us to capture and share our experiences on a scale never before possible. Instead of a single narrative by a lone author, collaborative storytelling involves many voices.

This project involved three key groups of collaborators. The first consisted of the 80-plus students at DePaul who were intimately involved in every step of the writing, editing, production and promotion of this book. I'm incredibly proud of them, and I'm awed by their passion, wisdom and skill. Special thanks are in order for the three first-rate research assistants who worked on this project: Erika Simpson, Lisa Applegate and Molly Pim.

The second collaboration was with the amazing creative team, cast, crew and staff at Steppenwolf, who transformed the stories that my students and I collected into a powerful theater piece. I regret that I can't recognize them all by name, but I do want to express my lasting gratitude to artistic consultant Kelli Simpkins, dramaturg Megan Shuchman and director Edward F. Torres, all of whom I cherish as theatrical mentors and creative co-conspirators. I also want to thank Steppenwolf Artistic Director Martha Lavey for her faith in the project—and in a first-time playwright. And finally, a huge and heartfelt thanks to my friend and fellow schemer, Hallie Gordon, the artistic and educational director of Steppenwolf for Young Adults, whose vision inspired this project and whose leadership made it a reality.

The third—and most important—group of collaborators was composed of the approximately 70 Chicagoans who lent their voices to this undertaking. For all of them, speaking with my students was a big leap of faith, and for many, it involved dredging up painful memories. For some, it even meant placing their own lives at risk. I am aware of the awesome responsibility that comes with collecting their stories, and I hope that my students and I have proved up to the task. In any case, I am grateful beyond words to all those who took part, and I regret that we could not fit more of their powerful stories into this book.

I want to offer special thanks to Joy McCormack, not only for sharing her story but also for her wisdom and collaboration on this project from the start. I'm also deeply grateful to other members of the MMV family, Siu Moy, Victor Valencia and Francisco Valencia Sr. And this project would not have been possible without community leaders who welcomed my students into their neighborhoods, including Jaime Arteaga, Max Cerda, Deanna Hallagan, Rev. Robin Hood, Father David Kelly, Diane Latiker, Mama Brenda Matthews, Edgar Ramirez and Jenice Sanders. And finally, I want to express my deep gratitude to John Zeigler, the managing director of Egan Urban Center at DePaul, whose knowledge of Chicago communities and relationships with local activists were invaluable to this effort, as were his wisdom, support, enthusiasm and friendship.

Many other people at DePaul also deserve recognition, beginning with my colleagues in the English Department. When I proposed the project to Anne Clark Bartlett, who was then department chair, she said, "Let's figure out how we can make this happen." I got the same response from Lucy Rinehart, who replaced Anne as chair and went out of her way on countless occasions to help me leap bureaucratic, logistical and financial hurdles. I am immensely grateful for her leadership, as well as for that of Craig Sirles and Michele Morano, the former and current director, respectively, of the Master of Arts in Writing and Publishing program. I also want to thank Cathy Clark and Jennifer Wright for saving me (and many others) from chaos on a daily basis. And I must give special recognition to two gifted colleagues, Chris Green and Jonathan Messinger, who joined me in teaching a series of classes that gave graduate creative-writing students at DePaul hands-on experience in developing, producing and launching a book. After their work in the classroom was complete, Chris and Jonathan donated their own time and expertise to the project. This book would not be possible without them.

Charles Suchar, dean of the College of Liberal Arts and Social Sciences, has been unfailingly supportive of this undertaking, as have others in his office, including Molly Bench, Susanna Pagliaro and Midge Wilson. Thanks are also due to Mark Laboe, Rubén Álvarez Silva and other members of the University Ministry at DePaul, as well as to Elizabeth Ortiz, José Perales and Miranda Standberry-Wallace at the Office of Institutional Diversity and Equity, and to Sara Miller-Acosta, Abena Apea, Cate Ekstrom and Paula Starkey at the University Office of Advancement. I am also grateful to Mary Devona, Marla Morgen, Anastasia Katinas and Jose Padilla at DePaul's Office of the General Counsel.

The project received extraordinary logistical, pedagogical and financial backing from the Irwin W. Steans Center for Community-based Service

Learning, an institution that makes me proud to teach at DePaul. I am indebted to Howard Rosing, Jeffrey Howard, Marisol Morales and the rest of the Steans Center's staff for their foresight, flexibility and steadfast support. The Beck Research Initiative for Women, Gender and Community—another project that makes me proud of DePaul—also provided vital financing and resources. I am deeply grateful to Beth Catlett and her colleagues at Women's and Gender Studies, and to Irene and Bill Beck and their family, whose belief in the power of positive action is inspiring.

This book was made possible by a grant from the Vincentian Endowment Fund at DePaul, where I am thankful to Rev. Edward R. Udovic and his staff. Additional support for printing and distribution came from the William & Irene Beck Charitable Trust, the Steppenwolf Theatre Company and Now Is The Time, a citywide effort against youth violence.

Funds for programming connected to this book came from the Richard H. Driehaus Foundation, where I am grateful to Peter Handler, Sunny Fischer and Richard Driehaus. I would also like to thank Robin Willard, Kathryn Eckert and Annie Tully at the Chicago Public Library, which co-sponsored events for this book, as well as hosting a tour of the theatrical version of *How Long Will I Cry?*

The goal of collaborative storytelling is to empower narrators and audience members to make connections with each other and with the broader world. So my final thanks—and my final plea—is to readers. Please share these stories (and this free book) with others, speak out about your own experiences, and stand up against bloodshed and injustice however you can. It will take many more voices—strong, loud and insistent—to change the narrative of violence in Chicago.

—*Miles Harvey*

The following groups are involved in anti-violence efforts in Chicago. We regret that we do not have enough space to list all the organizations that are working to make the city a safer and more equitable place. For more information about the services available to families of victims and to young people in need of legal services, gang-tattoo removal, shelter and other resources, please contact Chicago's Citizens for Change (chicagoscitizens-forchange@gmail.com), which is compiling a comprehensive guide.

Albany Park Community Center
1945 W. Wilson Ave., Suite 3000
Chicago, IL 60640
Phone: 773.583.5111
Website: www.apcc-chgo.org

The mission of Albany Park Community Center is to serve, support and educate diverse and multicultural community members as they determine their own path of growth and development. The organization envisions a vibrant community, in which members respect and celebrate diversity, use their skills and talents to help themselves and others live in safety and harmony and realize their hopes for a better life.

Alternatives, Inc.
4730 N. Sheridan Rd.
Chicago, IL 60640
Phone: 773.506.7474
Fax: 773.506.9420
Email: info@alternativesyouth.org
Social Media: http://www.facebook.com/AlternativesYouth or http://twit-ter.com/alternativesinc
Website: www.alternativesyouth.org

Alternatives is a comprehensive, multicultural youth development agency serving more than 3,000 young people and their families each year. Programs include counseling, leadership development and academic enrichment, as well as substance abuse and violence prevention.

Association House of Chicago
1116 N. Kedzie Ave.
Chicago, IL 60651
Phone: 773.772.7170
Fax: 773.384.0560
Social Media: https://www.facebook.com/AssociationHouse or https://twitter.com/ahchumboldt
Website: www.associationhouse.org

Based in the Humboldt Park neighborhood and offering programs and services locally and citywide, Association House helps participants gain independence through six service areas: community services, citizenship classes, child welfare, behavioral health, out-of-school time and El Cuarto Año alternative high school.

The Black Star Project
3509 S. Martin Luther King Dr., Suite 2B
Chicago, IL 60653
Phone: 773.285.9600
Fax: 773.285.9602
Email: info@blackstarproject.org
Social Media: https://www.facebook.com/pages/Black-Star-Project/98927762814
Website: www.blackstarproject.org

The Black Star Project is committed to improving the quality of life in Black and Latino communities of Chicago and nationwide by eliminating the racial academic achievement gap. The group's mission is to provide educational services that help preschool through college students succeed academically and become knowledgeable and productive citizens with the support of their parents, families, schools and communities.

BUILD
5100 W. Harrison St.
Chicago, IL 60644
Phone: 773.227.2880
Email: contactus@buildchicago.org

Social Media: https://www.facebook.com/BUILDChicago or https://twitter.com/buildchicago
Website: www.buildchicago.org

BUILD impacts communities by equipping at-risk youth with the life skills, training and resources necessary to emerge as leaders and active community change-makers. BUILD targets the at-risk demographic for participation and exposes them to multiple community resources, education, leadership training, mentoring and opportunities traditionally unavailable within their communities.

Chicago Area Project (CAP)
55 E. Jackson Blvd., Suite 900
Chicago, IL 60604
Phone: 312.663.3574
Fax: 312.663.5873
Email: info@chicagoareaproject.org
Website: www.chicagoareaproject.org

CAP empowers a broad base of community stakeholders to work together to improve neighborhood conditions, hold institutions accountable, reduce anti-social behavior by young people, protect children from inappropriate institutionalization and provide youth with positive models for personal development.

Chicago's Citizens for Change (CCC)
5600 S. Woodlawn Ave., 4th Floor
Chicago, IL 60637
Phone: 312.488.9222
Email: office@chicagosurvivors.org
Social Media: http://www.facebook.com/ChicagosCitizensForChange
Website: www.chicagoscitizensforchange.org

Chicago Survivors program's free 24/7 hotline: 855.866.6679

Founded by Joy McCormack, who tells her story in the final chapter of this book, Chicago's Citizens for Change aims to reduce youth violence through programs and partnerships that strengthen communities and promote restorative peace-making by supporting families and youth who have experienced loss due to violence. To ensure that no family walks this journey alone, CCC is committed to building a citywide response network to support families and loved ones of homicide victims and to providing opportunities for organizations, social services and justice systems to work together in a coordinated effort to serve Chicago's citizens.

Community Organizing and Family Issues/POWER-PAC
1436 W. Randolph St., 4th Floor
Chicago, IL 60607
Phone: 312.226.5141
Fax: 312.226.5144
Email: cofi@cofionline.org
Social Media: https://www.facebook.com/CommunityOrganizingandFamilyIssues
Website: www.cofionline.org

POWER-PAC is a cross-cultural, citywide membership organization of low-income parents. Its mission is to build a strong voice for low-income, immigrant and working families by uniting parents across race and community around issues of importance to families. POWER-PAC members are from throughout Chicago, including the neighborhoods of Austin, Englewood, Grand Boulevard, Humboldt Park, Lawndale, Little Village, Pilsen and West Town.

Cook County State's Attorney's Office - Victim Witness Assistance Unit
2650 S. California Ave., 1st Floor
Chicago, IL 60608
Phone: 773.674.7200
Website: http://www.statesattorney.org/index2/victimservices.html

The Victim Witness Assistance Unit was created in 1981 with the guiding philosophy that victims should be afforded their place in the system, informed about the status of the case, supported as the legal process proceeds and referred to outside agencies when additional help is needed. Besides providing in-person court support, victim-witness specialists co-facilitate a monthly support group.

Cure Violence

1603 W. Taylor St.
Chicago, IL 60612
Phone: 312.996.8775
Website: http://cureviolence.org or http://cureviolence.org/partners/illinois-partners/

Formerly known as CeaseFire, Cure Violence reverses the spread of violence by using the methods and strategies associated with disease control—detection and interruption, identifying individuals involved in transmission, and changing social norms of the communities where it occurs. The group was the focus of the acclaimed 2011 documentary film *The Interrupters*.

Dajae Coleman Foundation (DC3F)

P.O. Box 12
Evanston, IL 60204
Phone: 847.461.3223
Email: info@dc3f.org
Website: www.dc3f.org

The Dajae Coleman Foundation (DC3F) provides Evanston's youth with the opportunity to maximize their potential by creating an informed and mobilized environment, which aims to enhance their quality of life and develop them into men and women of integrity. DC3F offers programs that motivate the youth and instill positive values that help to guide them.

Demoiselle 2 Femme

9415 S. Western Ave., Suite 200
Chicago, IL 60643
Phone: 773.779.9371
Fax: 773.779.9471
Email: info@demoiselle2femme.org
Social Media: https://www.facebook.com/Demoiselle2Femme, https://twitter.com/demoiselle2femm, http://www.youtube.com/demoiselle-2femme
Website: www.demoiselle2femme.org

Demoiselle 2 Femme (D2F), French for "Young Ladies to Women," is a not-for-profit organization committed to providing holistic programs and services that support adolescent females in a successful transition to womanhood. T-awannda Piper, whose narrative opens this book, is the director of programs for the organization.

Enlace Chicago - Violence Prevention

2329 S. Troy Ave.
Chicago, IL 60623
Phone: 773.823.1062
Email: info@enlacechicago.org
Social Media: http://www.facebook.com/enlacechicago or https://twitter.com/EnlaceChicago
Website: www.enlacechicago.org

Enlace Chicago has one of the most comprehensive violence-prevention initiatives in the Chicago metropolitan area, providing services ranging from school-based prevention work to advocacy for reform in juvenile justice policy. Enlace is based in the Little Village community.

Gordie's Foundation

6430 S. Ashland Ave.
Chicago, IL 60636
Phone: 773.434.3920
Fax: 773.476.7526
Email: chmillgordie@sbcglobal.net
Social Media: https://www.facebook.com/pages/Gordies-Foundation/163496413678066
Website: www.gf28.org

Founded by Audrey Wright, whose story appears in this book, Gordie's Foundation provides ex-offenders with marketable vocational training that can be the springboard to a productive lifestyle change. The organization is based in the Englewood community on the South Side.

J-Def Peace Project
1436 W. 18th St.
Chicago, IL 60608
Phone: 312.834.9790
Email: jdefpeaceproject@gmail.com
Social Media: https://www.facebook.com/pages/The-J-DEF-Peace-Project/171459632918845

The J-Def Peace Project uses multidisciplinary arts to foster a peaceful community. Its goal is to continue the work of aspiring hip-hop artist Jeff Abbey Maldonado Jr., who was murdered in the Pilsen neighborhood in 2009. His father, Jeff Maldonado Sr., talks about the young man's life and legacy in this book. The mission of the J-Def Peace Project is to create public artworks with education, culture and peace.

Kids Off the Block, Inc.
11627 S. Michigan Ave.
Chicago, IL 60628
Phone: 773.995.9077
Fax: 773.264.3912
Email: dianekob@hotmail.com
Social Media: https://www.facebook.com/dianekob or https://twitter.com/KidsOffTheBlock
Website: http://www.kidsofftheblock.us

Founded by Diane Latiker, whose narrative appears in this book, Kids Off the Block provides at-risk, low-income youth positive alternatives to gangs, drugs, truancy, violence and the juvenile justice system.

Lazarus Jones Save Our Children Campaign
P.O. Box 257474
Chicago, IL 60625
Phone: 773.386.0750
Email: lazarusjonessocc@yahoo.com
Social Media: https://www.facebook.com/pages/Lazarus-Jones-Save-Our-Children-Campaign/129568373810731?ref=hl
Website: http://www.lazarusjonessocc.org/

Founded by Pamela Hester-Jones, whose story appears on these pages, the Lazarus Jones Save Our Children Campaign focuses on improving safety within our communities through support, counseling and educational workshops.

Marillac Social Center
212 S. Francisco Ave.
Chicago, IL 60612
Phone: 773.722.7440
Fax: 773.722.1469
Email: info@marillacstvincent.org
Social Media: https://www.facebook.com/MarillacSt.VincentFamilyServices or https://twitter.com/MSVChicago
Website: http://marillacstvincent.org/

Since 1914, Marillac Social Center has been serving the needs of the poor and working poor of the West Side of Chicago. Sponsored by the Daughters of Charity, Marillac Social Center provides vital programs and services in the areas of child development, social services, family services, senior services and youth programs.

Parents of Murdered Children, Inc. (POMC)
Little Company of Mary Hospital and Health Care Centers
2800 W. 95th St.
West Pavilion, Room 8536
Evergreen Park, IL 60805
Phone: 708.720.6104
Alt. Phone: 773.847.1613
Website: www.pomc.com/chicago/index.htm

Parents of Murdered Children, Inc. is a non-profit self-help support group for survivors of homicide victims. The group offers follow-up with supportive family services after the murder of a family member or friend. The Chicago Area Chapter of POMC holds monthly meetings, provides a telephone network of support, supplies information about the grief process, organizes a speaker's bureau and provides accompaniment for survivors who must attend court proceedings.

Precious Blood Ministry
P.O. Box 09379
Chicago, IL 60609
Phone: 773.952.6643
Fax: 773.952.6739
Email: nojail@aol.com
Website: www.pbmr.org

Located in the Back of the Yards neighborhood, Precious Blood Ministry works with young people 14 to 24 years old, many of whom are court-involved or are coming out of detention or incarceration. Precious Blood Ministry employs a restorative-justice program that tries to create a safe haven for young people, engage them and help them access whatever resources they need, including mentoring, job placement, housing and education.

Project H.O.O.D. (Helping Others Obtain Destiny)
6620 S. Martin Luther King Dr.
Chicago, IL 60637
Phone: 773.326.4215
E-mail: info@projecthood.org
Social Media: https://www.facebook.com/ProjectHood1 or https://twitter.com/projecthood1
Website: http://www.projecthood.org/

Pastor Corey Brooks, whose story appears on these pages, founded Project H.O.O.D. to build a community center and call attention to street violence on Chicago's South Side.

Project NIA
1530 W. Morse Ave.
Chicago, IL 60626
Phone: 773.392.5165
Email: mariame@project-nia.org
Social Media: http://www.facebook.com/pages/Project-NIA/218584157088 or https://twitter.com/projectnia
Website: www.project-nia.org

Project NIA supports youth in trouble with the law, as well as those victimized by violence and crime, through community-based alternatives to the criminal legal system. The group advocates for redirecting resources from youth incarceration to youth opportunities.

Purpose Over Pain
1210 W. 78th Place
Chicago, IL 60620
Phone: 773.234.8117
Email: purposeoverpain@gmail.com
Website: www.purposeoverpain.com

Purpose Over Pain was formed in 2007 by members of seven families who had lost children to senseless gun violence. The co-founders include Pamela Montgomery-Bosley, whose story is in this book. Purpose Over Pain works to assist families victimized by gun violence by helping with funeral expenses, offering counseling and directing them to support groups. Members of the group also lobby for common-sense gun legislation and speak at schools and community events about gun violence and what it does to communities.

Southside Together Organizing for Power (STOP)
602 E. 61ˢᵗ St.
Chicago, IL 60637
Phone: 773.217.9598
Email: southsidestop@gmail.com
Website: www.stopchicago.org

STOP is a community organization that fights for South Side residents on issues such as gentrification, displacement and health cuts, as well as youth incarceration and criminalization.

Strengthening Chicago's Youth (SCY)

Ann & Robert H. Lurie Children's Hospital of Chicago
225 E. Chicago Ave., Box 62
Chicago, IL 60611
Phone: 312.227.6678
Email: info@scy-chicago.org
Social Media: https://www.facebook.com/StrengtheningChicagosYouth or
https://twitter.com/SCY_Chicago
Website: www.scy-chicago.org

Spearheaded by Lurie Children's, SCY is a group of private and public stakeholders that takes a public-health approach to violence prevention, with a focus on policy, systems and environmental change. SCY believes that preventing violence before it occurs requires a balanced effort that addresses the complex factors underlying violence and builds on the assets of youth, families and communities.

UCAN

3737 N. Mozart St.
Chicago, IL 60618
Phone: 773.588.0180
Fax: 773.588.7762
Email: info@ucanchicago.org
Social Media: https://www.facebook.com/UCANChicagoland or www.twitter.com/UCANchicago
Website: www.ucanchicago.org

UCAN strives to build strong youth and families through compassionate healing, education and empowerment. UCAN aims to help prevent violence by focusing on non-violent conflict resolution strategies, mentoring, youth empowerment, leadership development and advocacy.

YMCA of Metropolitan Chicago -
Youth Safety and Violence Prevention
1608 W. 21st Place
Chicago, IL 60608
Phone: 312.587.2243
Email: mhelder@ymcachicago.org
Website: http://www.ymcachicago.org/programs/youth-safety-and-violence-prevention/

The YMCA of Metropolitan Chicago provides leadership and initiatives that help make neighborhoods safe through a unique combination of collaborative community organizing, education and training, family-wellness programs, and intensive youth and family outreach. Through the Youth Safety and Violence Prevention and Street Intervention Program, the Y integrates evidence-based prevention, intervention and reduction strategies and has a presence in 11 of Chicago's at-risk communities including Humboldt Park, Little Village, Logan Square, Pilsen, South Chicago, Bronzeville, West Lawn and West Garfield.

Youth Guidance
1 N. LaSalle St., Suite 900
Chicago, IL 60602
Phone: 312.253.4900
Fax: 312.253.4917
Email: info@youth-guidance.org
Social Media: https://www.facebook.com/youthguidance.chicago, https://twitter.com/YG_Chicago or https://www.youtube.com/user/YouthGuidanceChicago
Website: www.youth-guidance.org

Youth Guidance operates the Becoming a Man program, a school-based counseling, mentoring, violence prevention and educational-enrichment program that promotes social, emotional and behavioral competencies for at-risk male youth from Chicago's toughest neighborhoods.

Youth Service Project, Inc. (YSP)
3942 W. North Ave.
Chicago, IL 60647
Phone: 773.772.6270
Fax: 773.772.8755
Email: info@youthserviceproject.org
Social Media: http://www.facebook.com/pages/Youth-Service-Project/245115743727, https://twitter.com/YSPChicago, http://www.youtube.com/user/YouthServiceProject or http://www.youthserviceproject.org/?-feed=rss2
Website: www.youthserviceproject.org

Since 1975, YSP has worked with youth and families in the greater Humboldt Park community. The group offers programs in seven core areas: education, recreation, intervention, prevention, arts and culture, community building and diversion.

When the theatrical companion to this book premiered at Steppen-wolf Theatre Company in February 2013, it was part of a citywide call to action against youth violence and intolerance called Now Is The Time. This initiative, co-sponsored by the Chicago Public Library, promotes dialogue between young people seeking solutions to minimize violence and strengthen their communities.

Consider these questions for further discussion:

- In Miles Harvey's introduction to *How Long Will I Cry?*, he notes that Chicago is the most racially segregated city in the country. Do you think that there's a connection between racial segregation and youth violence? And how do you think racial tensions in Chicago could be abated?

- After the murder of 16-year-old Derrion Albert, Miles Harvey wondered what he could do—or what anybody was supposed to do—to tackle a problem as big, scary and complex as youth violence. How do you think one person, or one group of people, could make a difference (small or big)?

- Miles Harvey notes that in today's world, everyone is blogging, texting, tweeting, Friending–but nobody's really listening. One of the main goals of this book is to make people feel more connected with each other. What other sorts of stories would help people "hear" each other and would be inspirational to collect?

- Statistics show that nearly 80 percent of recent youth homicides (kids killed under the age of 21) took place in 22 low-income black or Latino communities on Chicago's South, Southwest and West Sides—even though just one-third of the city's population lives in those areas. What do you think the government should do about black-on-black and Latino-on-Latino crime? How about the police? How about people who live in these communities, and those who live outside of them?

- In which of the stories did you witness someone taking positive action? Was it action for themselves, action for their community or both?

- Whose story did you most relate to out of the people interviewed? Who did you find inspiring and why?

- In Max Cerda's story, he talks about first joining a gang for a sense of camaraderie. What are positive outlets a person can turn to when looking for camaraderie? As a society, how can we create constructive opportunities for young people searching for a sense of community as an alternative to joining a gang or turning to violence?

- In Diane Latiker's story, she mentions that when she was growing up, gangs were protectors of neighborhoods; they took care of innocent people. Do positive "gangs" exist today? If so, what do they look like?

- In Pastor Brooks' story, he sees the need for a community center in place of a hotel serving as a hub for criminal activity. Are there specific things that can be done in your community to reduce violence or criminal behavior?

- What are your fears surrounding violence in your neighborhood or community? Brainstorm a list of three solutions that could minimize your fears and help you feel safer.

- Where did you see examples of hope within these stories?

ABOUT THE EDITORS

Miles Harvey (editor) wrote the stage version of *How Long Will I Cry?: Voices of Youth Violence*, which premiered at Steppenwolf Theatre in 2013. He is also the author of *The Island of Lost Maps: A True Story of Cartographic Crime* (Random House, 2000) and *Painter in a Savage Land: The Strange Saga of the First European Artist in North America* (Random House, 2008). He teaches creative writing at DePaul University.

Alex Kotlowitz (foreword) is the award-winning author of three books, including the national best-seller *There Are No Children Here*. A producer of the documentary *The Interrupters*, he has published work in *The New York Times Magazine*, *The New Yorker*, *Granta* and on public radio's *This American Life*. He's a writer-in-residence at Northwestern University.

Chris Green (associate editor) is the author of two books of poetry: *Epiphany School* and *The Sky Over Walgreens*. His poetry has appeared in such journals as *Poetry*, *New Letters*, *Verse*, *Nimrod*, *RATTLE* and *Black Clock*. He recently edited the anthology *Brute Neighbors: Urban Nature Poetry, Prose & Photography*. He teaches in the English Department at DePaul University.

Jonathan Messinger (associate editor) is co-publisher of featherproof books. For more information about him and his work, visit shootthemessinger.com.

Jason Harvey (book designer) has been living and designing in the Chicago area for the past 20 years. His work focuses on book and website design and has been recognized by many design competitions including 50 Books/50 Covers, sponsored by the American Institute of Graphic Arts. To see more of Jason's work, visit www.jhbookdesign.com.

Carlos Javier Ortiz (cover photographer) won the Robert F. Kennedy Center for Justice and Human Rights Photography (2009) award for *Too Young to Die*, his multiyear examination of youth violence in the United States and Central America. In 2011, he received the Open Society Institute Audience Engagement Grant for his continuing work on that project. Recently he was awarded a grant from the Pulitzer Center on Crisis Reporting for his work on *Too Young to Die* and youth violence in Guatemala. His work has been published in *The Washington Post*, *Ebony Magazine*, *Le Monde Magazine*, *GEO*, and in numerous international print, broadcast and online venues.